Understanding & Mana Dyslexia For Dummie

Spotting Dyslexia Warning Signs

A person with dyslexia struggles on a long-term basis with written (and sometimes spoken) words, even though she's bright (or extra bright) in other areas. A whole cocktail of symptoms tells a psychologist that your child has dyslexia and you can find a list on the BDA website (www.bdadyslexia.org.uk) to help you further, but warning signs include the following:

- Enjoys being read to but has a lack of interest in letters and words at a young age.

- Inability to identify rhyming words (like *hat*, *pat* and *fat*) and word patterns (like *Bill*, *bear*, *bun*, *bed* and *ball*, which all begin with 'buh') at an early age.

- Difficulty remembering names of familiar objects, numbers, colours and shapes at an early age.

- Inability to remember sequences of numbers (like their telephone number) or letters (like the alphabet) or fast facts (like multiplication tables).

- Extreme difficulty with reading. A child with dyslexia may leave out little words (like *of*), misread small everyday words (like *they*) even though she reads some harder words, read similar-looking words instead of actual words (like *was* for *saw* and *horse* for *house*), read words that are similar in meaning instead of actual words (reading *little* for *small* or *lovely* for *pretty*) and read words that make no sense but have one or two letters that are in the actual word (like *tall* instead of *lot* because both words have *l* and *t* in them). A child with dyslexia may, for example, read 'There were a lot of roses growing all around Jane's house' as 'There was a tall flowers growing around Jane's horse'.

- Extreme difficulty with spelling. A child with dyslexia may transpose letters (*aleiv* instead of *alive*), leave out letters (*aliv*), add letters (*alieve*) and reverse letters (typically *b* and *d*). She may also write words phonetically (exactly as she hears them), producing spellings like *becuz*, *wur* and *thay*.

Chapter 3 has more information about the general signs of dyslexia seen in people of all ages.

Engaging in Memorising, Visualising and Rhyming

A child with dyslexia struggles to remember how words are put together in print, but rhyming and visualisation strategies can help her. When she turns letters into lively, more concrete characters, she can fix them better in her mind:

- Help your child with short vowel sounds by having her draw images into the vowels while saying their short sounds. For example, she can create an apple out of *a*; draw an egg inside the top part of *e*; convert a pen with a blob of ink on top into *i*; change *o* into an octopus; and draw an arrowhead on each of the two top ends of *u* so it represents 'up'.

- Help your child read and spell words like *late*, *hole* and *cute* by showing her the 'Bossy e rule': when *e* is on the end of a short word, it bosses the earlier vowel into saying its name (but stays silent itself).

- Help your child read and spell long-vowel words like *meet*, *neat*, *nail* and *boat* by teaching her this rule: 'When two vowels go walking, the first one does the talking (and says its name).'

You can read the full account of these and other memory-jogging strategies in Chapter 11.

For Dummies: Bestselling Book Series for Beginners

Understanding & Managing Dyslexia For Dummies®

Cheat Sheet

Picking Up Phonics

In straightforward terms, *phonics* means 'sounds of language' and your child needs to know these. One way to do this is the teaching method in which you show your child that letters and groups of letters represent speech sounds. Your child with dyslexia needs to get a firm grip on phonics so that she discovers order in words that otherwise seem to her like an arbitrary mix of letters. You can read the complete ins and outs of phonics in Chapter 12, but right here are four simple strategies to help you guide your child through phonics in the systematic, sequential way that experts recommend:

- Emphasise single letter sounds (rather than names) to your child. Play games like 'I spy with my little eye something beginning with "buh" or "cuh" or "ch"'. Ask your child to tell you words to continue a word pattern like *Bill*, *bear*, *bun*, *bed* and *ball* (all beginning with 'buh').

- Read rhymes and rhyming stories to your child, and sing rhyming songs so that you prime her for identifying word families like *pan*, *fan*, *man*, *can* and *tan*.

- When you introduce written words to your child, start with a simple two-letter word like *at* and show her how she can add letters to *at* to build a whole *at* word family (*bat*, *mat*, *cat*, *sat*, *fat*). Make this activity more fun, and easy to repeat, by having your child use a book-sized whiteboard and marker pens. Even better, have two sets of boards and markers so that you can do the same activity and you don't interfere with your child's board!

- Any time your child gets to know a word from which she can build a word family, build that family with her. Start her off with three-letter word families like *big*, *pig*, *fig* and *wig*; build up to middle-level families like *chop*, *stop*, *flop* and *shop*; and help her really think about tricky word families like *would*, *should* and *could*; and *fight*, *might*, *fright*, *tight*, *sight* and *flight*.

Having Some Multisensory Fun

Multisensory learning is the kind of learning method that suits children and adults with dyslexia best. In simple terms, *multisensory learning* is hands-on learning that engages a few of your child's senses (typically seeing, hearing, saying and doing) together at about the same time.

You can help your child with multisensory learning at home by having her play a lot of hands-on and physical games, say out loud the words she reads and writes and fit drawing and model building into homework assignments whenever she can. Additionally, when she first learns letters and words, have her:

- draw their shapes in different media, like sugar and pudding
- trace over them on unusual textures, like sandpaper
- construct 3D models of letters out of modelling clay

Chapter 14 has the full story on multisensory learning.

For Dummies: Bestselling Book Series for Beginners

Understanding & Managing Dyslexia

FOR

DUMMIES®

by Tracey Wood
and Katrina Cochrane

A John Wiley and Sons, Ltd, Publication

Understanding & Managing Dyslexia For Dummies®

Published by
John Wiley & Sons, Ltd
The Atrium
Southern Gate
Chichester
West Sussex
PO19 8SQ
England

E-mail (for orders and customer service enquires): cs-books@wiley.co.uk

Visit our Home Page on www.wiley.com

For general information on our other products and services, please contact our Customer Care Department within the U.S. at 800-762-2974, outside the U.S. at 317-572-3993, or fax 317-572-4002.

For technical support, please visit www.wiley.com/techsupport.

Wiley also publishes its books in a variety of electronic formats. Some content that appears in print may not be available in electronic books.

British Library Cataloguing in Publication Data: A catalogue record for this book is available from the British Library

ISBN: 978-0-470-74132-0

Printed and bound in Great Britain by TJ International, Padstow, Cornwall

10 9 8 7 6 5 4 3 2 1

About the Authors

Tracey Wood was born in England. She went to teachers college in Leeds and graduated with an honours degree in psychology and education. She taught in a special school for four years and loved it, but sunnier climes called and she left England for a backpacking vacation in Australia. Twelve years later she was still enjoying the warmth of Australia but had traded her backpack for a husband and two kids.

In Australia, Tracey earned a diploma in special education and a master's degree in education. For several years she ran a high school special education unit and then started her own reading clinic. In the 1990s Tracey moved (with her husband's job) to the San Francisco Bay area. She ran a reading and writing clinic; helped in her kids' school; led two scouting troops; instructed for the Red Cross; created her website, ReadingPains.com; and wrote her first book, *See Johnny Read! The 5 Most Effective Ways To End Your Son's Reading Problems.*

Still on the move, Tracey relocated to Toronto and wrote her second and third books, *Teaching Kids to Read For Dummies* and *Teaching Kids to Spell For Dummies.* While writing *Overcoming Dyslexia For Dummies,* she relocated again, to Boston.

Tracey is a literacy consultant and public speaker. She writes articles for magazines like *Big Apple Parent* and *Teachers of Vision,* has appeared on *Access Help TV* and national radio shows like *Parent's Journal* and *The Parent's Report,* and is committed to steering (albeit unsteadily) her two children through childhood with all their limbs and faculties intact.

Katrina Cochrane graduated in English and History in 1984 and worked for two airlines travelling the world before deciding in 1993 to retrain as a teacher. Having obtained her PGCE from Reading University, she worked as an English teacher at secondary level. As a result of coming across so many children with dyslexia and not having any knowledge of how to help them, in 1999 Katrina enrolled on the Dyslexia Institute's postgraduate diploma course. During the course she was offered a job teaching for them and has never looked back. In 2003, she was made Principal of the Egham Centre, working at their headquarters. In 2001, she completed her master's in education, her dissertation on the subject of creating a dyslexia-friendly school, and in 2007 her Certificate of Competency in Educational Testing.

Katrina enjoys running a busy centre which assesses and teaches both adults and children. She also gives courses for SENCOs, teaching assistants and parents, and is generally passionate about raising awareness of dyslexia. Katrina is also a tutor on the postgraduate training course for teachers.

Katrina is married and has two teenage sons – one with dyspraxia – who keep her very busy. She is a parent governor of Farnborough Sixth Form College and in her spare time(!) enjoys reading, especially cookery and diet books!

Dedication

This book is dedicated to Kevin, Alex and Oliver. Perhaps one day I will learn to cook!

Publisher's Acknowledgements

We're proud of this book; please send us your comments through our Dummies online registration form located at www.dummies.com/register/.

Some of the people who helped bring this book to market include the following:

Acquisitions, Editorial, and Media Development

Project Editor: Steve Edwards

Development Editor: Brian Kramer

Content Editor: Jo Theedom

Commissioning Editor: Wejdan Ismail

Publishing Assistant: Jennifer Prytherch

Copy Editor: Sally Osborn

Proofreader: Helen Heyes

Technical Editor: Jenny Summerton

Executive Editor: Samantha Spickernell

Executive Project Editor: Daniel Mersey

Cover Photos: © Digital Vision/Alamy

Cartoons: Ed McLachlan

Composition Services

Project Coordinator: Lynsey Stanford

Layout and Graphics: Samantha K. Allen, Reuben W. Davis

Indexer: Claudia Bourbeau

Special Help

Brand Reviewer: Zoë Wykes

Contents at a Glance

Table of Contents

Introduction

You've picked up this book because you're concerned about your child. He isn't keeping up in class, hates to read and makes spelling errors even in simple words. Is he dyslexic? Should you be asking for an assessment? What can you do to help him at home?

Or maybe you're flicking through these pages for yourself. When you were at school you felt stupid, and now you avoid reading and hate writing. You're wondering whether you should call yourself 'dyslexic' and, if you do, whether that may make much difference to your life. We hear you! You need straightforward, practical, positive advice.

We spend our (happy and ever-so-rewarding) working lives helping children and adults with dyslexia. We know that we change lives. Sincerely, warmly and rather proudly, we offer you this book so that you too can make a difference.

About This Book

In this book, we give you all the relevant information and leave out the rest. We don't bury you under a mound of theories, lose you in terminology or wear you out with alternatives. We don't preach, prattle or pretend that one definitive answer exists. Instead, we give you honest information about the stuff that matters. And we move you quickly from theory to practice.

You get hands-on activities your child can start straight away, strategies that are good for his whole lifetime and handy tips for dealing with daily problems (like how to help him get organised and keep his *b*s and *d*s facing the right way once and for all). For teens and adults, we give the lowdown on things like note taking, applying to college and succeeding in the workforce. And to keep you on the ball with current research, you get news about brain mapping, dyslexia therapies and the reading programmes most specialists prefer.

Whether you're just beginning to consider the term *dyslexia* or you've already done some research; whether you've got your child's Statement under way or you've never heard of a Statement; whether you want reassurance, practical strategies or legal details made easy, this book's for you. Surf through it or immerse yourself chapter by chapter, whichever suits you. The chapters in this book let you pick and choose, but they also follow a logical progression. The book contains so much information that you're sure to get the guidance you're looking for. And whatever your needs and interests, in the Part of Tens you get quick lists, each of ten items, of really handy stuff.

Conventions Used in This Book

To *he* or not to *he*? In this book we clean up that sticky dilemma by using *he* and *she* in alternate chapters. You can be sure that the book's for everyone, and after you're used to the idea of switching between *he* and *she*, you may well end up thinking that all other books should do the same.

In this book, we give you a lot of current prices for materials, therapy, tutoring and more. These prices can change over time, so use them as your guide rather than as set-in-stone facts.

We feature a few other conventions to help you work your way through this book:

- *Italic* points out defined terms or emphasises a word.
- **Boldface** text indicates keywords in bulleted lists and the action part of numbered steps.
- `Monofont` highlights web addresses.

When this book was printed, some web addresses may have needed to break across two lines of text. If that happened, rest assured that we haven't put in any extra characters (such as hyphens) to indicate the break. So, when using one of these web addresses, just type in exactly what you see in this book, pretending that the line break doesn't exist.

What You're Not to Read

A lot of books about dyslexia seem to revel in technical jargon. This book doesn't. It gives you the jargon, sparingly, and warns you in advance with the Technical Stuff icon so that you don't have to read a paragraph if you don't want to. Don't let the jargon scare you, though; it's there in case you need to assert yourself or write smart requests, applications and other formal stuff. The Technical Stuff icon also highlights info that's interesting but not crucial to your understanding of dyslexia.

As well as bits of jargon, you're going to see sidebars in this book (they're in the shaded grey boxes). Sidebars offer bonus or additional information that you don't *have* to read but may enjoy all the same.

Foolish Assumptions

Because you're reading this book, we're assuming the following about you:

✔ You want to help a child, or yourself, have a better understanding of dyslexia. You may be the parent of a child or a young adult who's having difficulty reading and may be dyslexic, or you may be a teacher looking for information so that you can help students with dyslexia and their parents. You may even be an adult looking for tips for yourself.

✔ You need plain-talking, down-to-earth guidance about things like your rights and the kinds of strategies that can make your life easier.

✔ You want pointers of how to get things right but not reams of jargon.

How This Book Is Organised

This book has seven parts, all filled to the brim with information about dyslexia.

Part 1: Figuring Out What Dyslexia Is All About

In this part, we establish exactly what dyslexia does and doesn't mean. The 'doesn't' part is important because, as many educators point out, the term dyslexia gets so overused that its meaning can be obscured. We also talk about the causes and types of dyslexia and give you an overview of the symptoms to watch out for at any age.

Part 11: Determining When to Get a Diagnosis

This part looks more closely at the signs of dyslexia. We examine your child's behaviour in the pre-school and school years and show you when and how to get an assessment.

Part III: Exploring Your Options for Schools and Programmes

Your child struggles every day in class, but would he do any better in another class or even another school? How much does private tutoring cost, and are some learning centres better for your child than others? How can you make sure that your child with dyslexia has a good Individual Education Programme (IEP), and what can you do to make schoolwork easier for him? And how can you work effectively with your child's teacher? In this part, we answer your big questions.

Part IV: Taking Part in Your Child's Tuition

Most tuition for dyslexia involves structured multisensory and phonics-based instruction. Not sure what we're talking about? That's fine. This part of the book explains everything in simple, straightforward terms that you can feel completely comfortable with. We also tell you about methods of memorising, visualising and rhyming to help your child read more fluently; show you how to establish a happy reading routine; and give you fun tips to help your child accomplish everyday tasks easily.

Part V: Moving beyond the Childhood Years

Anyone who's been through secondary school in the last few decades has heard (at least a little) about things like Personal Statements, voluntary work and UCAS forms. In this part we tell you what students with dyslexia do to make these kinds of things less formidable during the university application process. We also give you the lowdown on helping your child with dyslexia adjust to the teenage years and show adults with dyslexia how to be more successful in the real world.

Part VI: The Part of Tens

The Part of Tens is where a whole load of useful information gets boiled down to wonderfully easy lists. Here you get ten tools for making life easier for someone with dyslexia and ten dyslexia programmes.

Part VII: Appendixes

In Part VII, we leave you with a battery of tests so that you can determine your child's grasp on phonics skills, and we also include a handy reference guide to a variety of dyslexia resources.

Icons Used in This Book

The following icons highlight noteworthy information throughout the book.

This icon tells you that a piece of advice or an activity is good for adults as well as (or instead of) younger little beings.

You see this icon when we offer information that's really worth hanging on to.

Here's your alert to interesting but non-essential information (such as jargon). Skip ahead or brace yourself!

This icon means we're offering a golden nugget of handy advice, probably discovered at first hand.

Here's something you *don't* want to do. This icon warns you of the landmines that you may encounter.

Where to Go from Here

So you have this copy of *Understanding & Managing Dyslexia For Dummies* in your hands. Although one thing that people with dyslexia certainly are not is 'dummies' – anything but – you can use this book to gain a really good understanding of dyslexia. If you're not sure whether your child needs an assessment for dyslexia, you've come to the right place. Go to Chapter 3 to learn about general indicators of dyslexia, Chapter 4 for specific signs you may see during the nursery and infant school years or Chapter 5 for signs of dyslexia that surface (or don't go away) later in school. Chapter 6 has details on testing.

If your child's already been diagnosed as having dyslexia and is eligible for extra help at school, or a Statement, go to Chapter 8. If you know that your child with dyslexia doesn't qualify for a Statement and you want to know what options are left, go straight ahead to Chapter 9. To get straight into doing your own reading activities, open up at Chapter 13.

Not in that much of a rush? Great! You may enjoy a traditional journey through this book, starting at Chapter 1 and working through. Take your time, and especially mull over points that apply exactly to you. This is your map for guiding your child with dyslexia confidently forward.

Part I

Figuring Out What Dyslexia Is All About

In this part . . .

This book contains a tremendous amount of information, so in this part we help you get off on the right foot with some basic but essential facts. First, you find out what dyslexia really means (and what it doesn't mean). We cover its possible causes and the different forms it takes. Then, when you're up and running, we show you how your child's behaviour may indicate dyslexia, no matter how old he is. Got your water and sensible footwear? Off you go!

Chapter 1

Understanding the Basics of Dyslexia

A quick visit to a bookshop or newsagent can be overwhelming. So many promises, so little time. You may find yourself struggling to decide what topic has the most appeal: 'Sixteen foods to make you younger, happier and sexier', 'Ten minutes to a flat stomach' or 'Sleep yourself slim'. Wouldn't it be nice if this book offered you a similar approach to dyslexia, with topics such as 'Sixteen surefire ways to beat dyslexia', 'Ten minutes to perfect reading and spelling' and 'Bringing up a reader without lifting a finger'?

But in real life, people like to hear the truth. So in this book we give you the plain and simple truth about dyslexia – not the shortcut answers you find in the latest magazines. And everything starts in this chapter with a straightforward outline of what dyslexia really is, a simple sketch of how it shapes your child's life and a lightning tour of the programmes and help you can find in and out of the classroom.

Defining Dyslexia in Plain Terms

Plenty of children struggle with reading. Their parents get extra help for them, and after a few months they catch up. Sometimes the problem disappears suddenly without any intervention at all.

Dyslexia isn't like that. If you're wondering whether your child has reading problems or dyslexia, and what the difference is, here's the simple answer: a child with dyslexia has *enduring* and *unexpected* difficulty with reading and writing. She's bright, you give her loads of extra help, but she just doesn't get it. A boost of extra help doesn't make everything right for her because she needs a different kind of help over a longer time than just a few months. She probably learns to read and write at about age 10, but all through her life she needs to read and reread written text several times before she fully comprehends what she's read. In addition, when she writes important stuff, she needs to complete several drafts.

Watch out: misconceptions about dyslexia abound. Here's what dyslexia isn't:

- ✔ Stupidity
- ✔ Laziness
- ✔ Wilfulness
- ✔ Intentional distractibility

Research about dyslexia provides insight into its possible causes. For instance, it's thought that people with dyslexia use a different part of the brain to people without dyslexia when they read, and they use more of it. Dyslexia also tends to run in families. And some psychologists break dyslexia down into several types, including phonological dyslexia and visual dyslexia.

In Chapter 2, we give you the full story on the definition, causes and types of dyslexia. We also tell you about different conditions related to (and often mistaken for) dyslexia.

Dyslexia shouldn't prevent your child from achieving her goals or dreams. Plenty of professionals are dyslexic. They have strategies and routines that help them achieve high standards. Oh, and your child may like to know that famous people like Tom Cruise and Orlando Bloom (Hollywood actors) and Richard Branson (Chairman of Virgin Group) are just three of the many high-flyers who have dyslexia.

Focusing on the Symptoms of Dyslexia

Here's the thing about dyslexia. One teacher or psychologist may tell you your child lacks 'automaticity of language' or perhaps 'auditory perceptual skills', while another tells you she has 'SpLD' or 'specific learning difficulties', or 'dyslexia'. Some practitioners never use the term 'dyslexia', but psychologists who *do* diagnose it look for a fairly standard set of symptoms. Different symptoms reveal themselves at different ages.

The kinds of behaviours that indicate dyslexia in a pre-school child include the following:

- ✔ Starts to speak late (no actual speech until after age 2)
- ✔ Says muddled-up words (*aminal* for *animal* or *gabrage* for *garbage*)
- ✔ Can't tell you rhyming words (*cat/hat*)
- ✔ Can't tell the difference between letters and other symbols or squiggles

The kinds of behaviours that indicate dyslexia in a school-age child include the following:

- ✔ Writes words with letters in the wrong places, like *saw* instead of *was* and *vawe* instead of *wave* (called *transposing* letters)
- ✔ Reverses letters and numbers (especially *b* and *d*, *p* and *q*, and *3* and *5*)
- ✔ Writes so that her words are barely legible (letters are badly formed and the wrong size)
- ✔ Adds or leaves out small words when reading (which can totally change the meaning of the text)
- ✔ Has trouble retelling a story in the correct order of events

For now, the main thing to keep in mind is that dyslexia, unless it runs in your family, can hit you like a shot out of the blue. Your child seems fine or even advanced intellectually, so that you just don't expect her to stumble with reading and writing. That stumble, from which your child seems unable to recover, is what dyslexia typically looks like.

In Chapter 3, we give you an overview of dyslexia symptoms at any age. We focus on symptoms in pre-school children and what to do about them in Chapter 4, and on symptoms in school-age kids and how to take action in Chapter 5.

Keep in mind that undiagnosed teenagers and adults also show a few common signs of dyslexia, including an avoidance of reading and plenty of diversionary tactics for steering clear of handwriting. See Chapter 3 for details.

Deciding When to Have Your Child Tested

If you're worried that your child isn't getting the hang of reading, chances are that your fears are well founded. Seeking professional advice is better than wasting precious months wondering whether your concerns are valid. If your child does have dyslexia, or any other learning difficulty, the sooner you investigate the reason for this, the better.

That said, you can't whisk your child off to a psychologist for a dyslexia assessment much before she turns 5 because dyslexia's mostly about how well she reads and writes. When she starts school and struggles with the alphabet, speech sounds and text, that's the time to have her assessed quickly so that you can quickly start the intervention that can help her most.

If you do take your child for formal assessment, the tests that your child can undergo (depending on her age) include the following:

- ✔ Language tests
- ✔ Early screening tests
- ✔ IQ tests
- ✔ Performance tests
- ✔ A combination of attainment/ability and diagnostic tests

The person who usually runs a full assessment for dyslexia is a psychologist. Your local education authority (LA) employs an educational psychologist. Your child's assessment referral can come from the school or from you as a parent (called a *parental statutory assessment*). If you want an outside or second opinion, you can ask a private educational psychologist to assess your child. The British Psychological Society (www.bps.org.uk) can give you details of chartered psychologists in your area. In addition, Dyslexia Action (www.dyslexiaaction.org.uk) and Helen Arkell Centres (www.arkell centre.org.uk) have banks of chartered psychologists who can provide assessments.

For full details on testing, including how to prepare your child for an assessment and what to do with the results, check out Chapter 6.

Exploring Different Schools and Programmes for Your Child

Of course you want the best possible education for your child, but finding the best school for her becomes even more important after she's diagnosed as having dyslexia or if you think she doesn't get appropriate help from the school she's in. In Chapter 7, we help you figure out whether your child's current school is doing a good job and what kinds of help other schools may offer. We provide you with a list of questions to consider as you decide what kind of school you want your child to attend. We also introduce you to the services and staff members you find in the state sector and give you the low-down on the following forms of alternative schooling:

- ✔ Private schools with provisions for dyslexia
- ✔ Montessori schools
- ✔ Steiner (Waldorf) schools
- ✔ Special schools for children with dyslexia
- ✔ Home schooling

Under the 1993 Education Act and the Special Educational Needs Code of Practice, local authorities and schools must cater for children with special educational needs (SEN), including children with dyslexia. In Chapter 8 we give you the full story about SEN Statements, including the fine print on the document, and how to prepare for an appeal if you're unsuccessful in acquiring a Statement. This preparation includes gathering important documents and making sure that you have the correct support to guide you, such as Parent Partnership. We also cover the acts that govern SEN (the main one is the Education Act of 1993) and let you know your child's rights under these acts.

You have the legal right to a Statement if your child is found to have a learning disability that falls within the criteria that the LA set. Only a small number of children have severe enough needs to receive a Statement; the government recommends Statements for only 2 out of every 100 children. A Statement can also be issued for a child at a private school.

What if your child doesn't receive a Statement? Don't worry. In Chapter 9 we tell you how to secure help without one. In school, you can stay in close contact with your child's teacher and enrol your child in homework clubs, tutoring programmes and extra-curricular activities that make her feel confident. Outside school, you have several options for strengthening your child's reading abilities:

- ✔ Dyslexia centres
- ✔ Specialist dyslexia tutors
- ✔ Private, individual tutors
- ✔ General learning centres

Of course, you can also offer your assistance at home by helping your child manage her homework and setting her up with plenty of additional resources (including those we mention in Chapter 19).

Whether or not your child has a Statement, sometimes you may feel like you have absolutely no control over what your child does in class. The teacher assigns work, your child struggles with it and the process moves on like an avalanche you can't avert or escape. Well, we can help! You really *can* influence what happens to your child in school; you just need to know how.

In Chapter 10, we tell you how to team up with your child's teacher by having regular conferences, making all the accommodations you want seem beneficial to everyone and keeping a paper trail so that your nice manner has some power behind it.

Sounds easy? Well, maybe you've been lucky. At some point in your child's schooling you may find yourself worrying that your child's discovering more about frustration than anything else, and that's where this book comes in *really* handy. In these pages, you get step-by-step guidance for avoiding disputes with teachers and pressing your point reasonably, and you get places to go if you find yourself locked in combat anyway.

Helping Your Child with Activities at Home

You've probably heard advice that tells you to help your child with dyslexia at home by doing the following:

- Reading a lot of books with her
- Doing a lot of hands-on activities with her
- Telling her all the time how terrific she is

That advice is good. But it's a bit, well, obvious. And besides, it's vague. What *kinds* of books should she read? Should you think up your *own* stimulating activities (in between cooking meals, taking her to sports practice and, oh yes, going to work)? And what if your child knows you're telling her she's great simply because the parenting books tell you to say so? What do you do then?

In Part IV of this book, you get specific, practical advice on the following ways to take part in your child's individual programme:

- You can use great memorising, visualising and rhyming tricks to help your child grasp words fast. We cover these methods in Chapter 11, along with a list of 220 common sight words that appear frequently in all written text.
- A knowledge of phonics is crucial to reading effectively. In Chapter 12, we provide you with plenty of activities that help your child get the hang of sounding out words.
- Practice makes perfect, especially in reading. In Chapter 13, we give a variety of reading methods you can use with your child, including

setting up a reading routine, selecting the right books and handling your child's reading errors kindly.

✔ *Multisensory* is a buzzword in the world of dyslexia, but what exactly does that mean? In a nutshell, *multisensory* means 'using more than one sense – visual, auditory and kinaesthetic – together to do something'.

In Chapter 14 we explain the benefits of doing multisensory activities as part of your child's education.

✔ Even everyday activities such as staying organised, telling the time and following instructions can be difficult for a child with dyslexia. In Chapter 15, we show you how to help your child handle everyday tasks with ease and build her confidence, giving you simple and effective strategies to help that won't cost you a fortune.

Something especially great is that you get road-tested materials in these chapters. Instead of impractical suggestions and lists of books as long as your arm – books that the author may or may not have read – you get practical ideas and a manageable quota of recommendations that we've personally tested or had tested by other parents and teachers. How's that for *really* useful? Get your hands on the best books and kits around and, if your child's teacher hasn't seen them yet, give him the info!

Helping your child with dyslexia with reading and other activities at home has multiple benefits. The following are just a few.

✔ Your child may not start to find reading easy until about age 10. But she's smart and good at covering up, so the rest of the world may think that she's doing okay. That's where your help at home really counts. You can get a first-hand, close-up view of what's going on and inform the teacher. If you don't inform the teacher, and especially if your child can sound out simple words and knows a few sight words, her difficulties may not show up in school until much later (when all of a sudden pretty much everyone else but your child reads fluently).

✔ When your child goes through a hear-see-say-do routine (which we explain in Chapter 14) with new concepts, they stick in her mind better than when she does any one of those things on its own. The fancy name for this is *multisensory learning*, a buzzword in dyslexia circles. You can make learning multisensory at home simply by getting your child into useful habits such as saying out loud things she wants to remember and words she's copying down.

✔ Social and sporting interests may be especially important for your child with dyslexia because they may give her a chance to excel and be popular. You can help at home by establishing a schedule that's strict enough for homework to get done and flexible enough to cope with football finals and the occasional McDonald's.

Watching Your Child with Dyslexia Grow

When our children were little, we thought other people's bigger children were, well, big. They looked capable and self-sufficient. How wrong was that! The children in both our families are now older, and they need just as much help from us as they ever did – and, in many ways, more.

When your child's young, the issues you face as a parent can seem easy – how to divide a lump of Play-Doh among her friends and stop them from eating it, for example. As children get older, things get trickier. Should you force your shy child into a sports team for her own good and what should you do, if anything, about that heinous other child who's calling your daughter hurtful names?

Your child with dyslexia needs your help long after she stops eating Play-Doh. She has subject choices to make, examinations to take and social events to attend. She needs your guidance, and later, of course, she needs you gradually to hand the reins over to her. In Part V of this book, you get practical advice for almost everything. And if we have no idea about something, like where your child with dyslexia should study anthropology, we direct you to people who probably do know.

Chapter 16 is all about teenagers with dyslexia. We tell you how to help her foster her independence, learn to drive, handle school challenges and develop essential work skills.

In Chapter 17, we tell you about getting your child with dyslexia into university and how to apply for the Disabled Students' Allowance. You find out about writing a great Personal Statement for the UCAS form, researching the best universities and colleges and more.

Chapter 18 is where we deal with the challenges that adults with dyslexia face. We tell you about great techniques for adults and the rights you have as an adult with dyslexia in the working world.

Everything's here, so what are you waiting for?

Chapter 2

Pinpointing What Dyslexia Is (And Isn't)

In This Chapter

▶ Describing and defining dyslexia

▶ Delving into the causes of dyslexia

▶ Looking at dyslexia by type

▶ Comparing dyslexia to other disorders

Researchers have been studying dyslexia for years. They've found that dyslexia is almost certainly a brain issue, and they know how it shows itself in your child's behaviour. This chapter gives you a detailed picture of what dyslexia means in practical terms, banishes misconceptions about it, checks out its causes and compares it to similar conditions.

Understanding the Real Meaning of 'Dyslexia'

In the following sections, we provide a straightforward definition of dyslexia, clear up misconceptions about it and explain dyslexia's classification as a learning disability.

Looking at the straight facts

Dyslexia has an easy, literal meaning: trouble with words. Your child has trouble with any combination of reading, writing and spelling and perhaps with speaking and pronunciation as well. Children with dyslexia can be bright – parents read to them and they have good teachers, but unexpectedly they just don't get it.

The word *dyslexia* has Latin and Greek roots. The 'dys' part is Latin for 'difficulty' and 'lexis' is Greek for 'word.'

Your child may have other difficulties too. He may have trouble understanding directional instructions (left/right and up/down), remembering certain maths facts (sequences of numbers and multiplication tables) and recalling words when he's speaking. And for you, these difficulties may all come as a bolt out of the blue!

That's our in-a-nutshell description of dyslexia. Following are a few more key points about the nature of dyslexia:

- Dyslexia is a disorder that mainly affects your child's ability to read and write. A child with dyslexia typically has trouble recognising words, sounding them out and spelling them.

- A child with dyslexia often lacks other important language skills. He may have trouble recalling a sequence of spoken words or instructions and remembering words that he wants to use.

- Dyslexic people lack the ability to discriminate sounds within a word (called *phonological processing*).

- Dyslexia is a lifelong condition, but with skilled teaching, your child can learn to read (albeit sometimes later than other children) and minimise the impact that dyslexia has on his life.

- The exact cause of dyslexia is still not completely clear, but studies show definite brain differences between people with dyslexia and people without dyslexia. See 'Weighing up brain research' later in this chapter for more details.

- Dyslexia can affect your child's self-image. A child with dyslexia can end up feeling different and uncomfortable in the learning situation, 'thick' and less capable than he is, so your insight and support are especially important.

You can receive plenty of additional basic information about dyslexia from the organisations we list in Appendix B.

Moving away from common misconceptions

Children with dyslexia must learn to overcome, or at least get around, their problems, which includes learning about not just their own limitations and strengths but the attitudes and ignorance of people around them. Of course doing so is hard – at times it can be very hard – but if your child knows the devil he's dealing with, he has every chance of laying the problems to rest.

Make sure that your child understands that dyslexia is a brain issue as well as a learning issue. (Young children can understand if you tell them, for example, that a few of their brain wires take different paths than other people's.) This disability makes reading, writing, spelling and sometimes doing other things difficult, like telling left from right and retrieving words. (See 'Investigating the Causes of Dyslexia' later in this chapter for more details.)

But dyslexia *isn't* plenty of other things that people who don't know any better believe it to be. It's not anything to do with being:

- ✔ Distracted
- ✔ Lazy
- ✔ Slow
- ✔ Stupid
- ✔ Wilful

Indeed plenty of evidence demonstrates advantages in being dyslexic. People with dyslexia are often more creative and able to do things practically than other people and are usually good at problem solving. So you can see dyslexia as just another problem to solve.

And if your child's certain of what dyslexia is and isn't, he can let other people know too!

Classifying dyslexia as a 'learning disability'

Dyslexia is a *specific learning disability* (SpLD). The 'specific' part tells you that dyslexia specifically affects certain aspects of learning (in the case of dyslexia, reading and writing). Other specific learning disabilities include speech and articulation disorders, auditory processing disorders, non-verbal learning disability, dyscalculia (which affects maths), dysgraphia (which affects writing) and dyspraxia (which used to be called *clumsy child syndrome*), all of which can coexist with dyslexia.

The British Dyslexia Association (BDA) calls dyslexia a specific learning disability, and many schools talk *only* about a 'specific learning disability' (SpLD), not dyslexia. Why? Many local education authorities currently use the term SpLD in their documentation, so teachers in turn use it. You may find yourself in a strange situation: an independent psychologist tells you that your child has dyslexia, but all through the school system, you talk only of SpLD.

You probably need to use the term SpLD in school, but that doesn't mean you always have to use it. Maybe you don't like the 'disability' label. Maybe you feel that 'dyslexia' carries less of a stigma. Maybe you decide that when you're in your child's school, you talk about his 'specific learning disability' to keep people happy, but to keep yourself and your child happy, you use 'dyslexia' everywhere else. The most important thing is to recognise your child's own mix of ability and difficulty and then you can tell other people about it more easily.

The following bullet list covers some pros of using both terms:

- ✔ Teachers generally use the term SpLD.

- ✔ Most local education authorities use SpLD.

- ✔ Most specialists use SpLD.

- ✔ 'Dyslexia' can be like a designer-label learning condition; people think it's interesting and don't equate it with 'thick'.

- ✔ 'Dyslexia' is specific; it delineates your child from kids who are poor readers, writers or spellers for other reasons.

Investigating the Causes of Dyslexia

Current studies suggest that about 20 per cent of the population have a reading disability, and of those, most have dyslexia. Dyslexia occurs in people of all races, backgrounds and intellectual levels. In the next sections, we walk you, step by step, through insights that research and experience provide into the causes of dyslexia.

Weighing up brain research

The British Dyslexia Association (BDA) makes no bones about the origins of dyslexia. Umpteen studies show it and the BDA says it outright: dyslexia is neurological in origin.

So there you have it. Just about every expert now agrees that even though brain mapping is a relatively new scientific development, and even though you can't say how much of a person's brain map is a result of heredity and how much a product of environment, brain differences definitely show up between people with dyslexia and people without dyslexia.

Here's what the terrain looks like on a person with dyslexia's brain map:

✔ When a person with dyslexia reads, parts of his right brain hemisphere get really active, whereas when a fluent reader reads, he uses mostly his left hemisphere. The left side of a person's brain is the side all wired up for language. When a person with dyslexia reads, he uses the less efficient (for reading) right side of his brain, so he works harder at reading than a person without dyslexia does and takes a lot longer to read.

Researchers aren't sure yet of the neurological and chemical specifics of why this happens, but they know brain damage isn't involved. A person with dyslexia's brain isn't missing anything, it just works in a different way than that of a person without dyslexia. There may even be, as some people argue, a good reason for this. Many people say that people with dyslexia have accentuated spatial skills, such as the 'gift' of being able to see things in three dimensions (people normally see things in two dimensions). The high scores that people with dyslexia have achieved in tests of non-verbal ability can demonstrate this. Some people with dyslexia have made achievements in life perhaps because of their dyslexia and not despite it.

✔ When a person with dyslexia improves his reading skills (by being instructed in phonologic activities – see Chapter 12 for more details), his brain map starts to look more like that of a person without dyslexia.

✔ Not only do people with dyslexia use a different part of the brain when they read than people without, but they use more of it. In the October 1999 issue of the *American Journal of Neuroradiology,* researchers reported that when people with and without dyslexia performed the same oral language activities, those with dyslexia used nearly five times as much brain area. In effect, their brains had to work five times harder. As a result adults and children with dyslexia can get very tired by the end of the school or working day and remembering this is important. It may explain why children can be very resistant to doing homework when they've been at school all day.

Getting into genetics

A couple of things about the cause of dyslexia are clear:

✔ Dyslexia runs in families.

✔ People with dyslexia have a different kind of brain map than people without dyslexia (see 'Weighing up brain research', earlier in this chapter).

Researchers aren't so clear whether you inherit a dyslexic brain or your brain develops that way as a result of your not being able to read. This is a tricky area, all the more so because the brain's such a complex organ.

Famous people with dyslexia

Scores of talented, and of course perseverant, people have overcome dyslexia. They've achieved all kinds of things, including becoming famous writers! Here are just a few dyslexics who sidestepped the obstacles and became super-successful.

Inventors and scientists

✔ **Thomas Edison:** American. Invented the light bulb. Discovered the 'Edison effect', which led to the invention of the radio. Also held more than 1,000 patents for devices used in other inventions.

✔ **Albert Einstein:** Originally German but lived in Switzerland, Britain and the United States. Developed special and general theories of relativity and in 1921 received the Nobel Prize for Physics.

Business moguls

✔ **Steve Jobs:** Founder of Apple Computer. CEO of Apple and Pixar, the Academy Award-winning animation studio.

✔ **Richard Branson:** Entrepreneur. Published a magazine called *Student* at age 15 and shortly after in the 1970s established Virgin Records. Expanded his global empire to include an airline, trains, media – even wedding dresses. The Virgin brand currently embraces more than 360 companies and Branson is the 236th richest man in the world according to *Forbes.*

Politicians

✔ **Winston Churchill:** British prime minister. Led the country to victory through the Second World War.

✔ **John F. Kennedy:** Youngest US president ever elected. Served exactly 1,000 days before being assassinated.

Artists

✔ **Leonardo da Vinci:** Italian painter who painted in a realistic style. Famous also for being a gifted sculptor, inventor, mathematician, scientist and architect. Painted the *Mona Lisa.*

✔ **Pablo Picasso:** Spanish painter famous for using different styles like expressionism and cubism. Painted *The Three Dancers.*

Movies and music

✔ **John Lennon:** Famous as one of the 'Fab Four' and a solo artist. Just two of his songs with the Beatles are 'Strawberry Fields Forever' and 'All You Need Is Love'. Killed in New York in 1980.

✔ **Steven Spielberg:** Produced *E.T., Jaws, Jurassic Park* and many other brilliant movies.

Sports stars

✔ **Muhammad Ali:** Olympic light heavyweight boxing champion.

✔ **Jackie Stewart:** Scottish former racing driver. Competed in Formula One between 1965 and 1973, winning three World Drivers' Championships. Knighted in 2001.

Writers

✔ **Lewis Carroll:** British author of *Alice's Adventures in Wonderland* and *Through the Looking Glass.* Real name Charles Lutwidge Dodgson, lectured in maths at Oxford University.

✔ **Ernest Hemingway:** Often called the most influential American writer of the 20th century. Wrote *For Whom the Bell Tolls* and *A Farewell to Arms.* Shot himself after battling depression.

That said, most experts believe dyslexia has a genetic basis. The race is on to establish exactly which gene or genes are involved. Look out for more research on this topic, because figuring out the origins of dyslexia is clearly a hard nut to crack.

A couple of research teams both claim to have found a single dyslexia gene:

✔ In a 1999 issue of the *British Journal of Medical Genetics*, a team of researchers said they were first to discover a single dyslexia gene. They expressed hope that when their research is more developed, it will lead to children with a family history of dyslexia being genetically tested when they start school. You can read more at `http://news.bbc.co.uk/1/hi/health/440261.stm`.

✔ A gene called 'KIAA0319,' which is likely to be one of the causes of dyslexia in children, was discovered in Wales in 2005. Researchers at Cardiff University said, 'This is a major breakthrough and the first study to identify one gene which contributes to susceptibility to the common form of dyslexia.' You can read more about this study at `www.cardiff.ac.uk/newsevents/11554.html`.

To really keep your finger on the pulse of current research, visit Dyslexia Teacher at `www.dyslexia-teacher.co.uk` or the Dyslexia Research Trust that doctors John Stein and Sue Fowler have set up at Oxford University, at `www.dyslexic.org.uk`.

Breaking Dyslexia Down into Different Types

Getting people to classify your child as dyslexic can be hard enough, but sometimes you may face just the opposite problem. You may meet a psychologist or therapist who tells you not only that your child has dyslexia (which you're only beginning to get a good understanding of) but that he also has one of many kinds of dyslexia!

Just so you're one step ahead, here are the subtypes of dyslexia:

✔ **Phonological dyslexia:** Also called *dysphonetic* or *auditory dyslexia* or *dysphonesia*, this kind of dyslexia is the most common. If your child has phonological dyslexia, he has trouble identifying *phonemes* (sounds within words) and matching letters to sounds. He makes wild guesses and struggles to read nonsense words, and his spelling might be all over the place and may include impossible letter combinations like 'sfr'.

Most tests for dyslexia ask your child at some point to read nonsense words like *sluft* and *prenck*. That's so your child can't guess but has to sound the letters out. This particular exercise can single out whether a child has phonological dyslexia. (Take a look at Chapter 6 for more info about testing.)

✔ **Visual dyslexia:** This kind of dyslexia is also called *dyseidetic* or *surface dyslexia* or *dyseidesia*. If your child has visual dyslexia, he can sound out words, but has trouble with words that don't sound out regularly (such as *who* and *any*) and that he therefore has to learn largely by sight. He may read very slowly and spell phonetically (throo, skayt, dorter) without registering that the appearance of his words is wrong. To check for visual dyslexia, a psychologist asks your child to read a load of phonetically regular words (like *think*, *wishing* and *testing*) and irregular words (like *who*, *they* and *enough*) to check for obvious disparities in his reading of each kind. Visual dyslexia is not the same as visual stress (or *scotopic sensitivity syndrome*) where the letters can jump about on the page. Visual stress needs to be investigated by a specialist optometrist who can recommend coloured lenses or overlays.

✔ **Mixed dyslexia:** Also called *dysphoneidetic dyslexia*. This term refers to a combination of phonological and visual dyslexia. People with mixed dyslexia tend to have severe deficits in reading as well as cognitive functions such as visual motor integration, visual perception and working memory. Working memory (or short-term memory) affects all types of dyslexia and assessors use poor memory as an indicator of dyslexia.

✔ **Dysnomia:** Also called *semantic dyslexia*, *anomia* or *naming-speed deficits*. When psychologists describe your child with any of these terms, this means he has trouble finding his words. He can't always remember the right word, even though he knew it before, and instead he says 'the thingy' or another less appropriate or sometimes wholly inappropriate word.

Psychologists test your child for dysnomia by giving him a rapid automatic naming test. That's a fancy way of saying that they flash pictures of common objects (and colours, numbers and letters) at him and see how fast he names them, if at all.

✔ **Double deficit:** This term indicates that your child has phonological dyslexia *and* dysnomia. People with either type don't like to be asked to read out loud in front of others – although they may have been able to figure out a word they may be uncertain of how to pronounce it. Anyone dealing with a child with dyslexia should be aware of this.

✔ **Severe and mild dyslexia or dyslexic symptoms:** One last thing to remember about dyslexia is that whatever kind of dyslexia your child has, he can have it to a greater or lesser extent. And if he has mild dyslexia or only a few dyslexic symptoms, he may have difficulty getting additional help at school, even though it can affect him quite badly. (A psychologist can establish the extent of your child's dyslexia.) In Chapters 6 and 8, we go into detail about who does and doesn't qualify for extra – meaning over and above the usual – help at school.

Looking at Other 'Dys' Conditions Related to Dyslexia

Just when you thought we must've exhausted every possible long-winded term, here are a few more! Don't worry, the following section's brief, but these conditions are worth knowing a little about. They're conditions that are dyslexia-like but not quite dyslexia, if that makes any sense. The simplest way to introduce them is to say that the British Dyslexia Association calls them 'related disorders', and that's good enough for us!

Dysgraphia: Difficulty with writing

Dysgraphia means difficulty with handwriting, but – guess what? – it comes in three different types:

- ✔ **Dyslexic dysgraphia:** Your child's writing is often messy and illegible, especially when the text is complex. He often mixes lower and upper cases and doesn't use punctuation. He may hold pens and pencils with an unusual or awkward grip. Your child also does badly on oral spelling (spelling out loud), but can draw and copy written text relatively well and performs fine motor skills at normal speed. (Psychologists sometimes measure fine motor speed by asking your child to finger-tap.)

- ✔ **Motor dysgraphia:** Your child's writing is often messy or illegible. His copied text may be illegible too, and his spelling is probably erratic. His oral spelling is normal, but his drawing is usually problematic. His finger-tapping speed is abnormal. He gets tired when writing and usually holds pens awkwardly. Motor dysgraphia is due to poor muscle tone.

- ✔ **Spatial dysgraphia:** Your child's writing is illegible and so is his copied text. His oral spelling is normal. His drawing is terrible, but his finger-tapping speed is normal.

Psychologists usually classify dysgraphia as a condition separate from dyslexia but dyslexia often accompanies it. A child with dysgraphia has pronounced and enduring problems with writing. His writing is messy all the time, and without expert help over several months, it stays that way.

I've come across many children with dysgraphia who use a keyboard well because they're still faster on a keyboard than with handwriting. For some children with poor muscle tone, using voice-activated software may work well.

Dyscalculia: Difficulty with maths

Many dyslexics struggle with certain kinds of maths, a condition called *dyscalculia*. Dyscalculia is conspicuous because your child might manage perfectly fine with arithmetical tasks that don't require remembering strings of numbers. However, he struggles with:

- Copying maths problems
- Counting accurately
- Jotting down the wrong numbers in calculations
- Memorising maths facts
- Retaining maths vocabulary and/or concepts
- Reversing numbers

Many dyslexic children without dyscalculia have problems with maths. A diagnosis of dyscalculia is fairly rare, so a psychologist's diagnosis is essential.

Dyspraxia: Difficulty with motor skills

Dyspraxia used to go by the name 'clumsy child syndrome'. If your child has dyspraxia, he has trouble planning and coordinating his body movements and struggles with fine motor tasks like writing, buttoning his clothes and tying his shoelaces. He may have difficulty coordinating his facial muscles to produce sounds, so his speech may be garbled. His large motor coordination may be weak too, so he's conspicuously clumsy and weak at sports. The Dyspraxia Foundation has a useful checklist of symptoms and information about local support groups, which you can find on its website (www. dyspraxiafoundation.org.uk).

Researchers believe that dyspraxia, like dyslexia, isn't a result of brain damage but does start in your child's brain. They think that immature neuron development may be the culprit and are pretty certain that dyspraxia can't be cured (also like dyslexia).

Comparing Dyslexia to ADD and ADHD

Many children who have dyslexia have other conditions too. If your child has Attention Deficit Disorder (ADD) or Attention Deficit Hyperactivity Disorder

(ADHD), his main problem is with concentration and paying attention. He struggles to focus and to attend to what he's doing or who's speaking to him. He's often restless and fidgety and is likely to wander off when you talk to him. He's hard to keep on track in class and, with his unsettling behaviour, may stir up other children. The child who has ADHD and who exhibits signs of hyperactivity may well get more help than the child who has ADD and whose needs are less obvious.

The causes of ADD and ADHD aren't fully understood, and they affect some people more severely than others. The following sections give you the full story on these two conditions (Chapter 3 goes into more detail on the symptoms of dyslexia). If you want to find out more information on the difference between the two conditions, check out the Hyperactive Children's Support Group website at www.hacsg.org.uk.

Doctors or paediatricians look for more than just the following lists of symptoms. They look at your child's age, pattern of symptoms and degree of symptomatic behaviour. They look at how long symptoms have persisted. The following is only a rough guide. Contact your GP for a closer and clearer picture and ask for a referral to an appropriate specialist. You can also check out *AD/HD For Dummies* by Jeff Strong and Michael O. Flanagan (Wiley) or contact the National Attention Deficit Disorder Information and Support Service (ADDISS) on 020 8952 2800 or www.addiss.co.uk.

Only a child or adolescent psychiatrist, a paediatrician or paediatric neurologist or a GP can give your child a diagnosis of ADD or ADHD. Often, other professionals such as psychologists, speech therapists, teachers and health visitors contribute their observations to an ADD or ADHD diagnosis. These conditions are notoriously hard to pin down because all children display some of their characteristics sometimes, and a bored child or a child with dyslexia can have pretty much all the same symptoms. Many experts warn about over-diagnosing ADD and ADHD, so before you accept a diagnosis be sure that your child is inattentive even when he really loves what he's doing and hyperactive even when he's in a big space with fun activities on hand.

The www.adders.org website offers more information about the symptoms to look out for along with details of current research and contact details for local support groups.

And remember: doctors identify some children as having the combined type of ADHD, which means they have features of both inattention *and* hyperactivity-impulsivity.

Examining ADD

The Royal College of Psychiatrists has a complex formula for assessing your child, but its starting symptoms for Inattention ADHD or ADD are:

✔ Your child often misses details and makes careless mistakes in schoolwork.

✔ Your child has trouble staying on task.

✔ Your child often doesn't seem to listen to you even when you speak directly to him.

✔ Your child often fails to follow your instructions or finish tasks that he starts (and not because he's defiant or hasn't understood).

✔ Your child has trouble organising himself.

✔ Your child doesn't want to start tasks that he knows require concentration over time (like homework!).

✔ Your child often loses things (for example, he usually can't find school assignments, pencils or books).

✔ Most sounds, like small noises and cars passing outside a window, distract your child.

✔ Your child is generally forgetful.

Checking out ADHD

If your child has ADHD, he has ADD symptoms with some hyperactivity thrown in too. He's always restless. He's hyper. He's very hard to manage in a confined, controlled space like, oh yes, the classroom! To diagnose ADHD, the Royal College of Psychiatrists starts by looking for symptoms of hyperactivity and impulsivity.

✔ **Hyperactivity:**

- Your child fidgets. He flicks his fingers, waves his feet and squirms in his seat.

- Your child finds plenty of reasons for leaving his seat because to stay in it feels horribly hard.

- Your child runs when he really should be walking and climbs all over furniture when he's supposed to be 'behaving'.

- Your child has trouble with quiet play.

- Kind people describe your child as a 'live wire'.

- Your child generally talks, and talks and talks!

✔ **Impulsivity:**

- Your child has trouble waiting for his turn to talk. He often blurts out his answer because he just can't hold it in.

- Your child has trouble waiting for his turn in pretty much every situation.

- Your child is always interrupting or pushing in.

Names, names, names

When you talk to other parents whose children have problems in class, you're likely to hear about all kinds of disabilities, big and small, that you never knew existed. A lot of them may get confused with or coexist with dyslexia. Here are just a few of those numerous names:

✔ **Non-verbal Learning Disability (NLD):** Here's a disability that looks like the opposite of dyslexia! Your child has early speech, learns to read early and is excellent at spelling. He's conspicuously weak in motor and social skills and finds understanding what he reads hard. Why do you need to know about NLD when it's nothing like dyslexia? Because *some* of the symptoms can look the same. A child with NLD may, for example, have poor reading comprehension and awful handwriting!

✔ **Asperger Syndrome:** To all intents and purposes, this syndrome is a mild form of autism. A child with Asperger Syndrome may have symptoms of dyslexia, such as not understanding what he reads.

✔ **Semantic Pragmatic Disorder (SPD):** *Semantic* means meaning and *pragmatic* means being practical. Put them together and you have someone who doesn't understand everyday social and practical interactions. This disorder is like mild autism and is first identified as a conspicuous delay in speech and language development. So you can mistake it for dyslexia.

✔ **Hyperlexia:** This child is fascinated, at an early age, with letters, numbers and patterns. He learns to read, write and compute very early and looks like a genius. Unfortunately, although he may appear to have excellent reading skills, he has no understanding of what he's read. He's conspicuously weak in the areas of social interaction and oral language, and even though his reading and writing are advanced, he can be confused with a person with dyslexia because some people with dyslexia learn to read but struggle later on with moving to higher reading levels and writing and spelling.

With NLD, Asperger Syndrome and SPD, the child may take language literally and find it hard to 'read between the lines' from conversation or textually.

Chapter 3

Being Alert to Symptoms of Dyslexia at Any Age

. . . .

. . . .

*B*efore Katrina's first child was born, she vividly remembers buying every book on babies and childcare. Like any new parent, she was anxious that she would miss the vital signs that told her whether her baby had any serious disease. (She still has the dog-eared, credit-card-size checklist she used to carry in her purse that indicated whether a rash was an allergy or something more sinister like meningitis.) Luckily neither of her children succumbed to anything even vaguely life threatening – but at least she was prepared!

Experts often refer to dyslexia as a 'hidden disability' because it has no visible signs – no rashes, no headaches. However, you still need to be vigilant for symptoms of dyslexia. You need to focus on what's important and refer to a checklist so you don't forget anything.

In this chapter, we show you why you should look for signs of dyslexia at the first hint of reading trouble, and we give you details on the exact signs to look for at any age.

Understanding Why Looking for Signs Is Important

Educators agree that parents being involved with developing their children's reading (literacy) skills from an early age is a great idea and that this involvement is especially important when a child seems to be making a slow start. Many organisations such as the British Dyslexia Association (www.bdadyslexia.org.uk) or Dyslexia Action (www.dyslexiaaction.org.uk) have useful information on their websites about spotting the signs of dyslexia. If you notice the slightest hint that your child is struggling with reading, learning basic skills or shows a combination of other symptoms from their checklists, you must continue to look for signs that may indicate a more serious problem. The following sections explain why.

From the moment you notice your child behaving in ways that you think may possibly be symptomatic of dyslexia, jot them down. Later you may need to give a chronology of your observational information (especially to the educational psychologist who assesses your child – turn to Chapter 6 for assessment details), and this way you don't forget anything.

Appreciating that dyslexia is unexpected

Here's one important reason why you need to look for signs of dyslexia: dyslexia may be unexpected. Suppose that your child is bright, has a good vocabulary and, unless she's gone through a lot of failure, is often willing to try new activities. She's had all the opportunities you were able to put her way. She hasn't had any particular traumas. Despite all this, she just doesn't get reading and writing. You may be taken by surprise, shocked and horrified. You see other children, plenty of whom have barely any of the advantages your child has, surge forward. You see them start to read or write pretty easily and quickly progress to chapter books. But *your* child stays put. That's what dyslexia looks like – just what you really didn't expect.

But that's not all. Your child may show dyslexic symptoms late in her schooling. She's bright and resilient and picks up basic early reading skills, but later on, her rudimentary skills can't keep pace with the harder work she's given. Now you get the really big surprise. Your older child may have only a basic grasp of phonics and only a small repertoire of words she recognises instantly, and when she reads lengthy text, she has barely any comprehension. She's dyslexic, and up to now no one's picked it up.

When dyslexia shows up in older kids and even adults, it may be unexpected – not because the symptoms weren't always there, but because your child's strengths and coping strategies carried her through school and made her weaknesses virtually invisible.

Dyslexia shows itself in unique ways: each child has her own set of symptoms (from all the possibilities) and each symptom can vary in severity. Look out for an uneven pattern of skills and weaknesses. She may be really good at some things but really struggle at others. Even siblings with dyslexia may have very different strengths and weaknesses in academic performance, just as they do in other areas.

Being savvy about screening tests and what one teacher can do

If your child struggles with reading and writing, looking for signs of dyslexia is important because you may be the only one to spot or at least probe into them. 'But that's the school's job,' we hear you say. Well, yes and no. Your child does undergo baseline assessments when she first enters full time education. But suppose that your child:

- ✔ Does OK in initial baseline tests but starts struggling later on.
- ✔ Scrapes through the tests even though she struggles in class.
- ✔ Does fine on what the tests measure but has trouble with other skills that aren't tested.

All these things can happen, so keeping a close watch is in your child's best interests. And don't forget that teachers handle struggling kids in different ways too. Your child may have a terrific teacher who's sensitive to her difficulties and confident enough to speak up about them, but what if your child's teacher:

- ✔ Mistakes your child's problems as being within the acceptable range.
- ✔ Is busy keeping every child in line and can't give your child much attention.
- ✔ Believes that dyslexia doesn't exist (sounds far-fetched but it happens!).
- ✔ Believes (mistakenly!) that your child really can catch up in time.
- ✔ Believes that your child is either not capable or is being lazy.

You definitely need to monitor your child's progress (or lack of it) and jot down what you see. You can then go to the teacher with your observations in hand and ask for help. And if help doesn't seem to materialise, go right back and ask again. If you can't work things out with the teacher, see the SENCO (special educational needs coordinator) and the head teacher. After that, your next stop is your local education authority.

If your child isn't 'getting it', you're probably right to be concerned. But you don't sound convincing to the teacher if you just say, 'She isn't getting it.' You need to identify a cluster of specific weaknesses, because that's what the professionals do. Educational psychologists who assess children for dyslexia refer to a list of symptoms. If your child shows a cluster of them, she may be dyslexic and need to take a battery of tests to get the definitive answer (we talk more about tests in Chapter 6). But the starting point's when you see that she shows dyslexia-like behaviours pretty much all of the time. And *you* can spot those behaviours probably better than a psychologist can, because you see a billion times more of your child than he does.

Avoiding the 'wait awhile' trap

You want us to tell you the precise signs of dyslexia, and of course we do that later in this chapter, but first we have some important advice for you in case you get cold feet about taking your list of dyslexia-like behaviours to the school.

Parents of children with dyslexia frequently wait awhile before getting extra help – and later regret putting their request off. Your child makes the quickest gains in reading from Reception to Year 2. She's like a sponge at this time, ready and willing to learn a lot. Later, her first enthusiasm wanes, especially if she's struggling, and getting to grips with reading takes her much longer than other kids require. Don't wait. If you feel something's wrong, trust your gut instincts, even if someone tells you to wait awhile and let development take its course. A struggling child doesn't suddenly find that everything makes sense after all. She doesn't catch up. Her problems just get worse, and then you have a job that's harder and takes longer.

Noticing Your Child's Late Development at Nursery

Your child starts talking late. She has trouble naming shapes and colours and doesn't understand nursery rhymes. She's not all that interested in stories and often walks off halfway through them. Should you worry? Maybe. Should you look for other signs and go to see a professional? Certainly. However, even if your child is a confident speaker but has trouble tying her shoelaces, knowing her right from left or reciting nursery rhymes, then there could still be a difficulty. Each child is different, but if you catch your child's difficulties when she's still at nursery, you have a great chance of helping her get up to par by the time her progress really counts, in Years 1 and 2. I've found that many nursery teachers correctly spot those children who are later diagnosed with dyslexia higher up the school.

The following list gives you the kinds of behaviours that educational psychologists have in mind when they look for clusters of symptoms that indicate dyslexia in your nursery-age child. We cover these symptoms (and what to do if you see them) in more detail in Chapter 4.

- ✔ She starts to speak late (no actual speech until after age 2).

- ✔ She says muddled-up words (such as *aminal* for *animal* and *hopistal* for *hospital*).

- ✔ She doesn't understand what you say until you repeat it a few times.

- ✔ She can't follow more than one direction at a time.

- ✔ She can't remember words.

- ✔ She takes a while to get words out.

- ✔ She can't consistently name the letters of the alphabet.

- ✔ She doesn't enjoy being read to.

- ✔ She enjoys being read to but shows no interest in words or letters.

- ✔ She has weak fine-motor skills (in activities such as drawing, tying laces, cutting and threading).

- ✔ She can't tell you rhyming words (*cat/hat*).

- ✔ She can't distinguish between letters and other symbols or squiggles.

- ✔ She can't recognise her own written name.

A psychologist assessing your child may also ask you whether your child has, or has had, a lot of ear infections or has had grommets fitted. Ear infections aren't a sign of dyslexia, but some people believe them to be a complicating factor that can make dyslexia worse.

Watching Your School-Age Child Fade

She can't read. She reverses and mixes up the order of letters when she writes words. She can't remember the alphabet. These are classic signs of dyslexia in your child when she's in primary school. You may notice the following behaviours in your child's cluster of dyslexia symptoms:

- ✔ She doesn't show a dominant handedness until about age 7.

- ✔ She has immature speech, saying words like 'wed' (red) and 'gween' (green).

- ✔ Her writing has lots of crossings out and may be messy. She can't tell you the sounds of the alphabet.

- ✔ She's bright and has good oral abilities but is unexpectedly weak at reading.

- ✔ She talks with an advanced vocabulary when she can't recall simpler words, saying things like 'We're going to the food distributor'.

- ✔ She frequently uses words like 'umm' and 'thingy'.

- ✔ She writes words with letters in the wrong places, like *saw* instead of *was* and *vawe* instead of *wave* (called *transposing* letters).

- ✔ She reverses letters and numbers (especially *b* and *d*, *p* and *q* and *3* and *5*).

Letter and number reversals are common in all children, including those who don't have dyslexia, up to about age 7. So what's the difference between a child making mistakes that are nothing to be concerned about and mistakes that may indicate dyslexia? A child with dyslexia makes mistakes just as often as she doesn't, and she continues making them in Year 2 and beyond:

- ✔ Her writing is barely legible (letters are badly formed and the wrong size).

- ✔ She's confused about directionality, such as left/right, up/down and front/back.

- ✔ She doesn't follow through with multiple-step chores.

- ✔ She's below her chronological age in reading and/or writing and spelling (as confirmed by her teacher, school tests or tests done by a specialist or psychologist).

✔ She adds or leaves out small words when reading (which can totally change the meaning of the text).

✔ She has trouble retelling a story.

✔ She complains of words moving or running off the paper.

✔ She complains of dizziness, headache or stomach ache while reading.

✔ She receives grades that don't match her intelligence or effort.

To determine whether your child's grades match her potential, you need to have her assessed by a psychologist. You may be able to see this pretty clearly without a test, though, and of course the teacher can let you know what he thinks.

✔ She can't remember the months of the year in sequence without going through them all.

✔ She can't remember facts like multiplication tables, days of the week, dates and names.

Your child also may show you signs of her dyslexia that have no direct connection to reading and writing. Her attitude, behaviour and all-round manner speak volumes. For example, she just figured out what the special needs table (a table in a class specifically for children with special educational needs) really means and she feels stupid, not as good as the other kids, and angry or frightened. How would *you* react? Here are some typical behaviours you may see:

✔ Your child looks and acts unhappy.

✔ Your child seems too quiet; she's practically invisible.

✔ Your child stirs up plenty of trouble at home and in school.

✔ Your child may be disorganised.

For more about dyslexia symptoms in school-age kids (and what to do about them), check out Chapter 5.

For a personal account of a mother discovering that her son has dyslexia, read *Reading David* by Lissa Weinstein (Perigee Books). Two aspects of the book make it unusual: the author is an educational psychologist herself but still missed (or denied) the signs, and the author's son, David, who's still in school now, gives his perspective.

Beware of report card rhetoric

The other day Tracey, whose daughter has dyslexia, was with a friend looking through her photo albums. One album spanned her daughter's elementary school years, and in it were old school reports. Her friend said, 'Check these out. They all say pretty much the same thing.' On every report a handful of words and phrases repeated themselves – *struggles, tries hard, slow, kind, helpful, a pleasure to teach.* 'You know, she really did try and try,' her friend sighed.

Harsher words may proliferate on your child's report – words like *lazy, inattentive, distractible, careless, immature* and *daydreamer.* Don't let them get to you. These words are characteristic of the reports that undiagnosed children with dyslexia get. Daydreaming is a common symptom of dyslexia – the child cuts off, probably because she finds it hard to process all the information (slow processing speed is assessed during a psychological assessment). So, as a parent, take these words on reports seriously and see them as warning signs of dyslexia, especially if you know that your child has been trying and hasn't been lazy.

The important thing is to remember that your child is doing her best in the face of adversity and that the teacher's words (though unfair and worth calling him to task on) are a very good reason to get an assessment. Make sure you talk to your child. Let her know that you don't think she's lazy or stupid and that you're trying to get her the help she needs. Let her know that you believe in her ability to learn and if she's co-operative think of fun things to do with her to help her understand and learn at home.

Recognising Signs of Dyslexia at Older Ages

Many adults wonder if their unsuccessful (and maybe unhappy) days at school were due to undiagnosed dyslexia. Teens can find themselves wondering the same thing, because even though dyslexia is now a recognised disability, children who have mild dyslexic symptoms, plenty of other strengths and good coping strategies may still go undiagnosed. In the following sections, we talk about the specific dyslexic symptoms that crop up in teens and adults.

Seeking out signs in teenagers

If your teenager dislikes school, doesn't do her homework and hardly ever picks up a book, dyslexia may be the reason – especially if this started when she was younger. Sometimes, identifying what is normal teenage behaviour and what could be undiagnosed dyslexia is difficult. Teenagers with dyslexia may go to great lengths to avoid reading and writing, find ways to cover up their reading failure and worry no end about it. Here's a quick rundown of things you may see your teenager with dyslexia doing:

- ✔ She avoids reading and writing.

- ✔ She guesses at words, skips small words and has little comprehension.

- ✔ She muddles the order of letters inside words in writing or leaves letters out completely.

- ✔ She starts to dislike school, even though she seemed to be doing fine before.

- ✔ She doesn't do homework, and her teachers are concerned or critical.

- ✔ She tells you that she's 'stupid' or 'couldn't care less'.

- ✔ She's more anxious and self-conscious than before (though you may have thought that was hardly possible!).

- ✔ She withdraws and doesn't want to get involved in as many social events (like birthday parties and sleepovers) as she used to.

- ✔ She becomes aggressive, abusive or anti-social (and worrisome) in other ways.

For information on helping your teenager succeed in high school and apply for college or university, check out Chapters 16 and 17.

Acknowledging adult symptoms

Adults with dyslexia may have learned to live with their difficulties. Whether they're open about their dyslexia, or even know they have dyslexia, is a different matter. Some adults tell everyone about their dyslexia, ask for accommodations at work and even joke about their mistakes at home. Some hide their dyslexia and go to great lengths to keep it under wraps. They don't trust to other people's understanding and don't want to lose their jobs or be thought of as 'mental cases' (a term that a friend of Tracey's, who has dyslexia, used!). Others don't know they're dyslexic.

The stereotypical adult with dyslexia may exhibit some or all of the following behaviours:

- ✔ She avoids reading out loud and reading complex text or avoids writing formal and long pieces of text, such as reports.

- ✔ She types letters in the wrong order.

- ✔ She transposes numbers and dates, especially 3s and 5s.

✔ She can't fill out forms, especially in front of others.

✔ She's adept at hiding her illiteracy by doing things like ordering what friends eat at restaurants to avoid reading the menu.

✔ She may have low self-esteem and/or a bad attitude.

✔ She has good days and bad days.

✔ She has organisational difficulties, such as coping with appointment diaries or keeping a tidy desk at work.

✔ She left school as early as possible.

✔ She holds a job below her potential and/or changes jobs frequently. She can also turn down promotion because she's afraid she won't cope with the demands of the job, even though she is practically very good at the job.

✔ She misses minor details at her job and finds it hard to spot mistakes she has made in her own writing.

✔ She can't play sports due to poor coordination.

✔ She may find it hard to read to her children.

Here are a few ordinary, everyday bits of information that an adult with dyslexia may be unable to read:

✔ Figures on a pay slip

✔ Instructions on prescription medicine

✔ Numbers in a telephone directory

✔ The menu in a restaurant

✔ Traffic signs, street names and maps

✔ Their emails

✔ Letters, books and homework that a child brings home from school

✔ TV schedules

✔ Instructions for building and using new toys or equipment

Adults with dyslexia have to recruit help and work out clever coping strategies every day of their lives or they face being isolated in a reading world. Check out Chapter 18 for additional signs of dyslexia in adults and tips on succeeding in the real world.

Dyslexia: A special burden for teens

When you talk to people with dyslexia and read dyslexic message boards, you find truckloads of personal anecdotes and figures about the pressures of secondary school. Some people talk about the terror of being asked questions that they feel they can never answer; others discuss the humiliation of not feeling bright.

For a few teenagers, the humiliation becomes too much. The strain and frustration of under-achieving can cause teens with dyslexia to be reluctant to go to school, to throw temper tantrums before school or to play truant. Cheating, stealing and experimenting with drugs can also result when children regard themselves as failures. Youngsters with learning disabilities constitute a disproportionately large percentage of both adolescent suicides and the prison population. Dr John Rack, Head of Psychology at Dyslexia Action, carried out extensive research for his report, *The Incidence of Hidden Disabilities in the Prison Population,* published in 2005. His report suggested that 20 per cent of the prison population had some form of hidden disability that 'will affect and undermine their performance in education and work settings'.

Your teenager may bury her dyslexia under a heap of defiant or self-abusive behaviours. Don't allow these secondary behaviours to bring you down or divert you – or fool you into thinking that your teen is just about adult enough to pull herself back on track. She needs you or another caring adult to show her that you believe in her, that academic skills aren't the only thing that matter. Concentrate on her strengths and help her to overcome her weaknesses (and seek professional help).

Referring to Your Family's History

If you have someone with dyslexia in your family, your child is more likely than other kids to have dyslexia. Dyslexia runs in families. Whether your family's black or white, well educated or minimally educated, rich or just getting by makes no difference. Dyslexia skips past race, gender and socioeconomic barriers – and money and position don't get you a cure either. No cure exists.

Here are some interesting snippets about family patterns regarding dyslexia:

- Many studies show the tendency for dyslexia to run in families. If one of your parents has dyslexia, you have an increased chance of having dyslexia yourself. Figures on this 'increased chance' range from 25 to 75 per cent. Because of various factors (like whether a child receives good instruction and is specifically called 'dyslexic'), a more accurate prediction really isn't possible.

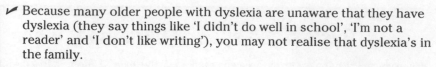

✔ Because many older people with dyslexia are unaware that they have dyslexia (they say things like 'I didn't do well in school', 'I'm not a reader' and 'I don't like writing'), you may not realise that dyslexia's in the family.

✔ Researchers can make predictions about the degree of dyslexia a person may have by looking at inherited brain differences. Most experts agree that people with dyslexia share a certain kind of brain activity (different parts working better or worse) and that when you map this, certain topographies suggest more trouble than others!

If you struggled at school or know that you have dyslexia, or if someone else in your family fits that bill, watch your child for symptoms of dyslexia right from an early age. If she doesn't have dyslexia, you lose nothing by watching her, but if she does have dyslexia, you gain valuable insight and time. You may even be the only person to spot that your child needs extra help and then you spare yourself that awful 'I should've known' kind of hindsight.

Part II
Determining When to Get a Diagnosis

'You.... are.... both.... complete....
blithering.... idiots.... so.... there..'

In this part . . .

What's the difference between dyslexia and a simple reading delay? When do most kids start to read independently? The teacher says your child's doing fine, but should you request a dyslexia assessment anyway? This part of the book gives you answers to these and other questions you may have. In addition, it offers a clear view of what dyslexia looks like in pre-school and school-age children and walks you through the complete dyslexia assessment process.

Chapter 4

Watching Your Child Carefully at a Young Age

In This Chapter

▶ Monitoring your child's early behaviour

▶ Helping your child with pre-reading activities

▶ Preparing your child for school

As any parent knows, nothing is as bleak as worrying about your child – except for worrying about him for a long time. That's why this chapter helps you move quickly from concern to action. Here you get a picture of what your pre-school child's development looks like and what kinds of behaviour may signify a potential problem. Then we give you games and activities to do at home that strengthen the skills a child with dyslexia typically struggles with, and we cover specific abilities that your child should have before he enters school.

Keeping a Close Eye on Early Skills

Your child's pre-school years are a magical time. You get to marvel when he begins to walk and speak, and just about every day he gains a new skill. Do you need to think about dyslexia now? If someone in your family has dyslexia, and/or if your child doesn't seem to be cruising past typical developmental milestones, you do.

Your child can be diagnosed with dyslexia before Year 2 or age 8, but generally around 7 is the optimum age. Assessors can use tests like the Dyslexia Early Screening Test (DEST) with children as young as 4 years old to look for weaknesses in skills like rhyming, phonemic awareness, immediate recall, hand–eye coordination, sound discrimination and shape formation. A child has to exhibit several of these at a severe level to be determined as at risk. (See Chapter 6 for testing info.)

What you can definitely do before school starts is be primed for potential problems, give your child plenty of play that develops his phonemic awareness (see 'Listening out for phonemic awareness', later in this chapter, for details) and if your child needs it, get him some speech therapy. If you're concerned, approach your GP for a referral to a speech and language therapist through the NHS.

In the following sections, we give you the lowdown on language, hearing and vision difficulties that may signal a bigger problem. We also delve into the fine motor and pre-reading skills to monitor in your pre-school child.

Talking late and unclearly

Delayed speech may be a red flag for dyslexia. If your child isn't speaking by age 2 or older, you want to be watchful of his progress with reading when he starts school. Delayed speech doesn't mean your child is dyslexic, but it does alert you to watch for later, more definitive signs (I talk about signs of dyslexia in older kids in Chapter 5).

Even before school starts, you should have your late talker's hearing checked (see the next section), and in addition you may want to consult your GP for referral to a speech and language therapist, just to make sure that your child's jaw and mouth muscles are developing properly (if not, facial exercises can help).

Five per cent of children enter school with difficulties in speech and language. If your child has muddled and unclear speech when he starts to speak, keep an eye on him. Does he typically say things like 'aminal' for 'animal' and 'bisghetti' for 'spaghetti'? Does he stutter and fumble for his words? If so, consult your health visitor or GP.

The following are a few more language problems that may indicate dyslexia and need the evaluation of a speech therapist:

✔ Is your child's receptive speech slightly off the mark? (*Receptive speech* is your child's ability to understand other people's speech.) Can he understand what's being said to him without you having to repeat it several times? Does he have trouble understanding the difference between 'under' and 'over', or 'in front' and 'behind'? This kind of confusion, especially over directionality, is another early indicator of dyslexia that speech therapy can help with.

✔ Is your child slow to name familiar objects? Many people with dyslexia struggle all their lives with word retrieval. They know what they want to say but can't pluck it from their brains. They end up using sentences like 'Can you pass me the thingy?' much more frequently than other people do.

Not dyslexia, but DVD

May your child have what speech therapists called developmental verbal dyspraxia (DVD) or *childhood apraxia of speech* rather than dyslexia? According to the American Speech-Language-Hearing Association, a child with this condition knows what he wants to say but can't get his brain to move his lips, jaw and tongue in readiness. The following signs may indicate DVD in your young child:

✔ He doesn't coo or babble in infancy.

✔ He may have feeding problems in infancy.

✔ Saying his first words takes him a long time, and some sounds are missing.

✔ He makes only a few consonant sounds.

✔ He replaces difficult sounds with easier ones or leaves out sounds altogether. (All children do this, but a child with developmental apraxia of speech does it often.)

Find out more (and guard against a possible misdiagnosis) by logging on to Afasic (www. afasic.org.uk), a UK charity that gives useful information and training for parents and professionals as well as raising awareness about speech and language impairments.

✔ Stammering is an involuntary blockage of normal speech patterns and isn't linked to dyslexia. That said, if your child hesitates while trying to find words and has a sort of stammer because he can't recall the words he needs, this is a warning sign of dyslexia.

✔ Poor letter articulation is a possible warning of dyslexia. If your pre-school child says 'wed and gween' instead of 'red and green', listen up. Poor articulation isn't a big deal now but becomes a red flag if he still talks that way by about Year 2.

The Royal College of Speech and Language Therapists is the professional body for speech and language therapists. You can contact them on 020 7378 3012 or at 2 White Hart Yard, London SE1 1NX. The RCSLT website (www. rcslt.org) gives details of speech and language therapists but you can't be referred through the website. Instead, you need to go to your GP, health visitor or school for a referral. Alternatively, you can find details of private therapists' locations and specialisms on the Association of Speech and Language Therapists in Independent Practice website (www.helpwithtalking.com).

Battling ear infections

A big dyslexia warning sign to look out for in children under age 5 is recurring ear infections. Ear infections in themselves don't mean your child is dyslexic, but many children with dyslexia have a history of ear infections. The infections don't cause dyslexia, but almost certainly make the condition worse by impairing your child's ability to hear speech sounds at a time when he should be making the most progress with auditory processing.

The funny thing about your child's hearing is that it has what you might call everything and nothing to do with dyslexia. Experts pretty much agree that although dyslexia is all about hearing sounds (in a phonetic sense rather than sounds as in a drum beating), it's not a straightforward hearing impairment. A child with dyslexia *hears* sounds okay, but he *processes* them all wrong. In other words, he may not translate the sound he hears into the alphabetical symbol it represents.

Dyslexia is thought to be a *phonemic* rather than a hearing disorder. Your child's ears work fine, but when he identifies and makes sense of sounds (in his brain), he goes wrong. He doesn't distinguish between sounds (or *phonemes*) inside words in the same way that other children do. This kind of awareness is called *phonemic awareness*, and some experts consider the lack of it the number one feature of dyslexia. A child who lacks phonemic awareness may not be able to hear the difference between words like *tot* and *top*, *cot* and *cut* and *tin* and *Tim.* For more details, see 'Listening out for phonemic awareness', later in this chapter.

Babies are given routine hearing tests within 48 hours of being born. As he gets older, your child should have regular hearing checks at school or at your doctor's surgery. If you have concerns about your pre-school child's hearing, consult your GP immediately.

Seeing a range of vision problems

Your child's vision is another factor (like his hearing, covered in the previous section) that may complicate but doesn't cause dyslexia. Many children with dyslexia complain of seeing wobbly, fuzzy or moving letters. However, he *still* has trouble matching sounds to letters. Your child with dyslexia may have vision problems and you can consult an optometrist to investigate this further. Usually, your child's visual difficulties can be treated by using coloured filters or with eye exercises or lenses, but his dyslexia is primarily a brain-based phonemic-processing issue.

Many symptoms of vision problems are the very same symptoms that suggest dyslexia, so you need expert help in fathoming out the right diagnosis. Your child may have dyslexia, or vision problems, or dyslexia *and* vision problems or perhaps something different again! Your child may have a vision problem if you notice that he does any of the following:

✔ Enjoys being read to but shows no interest in words and letters

✔ Loses his place along lines of print

✔ Gets eye strain or red or watery eyes when he looks at books

✔ Complains of blurred, double or moving print

Looking out for lazy and turned eyes

If your child has an undetected vision problem, he can develop symptoms that look like those of dyslexia. If he has dyslexia already, a vision problem makes things worse. Even when your child gets regular vision tests, problems can go undetected and parents may be so accustomed to seeing a symptom, like their child having a slight head tilt when he looks at books, that they no longer notice it. Here is some information about two really common eye problems:

 ✔ *Amblyopia,* or lazy eye, is when one of your child's eyes doesn't work as well as the other. About 3 per cent of children under age 6 have amblyopia. Treatment usually includes eye exercises and an eye patch, but if you don't treat it early, your child may have poor vision into adulthood. If your child squints or closes one eye to see, has generally poor vision and/or complains of eye strain or headaches, he may have amblyopia.

 ✔ *Strabismus,* or *deviating eyes,* is when your child's eyes don't look towards the same object together. The turn can be constant or intermittent, and if it's intermittent, it may be hard for you to detect.

Early examination is especially important if any other member of your family has had amblyopia or strabismus before.

For more information, visit your GP or local optician. For a directory of specialist optometrists in your area, visit the Institute of Optometrists (www.ioo.org.uk) or NHS Direct (www.nhsdirect.nhs.uk).

 ✔ Squints, frowns or rubs his eyes while looking at books and when in bright sun or fluorescent light

 ✔ Tilts his head or holds his book too closely when he looks at books

 ✔ Covers an eye to look at print

 ✔ Has trouble spotting items that are alike and different

 ✔ Avoids close-up tasks

 ✔ Is easily distracted

 ✔ Has a short attention span

 ✔ Needs a lot of breaks from paper-and-pen activities

 ✔ Tires quickly when he draws and traces

 ✔ Has trouble copying and tracing shapes and letters

 ✔ Reverses letters and numbers

 ✔ Complains of headaches

 ✔ Has poor hand–eye coordination

 ✔ Appears awkward or clumsy

An optician can tell you some sobering statistics:

- ✔ About one in every five school children has an undetected vision problem.

- ✔ A school's vision screening test doesn't pick up every kind of vision problem.

- ✔ Your child can have 20/20 eyesight (meaning normal distance vision) and still have problems coordinating both his eyes as a team, tracking print across a page without losing his place or adjusting focus when he looks from near to distant things.

Even though experts are pretty certain that vision problems aren't the cause of dyslexia, some dyslexia treatments (such as the Irlen Method) pay special attention to correcting your child's visual tracking (following words along lines of a page). We talk about these dyslexia treatments in more detail in Chapter 20.

Having trouble with playing and dressing

Children with dyslexia commonly have poor hand–eye coordination and fine motor skills. A child with dyslexia may have trouble throwing and catching, and tasks like tying his shoelaces, buttoning his shirts or threading beads may not be easy and cause him distress He may be late to develop a dominant hand too. He may switch between his right and left hand to write, catch a ball or do other hand tasks, and he may not become right- or left-handed until about age 7. Even then, he may use one hand for writing and the other for catching!

Plenty of children have poor hand–eye coordination and go through a time of being *ambidextrous* (able to use both hands), so (as with all the signs we mention here) these behaviours are only potential indicators of dyslexia. They don't indicate dyslexia for sure unless they persist at school and form part of a cluster of symptoms (see Chapter 5 for dyslexia signs in school-age children).

Displaying weak pre-reading skills

Certain additional pre-reading problems can be potential symptoms of dyslexia. If your child struggles with several of the pre-reading behaviours we list here right through Year 1, and he's otherwise bright and responsive (so you're surprised by this struggle with language skills), ask for an assessment. We walk you through the dyslexia (or 'learning disabilities') assessment process in Chapter 6. You can also try some of the activities we feature in the next section to help your child strengthen his pre-reading abilities.

✔ **Your child can't identify sounds inside words.** By the time they go to school, most children can tell you when words sound alike or different. They can give you a string of 'buh' words, like ball, balloon, bench and bun, and enjoy alliteration ('an alligator ate Alice'). A child with dyslexia usually doesn't understand what the fuss is about. He doesn't hear the pattern in the 'buh' words or may not appreciate the fun in alliteration.

✔ **Your child can't tell you rhyming words.** Most children can rhyme by the time they go to school. They can anticipate rhyming words on the ends of verses and happily tell you a few of their favourite nursery rhymes. A child with dyslexia usually doesn't do this. Rhyme is something he just doesn't get.

✔ **Your child isn't interested in words or letters.** Pre-school children usually enjoy writing letters and their name all over the place. A child with dyslexia usually doesn't.

✔ **Your child can't identify letters from squiggles.** A child with dyslexia takes longer to get to know letters than other children do. By the time he starts school, he usually hasn't learnt to identify all the letters and may confuse letters with each other, or letters and random squiggles with each other.

✔ **Your child can't retell a simple story.** Small children can tell you a story, albeit in an extended, roundabout way. They're not succinct or sophisticated, but they get there. A child with dyslexia usually doesn't get there. He finds it hard to recall sequences of events, so retelling a story is virtually impossible for him.

✔ **Your child isn't interested in hearing stories.** Some children with dyslexia don't enjoy hearing stories. They don't follow plots, don't understand wordplay and may walk right off in the middle of a story that other kids are begging for more of.

✔ **Your child can't write or recognise his own name.** A child with dyslexia may be unable to write or recognise his own name by the time he starts school.

Engaging in Pre-Reading Activities at Home

In the previous section, we touch on a few pre-reading difficulties (like not hearing rhyme or recognising letters) that can be indicators of dyslexia. But what practical strategies can you put to use at home to address them?

Plenty of language activities prepare your child for reading. You can loosely classify them as activities that build the following skills:

✔ **Print awareness:** When your child understands that print runs left to right and top to bottom, he's primed for following sentences in pages of text. Your child with dyslexia needs plenty of print awareness because directionality (left to right) is especially tricky for him.

✔ **Phonemic and phonics skills:** Before he can read, your child must get a few skills under his belt, such as phonemic awareness (hearing sounds in words) and phonics (matching letters to those sounds). At nursery, you want your child to do a whole bunch of singing, rhyming and saying different letter sounds so that he develops phonemic awareness and, from that, solid phonics skills.

We delve deeper into these areas in the following sections.

Developing print awareness

When children start school, some have no idea how to hold a book or follow along the lines and pages. *Your* child knows which direction written words run in, how chapters break a book into sections, how books tell you things and that they're written by authors, because you read to him. Print awareness is a relatively easy thing to help your child with – you simply read to him and point out the direction of the text, the parts of the book and so on – but is an important precursor of reading nevertheless. You can also produce or download (from websites such as www.bbc.co.uk/skillswise) fun dot-to-dot or tracking exercises that go from left to right to help your child develop print awareness.

Focusing on phonemic and phonics skills

Your child needs to get on top of *phonics*; that is, being able to sound out letters and words. To do that, he must develop a bunch of sequential skills that start with phonemic awareness. People get pretty technical about 'phono' terms, but of course we give you the simple explanation right here:

✔ **Phonemic awareness:** Before you give your child any instruction in the letters of the alphabet, he must be aware that words are made of chunks of sound. This appreciation of sounds is *phonemic awareness*.

✔ **Phonological awareness:** This is about sounds too – only more of them! When your child has phonological awareness, he has a fairly sophisticated appreciation of sounds. He can identify many chunks of sound, like prefixes (*un-aware*, for example) and rhymes (in word families like *make*, *take*, *rake* and *sake*, the *ake* part is called a *rhyme*).

- ✔ **Phonics:** After your child is aware that spoken words are made of sounds, he needs to discover that written letters and chunks of letters represent those sounds. This attaching of letters to sounds is *phonics.*

- ✔ **Morphological and orthographic awareness:** At the same time as your child gets comfortable with regular, easy-to-sound-out words like *cat* and *dog*, he has to get to know a few harder words. Words like *who* (which don't sound out) are pretty hard, and so are words like *brought* and *niece* (which have unusual sound-spelling chunks). And then there are prefixes (like *un*, *dis* and *pre*), suffixes (like *able*, *tion* and *ly*), contractions (like *can't* and *don't*), and stuff like that to learn! The prefixes and suffixes kind of learning is called *morphological awareness* (recognising the parts of words that convey meaning), and getting to know which letters typically come together and look right (like *ck* but never *kc*) is called *orthographic awareness.* (Chapter 11 has full details on memorising and rhyming tricks to help with difficult words.)

Some people also talk about 'phoneme grapheme correspondence'. The *phono* part means sounds and the *grapheme* part means written appearance, so the whole thing is recognising the written form of the sound.

The following sections focus on skills you can work on with your pre-school child: phonemic awareness and phonics.

Listening out for phonemic awareness

Your pre-school child is initially at the phonemic awareness stage, so you need to help him hear the sounds that words are made of. What's your best approach?

The following activities are great for helping to develop your child's phonemic awareness:

- ✔ Help your child hear the sounds in songs and rhymes by leaving key words out when you sing them. Your child provides the words using the rhyme as his guide.

- ✔ Have fun with alliteration ('The dotty dinosaur danced with doves') and read rhyming stories. Visit your library to find a good selection and ask the librarian for suggestions. Even if a librarian can't answer your question off the top of her head, she has lists of award-winning books and classics that she can print for you.

- ✔ When your child is at the computer, encourage him to play games that make him listen carefully. For a CD-ROM that's specially designed to fine-tune your child's auditory discrimination and phonemic awareness, check out the Earobics programme. The at-home version for children up to Key Stage 1 (4–7 years old), called Step 1, is PC and Mac compatible and costs £43 plus VAT from www.dyslexic.com. Find out more by logging on to www.earobics.com or www.donjohnson.co.uk.

Acquiring phonics skills

After your child gets the idea that words have sounds inside them and can come together in cute rhyming patterns, like 'I saw a bear on the stair in his underwear', he's ready to match sounds to letters.

You help your child remember the shapes and sounds of letters by having him get his hands on them; a child with dyslexia learns well when you help him use all of his senses, not just his vision and hearing. Have him draw letters in shaving foam, make them from modelling clay and trace them on your back with his finger. Help him remember the sound each single letter of the alphabet makes by associating the letter to an object or character. (I give more phonics exercises in Chapter 12 and multisensory exercises in Chapter 14.)

When your child gets to know a letter as a story character, he remembers it better. For example, the letter *a* can become Annie Apple, who looks like the letter *a* with a stalk and leaf attached and takes part in stories and songs. Annie Apple is part of a programme called Letterland, which originated in the UK and is used in countries all over the world. It's an extensive kit of books, tapes, CDs, CD-ROMs and flashcards, but you can get plenty of mileage from the basic soft-cover ABC book (£4.99) and the Alphabet Songs CD (£6.50). Check out Sammy Snake, Eddie Elephant, Clever Cat and a bunch of products at www.letterland.com.

Before you use these products, you may want to check with your child's school. If teachers already use Letterland, Jolly Phonics, (www.jolly learning.co.uk) or any other similar programme, they probably want you to use the same thing too.

Preparing Your Child for Nursery School

You want your child to be as prepared as he can be for nursery. If you notice him doing things like wandering off when you read him stories, even really interesting ones, and having no interest in writing his own name, you especially want to make sure that his other skills are more developed (so you have less to keep a watch over). The next sections let you know what nursery teachers hope to see in their new charges (on top of all the pre-reading stuff we go through in the previous sections).

Stirring up good feelings about school

In a perfect world, your child starts nursery by bouncing straight into the classroom and emerging hours later, radiant and replete with newly acquired knowledge! If he doesn't quite cut that kind of figure, here's the basic feeling-good-about-school standards that his teachers hope for:

Telling little kids the honest truth

Your child may show symptoms of dyslexia, like poor fine motor coordination, before he starts school. He may understand that he's not quite as skilled as friends the same age. If that's the case, he's probably more than a little nervous about starting school. You need to prepare him by giving him accurate information. When you tell your child about school and take him to school orientation days, be honest with him. Saying things like 'It'll be easy' and 'You're a big boy now' may not be quite what he needs to hear.

Feeling good about school can be tricky – even for older children. A friend of Katrina's made her child's start at his new secondary school easier by getting permission to escort her child to his form room before school re-started that September. By visiting his school without mobs of other children, he lost his anxiety about getting lost on the first day. Katrina's friend also colour coded a map of the school and her son's time-table, further easing his transition from a small primary school to a very large comprehensive.

- ✔ Your child knows roughly what routine to expect in class.
- ✔ Your child understands that the teacher is there to help him.
- ✔ Your child understands that other children want to be his friends.
- ✔ Your child is mostly excited to be there.
- ✔ Your child has no real separation anxiety.

Helping your child with language skills

If you suspect that your pre-school or school-age child has dyslexia, look closely at his language skills. Teachers hope for the following skills, and a child with dyslexia typically needs to work on at least three of them:

- ✔ Identifying the beginning sound of some words
- ✔ Recognising rhyming sounds
- ✔ Identifying some alphabet letters
- ✔ Recognising some common sight words, like 'stop'
- ✔ Telling you a simple story
- ✔ Recognising his written name
- ✔ Trying to write his name

For tips on strengthening basic language skills, see 'Engaging in Pre-Reading Activities at Home', earlier in this chapter.

Nurturing other academic skills

Some children with dyslexia struggle to remember sequences of numbers and directional concepts (like under and over). From the following list you can see that these skills feature fairly prominently in nursery school, so the more practice you give your child before he starts school, the better:

- **Understanding general times of day:** Is it morning or late afternoon? Most children have trouble with times of day, but a child with dyslexia may be more confused than most. Unless it's actually dark or he's just got up, he can't tell you whether it's morning, afternoon or evening, let alone what hour. Talking about time in terms of 'sleeps' helped with my children. Saying things like 'after you've had three sleeps' is more meaningful to a child than 'in three days' time'. See Chapter 15 for tips on helping your child figure out time.

- **Understanding directions such as up, down, in, out, behind and over:** Behind or in front, left or right – which is which? That's the kind of question that can plague someone with dyslexia all his life. Playing fun games such as hiding something and then saying 'it's under the table' can help with this. Many adults with dyslexia like doing practice runs when they leave familiar territory because they know that they have little hope of following directions for getting safely back. See Chapter 15 for help with directions.

- **Counting up to 10:** Many toddlers can count up to 10, and by the time they start school nearly all children manage this. A child with dyslexia may not. He can't keep the sequence in his short-term memory. See Chapter 9 for tricks on introducing simple mathematical concepts to your child.

- **Recognising shapes (square, circle, triangle and rectangle):** The fact that your pre-school child can't tell a circle from a square, or that he can't remember the name of the shape although he recognises that it's different, may be one of the first things that sets your alarm bells ringing. See Chapter 9 for tips on helping your child pick out shapes.

- **Tracing basic shapes:** Most small children can trace around shapes soon after they learn to hold a pencil. A child with dyslexia typically draws as much off the shape as on it.

- **Naming colours:** Children with dyslexia may have trouble naming colours. Psychologists testing young children for dyslexia usually include a rapid naming test in which your child is asked to quickly name colours, objects, numbers and letters. To help your child remember these classifications, spend several days on one colour, such as red, before introducing others (one at a time). The name rather than recognition of the colour may cause the problem so ask questions such as 'is it red like your jumper?'

✔ **Sorting items by colour, shape and size:** If colours and shapes are hard for your child, sorting pictures by these features is extra hard. Many children later diagnosed with dyslexia had this kind of problem early on.

✔ **Identifying parts of his body:** If your pre-school child always has trouble naming his body parts, watch his progress carefully to see whether other dyslexia signs appear. Playing games such as 'heads, shoulders, knees and toes' can help with this.

Encouraging fine motor skills

Children with dyslexia often have trouble disciplining their pencils. They have a hard time writing letters, their fingers get all tangled up in scissors and threading beads and pasta tubes onto string can be a nightmare.

For a preview of the kinds of small, fiddly hand-movements, otherwise known as *fine motor skills*, that teachers love to see in your child, check out this list:

✔ Your child puts simple puzzles (up to 12 pieces) together. (You can make these yourself by cutting up pictures and sticking them onto card. Start by making the shapes fit together very easily.)

✔ Your child uses scissors correctly. (You can buy training scissors that guide the fingers to help with this.)

✔ Your child draws and traces with pencils.

✔ Your child can fasten buttons and zips.

✔ Your child can unscrew lids from child-sized jars of craft materials.

The only way for your pre-school child to get better with fine motor skills is to do more of them. He needs to squeeze clay, pick up beads, fit jigsaw pieces into place and get his finger and hand muscles pumping. For a smorgasbord of things to do with sandpaper, modelling clay and gloop (a soapy, ooey, gooey mix you make yourself), go to Chapter 14.

You can shop online for resources, toys and games designed especially for children with special needs at LDA Learning (www.ldalearning.com).

Showing your child what's sociable

Dyslexia isn't a behavioural disorder. Your child doesn't behave badly or unusually because he has dyslexia – but he may, of course, act up or draw attention to himself in other ways if he's frustrated, infuriated or demoralised as a result of his dyslexia. Your child's teacher naturally (and idealistically!) hopes that all the children in her class have the following basic social skills:

- ✔ Your child uses words, not fists.
- ✔ Your child speaks clearly.
- ✔ Your child plays with other children.
- ✔ Your child follows simple directions.
- ✔ Your child can tell you what he needs and wants.
- ✔ Your child waits his turn.
- ✔ Your child goes to the toilet by himself.
- ✔ Your child is inquisitive and asks questions.
- ✔ Your child enjoys hearing stories.
- ✔ Your child says 'please' and 'thank you'.

Putting your child in charge of his personal information

A child with dyslexia may struggle with remembering sequences of numbers, like telephone numbers. Here are the essential things that teachers hope your child knows:

- ✔ His full name
- ✔ His age
- ✔ His address and telephone number
- ✔ His family members' names

Chapter 5

Acting Quickly with Your School-Age Child

In This Chapter
▶ Understanding the importance of early intervention
▶ Recognising symptoms at home
▶ Working with the teacher to help spot dyslexia signs

When your child goes to school, you can't help wondering how she compares to classmates. Is she keeping up? Does she have the same strengths and weaknesses as her friends? Is she really a little slower to read than her sister was, or is your memory hazy? In this chapter, we tell you what do and don't constitute reasons for having your school-age child assessed for dyslexia.

Responding Quickly to Reading Problems

If a teacher tells you your 5-year-old child isn't developmentally ready to read, he may be right. But if he says the same thing when your child's 7, and you can see your child has a deep and enduring confusion with words, he's wrong.

Children with dyslexia don't suddenly just 'get it' – not without the right intervention, anyway – but continue to struggle while the majority of children overtake them. Their acute difficulty with written text is obvious at ages 5 to 7, when nearly all the other kids are easily 'getting it'. Without intervention, the learning gap between your child with dyslexia and her classmates just grows and grows.

Difficulties caused by dyslexia don't get better on their own. The quicker you treat your child's dyslexia, the quicker and easier she can make headway, and the longer you wait to treat your child's reading problems, the more they compound. She misses out on the language-extending effect that reading facilitates.

This is because if she misses out on all the knowledge classmates are gaining through their reading, her marks drop, and she dislikes school because every classroom subject requires at least some reading.

All this makes sense, and a lot of research supports it. From two major studies conducted in the US – the 1999 Roper Poll Study and the 2002 Teaching Children to Read report – and other studies on how children read and what happens when they struggle, here's what we know for sure:

- ✔ Parents typically don't have enough confidence in their own judgement to act quickly on their child's reading problems, often waiting over a year before getting extra help.

- ✔ With intensive reading instruction, 95 per cent of struggling children age 9 or below can achieve average reading levels.

- ✔ A quick response to your child's reading problems is critical because older children don't learn to read as quickly or easily as the under-10 age group. Only 25 per cent of children age 10 and over ever catch up with their peers.

- ✔ Reception and Year 1 are the best grades of all for reading intervention. With intensive instruction, a child in Reception catches up to her peers four times more quickly than a child in Year 4 does.

Some alternative schools, like Steiner schools (see Chapter 7 for details), don't formally teach children to read until after age 7. This isn't a problem for children without dyslexia because in earlier grades they learn a lot of pre-reading skills, so they're well primed for a quick start. Your child with dyslexia, however, doesn't make this quick start and needs extra help.

So what's the moral of this story? Keep an eye on your child for symptoms of dyslexia (which we cover in the rest of this chapter) and talk to other people, such as teachers. Effective intervention may take care of the problem but if it doesn't, then think about assessment. The type of assessment depends on the age of the child – the older the child, the greater the need to consider assessment as a matter of urgency. You can start helping your child before assessment though, because anything that helps a child with dyslexia to learn will be useful, so starting straight away won't harm her. We talk at length about tests in Chapter 6.

When you give children extra help with reading, the young ones usually do best. Children under 7 make the best progress, and children at ages 7 to 10 do well too. After age 10, however, only 25 per cent of children ever catch up with their peers. Argh, what if your child's 10, 11, 12 or older? Don't panic. The statistics sound alarming, but you're reading this book, so you're obviously a person who gets things done. Your child can learn to read at any time, but the key, as with all things worth doing, is to practise consistently and frequently. Your older child needs to work harder and longer than if she starts her remediation at age 5, but she can still achieve the same end. Chapter 2 has the scoop on symptoms you see in older kids and teens; and after you determine that your older child or teen does have dyslexia, check out Chapter 16 for ways to help her succeed.

Noticing Dyslexic-like Behaviours at Home

If you're not sure whether your child struggles enough with reading and writing for you to worry, she can probably provide you with the answer. Children who struggle in class soon realise that they're low performers and find ways to internalise or externalise their hurt.

If your child is struggling, you can use the ideas in this book to help her while you investigate the cause. In the next sections we talk about ways to deal with three fairly typical behaviours your child with dyslexia may display at home: unhappiness, disorganisation and, of course, the continual struggle with words.

Your own observations of your child's behaviour are just as important as observations the teacher makes and test results. Many dyslexic-like behaviours are things you see at home and you're in the best position to notice whether your child's beginning to display the symptoms, which may show up in other ways too, such as a dislike of school or an avoidance of reading. Your child usually puts on her best face for the teacher, so if you jot down that your child tells you she's sick every morning before school but makes a quick recovery at the weekend, you can confidently let her teacher know. Note specific incidents and dates so that you have a full-colour picture of how your child's doing. That way, if the teacher says something like 'But she's so happy in class', you don't start doubting your own memory. Of course, write down the good things too, so that you can see whether certain times in school are better for your child than others.

Struggling with written words

Children with dyslexia always struggle with written words. Your child probably dislikes reading, making mistakes like reading *was* for *saw* and *horse* for *house*, and skipping right past small words like *it*. When she writes, she's likely to put letters in the wrong order inside words (called *transposing*), leave out letters altogether (called *omissions*) and face letters like *b* and *d* the wrong way (called *reversals*). These actions are all typical signs that your child may have dyslexia. (Some children without dyslexia do sometimes reverse letters but tend to grow out of this by the age of 9.) The longer your child continues to do these things the more you should be concerned. We go into more detail about these and other word-based signs in 'Struggling with reading' and 'Writing with difficulty', later in this chapter.

The information you probably want most from this book is how to help your child develop her reading and writing skills. We devote whole chapters to those answers too (see Part IV), but so that you have an outline of the important points in simple terms, here's what the research says:

✔ Your child needs to do plenty of phonemic and phonics activities because she lacks skills to match letters to sounds. (*Phonemic activities* teach your child that words are made of sounds. *Phonics instruction* shows your child how to match letters and letter combinations to those sounds.) We give you a wide variety of phonological activities to try in Chapter 12.

✔ The best instruction for children with dyslexia is structured, systematic and explicit instruction in phonics, delivered through multisensory activities – in other words, activities that involve auditory (hearing), visual (seeing) and kinaesthetic (doing) skills (check out Chapter 14 for more about these activities).

Feeling unhappy

If your child knows she's at the bottom of the class in reading, doesn't like going to school and dreads getting certain types of homework, what can you do about it?

You can tackle her unhappiness by talking it over with her. Let her know that you realise she feels humiliated because she can't read like the other children (even those who don't seem as bright as her), that you know she tries hard and that you want to help. Together you can pinpoint her specific difficulties, do reading and writing exercises to help reduce her problems and, if necessary, get an assessment for dyslexia. (We give you more details about building your child's self-esteem with positive talk in Chapter 15.)

And, perhaps most immediately helpful to your child, you can tell her about dyslexia and the many gifted and famous people who have it. Children with dyslexia nearly always say that when they realise clever and talented people have dyslexia too, they feel empowered, inspired and happier! (See Chapter 2 for a list of famous people with dyslexia.)

Being disorganised

Every child with dyslexia is different and the nature of their dyslexia varies in severity. However, your child may well have a messy notebook, desk and locker at school, especially if she has dyspraxic-type difficulties. At home her whole daily schedule may be slightly off course. She may have trouble getting ready on time, turning up where she's supposed to be and doing things you ask her to do.

The best advice parents of children with dyslexia say they have for helping a child with her disorganisation is to forget about fighting it. Your child's unlikely to wake up one day with a perfectly organised mind and military-like habits to match, but she *can* harness every helping device known to civilisation. In Chapter 15 we talk at length about understanding clocks and calendars, establishing and keeping a morning routine and other things to help with organisation. For now, however, you just need to know that, while your child may never be a virtual Mary Poppins, she can at least be a girl whose wall chart or pocket organiser and mobile phone pretty much organise her life for her!

Asking Your Child's Teacher to Look for Dyslexic-like Behaviours in Class

You need to be able to talk about dyslexic-like behaviours with your child's teacher so that he doesn't brush off your child's difficulties as her not being 'developmentally ready'. You can easily mistake dyslexia for more superficial reading problems, so if you're at all uncertain, tell the teacher what you're thinking (and the dyslexic symptoms you see) so that you're both on the same page.

You want your child's teacher to help you monitor your child's behaviour and pinpoint where she needs help. Start by telling him what behaviours you notice in your child and how persistent they are. Phrase what you say in terms of your child (for example, many teachers have an overemphasis on dictation work or copying from worksheets, so try saying 'Jane has particular trouble reading long worksheets'). Ask the teacher what he's observed and what test results and examples of your child's work he can show you. Jot down what he tells you, what you tell him and what you ask for. The paper trail you start now comes in handy later on as a baseline, so date all notes and put everything you discover into a single, at-a-glance document (with headings and bullet points).

In the next sections, we take a close look at your child's reading, writing and spelling and then list other symptoms her teacher can look out for in class. If the teacher's receptive to your comments, you may want to give him a copy of these symptoms so that he can simply check off any he sees. (We provide more information on working effectively with your child's teachers in Chapter 10.)

An indicator of dyslexia that the teacher doesn't see, but that you can tell him about, is family history. If someone in your family has dyslexia, your child's chances of having it increase greatly. See Chapter 2 for more details on the link between dyslexia and family history.

Struggling with reading

When you take a close look at the way your child reads, you see that what at first looks like a big muddle in fact has patterns. A child with dyslexia makes particular kinds of reading errors and may do some – but not necessarily all – of the following:

- She reads a word on one page but doesn't recognise the same word on the next page or the next day.

- She reads single words (without story line or other clues) slowly and inaccurately.

- She misreads words as other words with the same first and last letters or shape, saying things like 'form' instead of 'from' or 'trial' instead of 'trail'.

- She adds or leaves out letters, saying things like 'could' instead of 'cold' or 'star' instead of 'stair'.

- She reads a word that has the same letters but in a different sequence, like 'who' instead of 'how', 'lots' instead of 'lost', 'saw' instead of 'was' or 'girl' instead of 'grill'. And when she makes these kinds of mistakes without pausing or trying to figure out whether what she's reading makes sense, this clues you in that she's not comprehending what she's reading.

- She confuses look-alike letters such as *b* and *d*, *b* and *p*, *n* and *u* or *m* and *w*.

- She substitutes similar-looking words, like 'house' for 'horse', even though they change the meaning of the sentence.

- She substitutes a word that means the same thing but doesn't look at all similar, like 'trip' for 'journey' or 'cry' for 'weep'.

- She misreads, leaves out or adds small words like 'an', 'a', 'from', 'the', 'to', 'were', 'are' and 'of'.

- She leaves out or changes suffixes, saying, for example, 'need' for 'needed', 'talks' for 'talking' or 'soft' for 'softly'.

- She reads out loud with a slow, choppy intonation. Her phrases aren't smooth and she often ignores punctuation.

- She may be visibly tired after reading for only a short time.

- Her reading comprehension's poor because she spends so much energy trying to figure out words. Her listening comprehension's usually much better.

- She may have trouble *tracking* (following words and lines across pages). She skips words or whole lines of text.

- She tries to avoid reading or other close-up text-based tasks and has plenty of excuses on hand for why she can't read right now.

- She has lots of distraction activities, such as needing snacks, going to the toilet or taking breaks between very short bouts of actual reading.

- She complains of physical problems when she reads, like eye strain, red or watery eyes, headaches, dizziness or a stomachache.

- She squints, frowns, rubs her eyes, tilts her head, covers one eye to read or holds books too close to her eyes.

- She complains of words moving or running off the paper.

Writing with difficulty

A child with dyslexia usually shows a huge difference between her ability to tell you something and her ability to write it down. She tends to do the following:

- Avoid writing.

- Write everything as one continuous sentence.

- Not understand punctuation. She doesn't use capitals or full stops, or uses them randomly.

- Not understand the difference between a complete sentence and a fragment of a sentence.

- Misspell many words even when she uses only very simple ones and is 'sure' she knows how to spell them.

- Mixes up *b* and *d*, *m* and *n* and other look-alike letters.

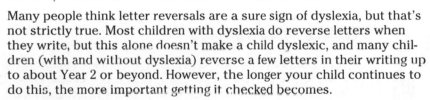

Many people think letter reversals are a sure sign of dyslexia, but that's not strictly true. Most children with dyslexia do reverse letters when they write, but this alone doesn't make a child dyslexic, and many children (with and without dyslexia) reverse a few letters in their writing up to about Year 2 or beyond. However, the longer your child continues to do this, the more important getting it checked becomes.

- Take ages to write.

- Write illegibly.

- Use odd spacing between her words. She may ignore margins completely and pack sentences tightly on the page instead of spreading them out.

- Use a mix of print and cursive and/or upper and lower case.

- Not notice her spelling errors. She reads back what she wanted to say, not what she actually wrote.

- Use both hands for writing up to about age 7. Most children choose a dominant hand at about age 5.

If your child does many of the things we list here and writing's her conspicuous Achilles' heel, she may have *dysgraphia* (also called a visual-motor integration problem), a kind of dyslexia characterised by poor, often illegible, handwriting. Chapter 2 has the full story on dysgraphia.

Making predictable spelling errors

Typically, a child with dyslexia spells far worse than she reads. Her spelling looks like the 'inventive' kind teachers expect to see in emergent readers at Foundation Stage even when she's well past that. She has particular difficulty with vowel sounds and often leaves them out. With much effort, she may be able to memorise Monday's spelling list long enough to pass the spelling test on Friday, but she can't spell the same words a few hours later when she wants to write them in sentences.

A child with dyslexia also does the following:

- ✔ Misspells frequently used words, like 'they', 'what', 'where', 'does' and 'because', despite practising and practising.
- ✔ Misspells words even when she's copying them from the board or a sheet.
- ✔ Has erasures, crossings out and undetected errors all through her writing.

Coping with other classroom tasks and issues

If your child has dyslexia, her teacher should spot many of the reading, writing and spelling errors we list in the previous sections. Other things may be conspicuously out of line with your child's intellect and bright personality:

- ✔ Noticeable and unexpected low achievement
- ✔ Conspicuous disorganisation
- ✔ Distractibility or a short attention span
- ✔ Hardly any sense of direction
- ✔ Persistent left/right confusion
- ✔ Difficulty making sense of instructions
- ✔ Difficulty remembering words and learning new words
- ✔ Immature speech (such as 'gween' for 'green')

- ✔ Inability (sometimes) in understanding what others say to her

- ✔ Difficulty finding appropriate words in telling stories

- ✔ Trouble with time, counting and calculating

- ✔ Difficulty sequencing days of the week and months of the year

- ✔ Failure to finish work on time

- ✔ Appearance of being lazy, unmotivated or frustrated

- ✔ Awkwardness or clumsiness (this could be an indicator of dyspraxic-type difficulties which often overlap with dyslexia)

Behaving unusually

The following sections cover problematic behaviours a child with dyslexia may display at school.

Acting invisible

Children with dyslexia develop all sorts of strategies to cover up their weakness in reading and writing. Being an obliging, sweet-natured, no-trouble child who blends into the background at school is one of them. When teachers describe your child in too-good-to-be-true terms, beware! Many children with dyslexia manage to go through whole years in school without being noticed. They become masters of cover-up, and no one realises what's going on. This is all very well in the short term but has disastrous long-term consequences, such as when your child fails school tests and you've wasted precious time when you could've been giving her extra help.

So if your child's practising the art of invisibility in class, help her learn new things. She needs to develop *phonemic awareness* (the awareness that a limited number of chunks of sound make words – see Chapter 12 for more details) and asking-for-help strategies.

Making trouble

A group of children are sitting outside the head teacher's office, and your child's one of them. She's in trouble for misbehaving, acting silly or giving the impression she just doesn't care.

Children commonly react to academic failure by failing in behaviour. Why? Because then all eyes are on your child's bad behaviour and not on her failure in reading and writing. She's labelled as unruly, but that's much easier for her to bear than teachers thinking of her as 'thick'. Watch out for bad behaviour. Remember that bad behaviour's a symptom of something deeper. And whatever you do, don't take it personally!

Pinpoint bad behaviour and nip it in the bud before it gets out of hand or becomes a habit for your child. Does the behaviour happen at certain times, only during some lessons (like reading time) or in reaction to a certain set of conditions? Don't focus on the 'behaviour problem' but instead, work as a team with the school to determine the real root of the behaviour.

When your child drives you and everyone else crazy and you feel like she's dragging your whole family down, remember that bad behaviour masks other things. Your child's stressed, and her misbehaviour's a way of showing it. She doesn't really mean to hurt you; she's just hurt, angry and frightened. Try to break the problem down into small bits and tackle one bit at a time. Look for practical solutions. Don't blame her – or yourself.

Having the gift of dyslexia

Many talented people have dyslexia, which leads some people to regard dyslexia as a gift. They say that the incidence of dyslexia among gifted people is higher than in the general population and that people with dyslexia tend to have scientific, engineering and/or creative types of talent.

We just need to alert you to the fact that your child can be both gifted and dyslexic at the same time. Whether her dyslexia enhances or stymies her talents is a whole different matter. The dyslexia-is-a-gift contingency maintains that people with dyslexia do excel in certain areas:

✔ They're good at hands-on learning and seem, almost intuitively, to figure out how to do things.

✔ They have strong graphical visualisation skills and can visualise objects in a moved or altered state.

✔ Children with dyslexia can sometimes tend to excel in constructing models, colouring and drawing.

✔ At an early age they're extra curious about how things work and often love to tear things apart and rebuild or fix them.

✔ They sometimes love to invent things and have mechanical talent.

✔ They have vivid imaginations. They're creative and sometimes known for their artistic ability.

✔ They can view the world from different points of view. However, they can process so much information that if they don't filter it, what begins as a talent can end up being a tangled mass of confusion.

Chapter 6

Testing Your Child for Dyslexia

• •

In This Chapter

▶ Clarifying when you need a test

▶ Finding out about different tests and administrators

▶ Getting your child ready to undergo testing

▶ Making good use of test results

▶ Deciding not to test

• •

You've watched your child struggle with homework, seen other kids out-strip him in class and at times wondered whether his teacher's too busy to see what's really going on. Now you want answers:

✔ What exactly is my child struggling with?

✔ Does he have dyslexia?

✔ How do I have him tested?

✔ If he takes a test, does he get extra help?

In this chapter we give you the answers to these questions and more.

Before you even get started with having your child tested for dyslexia, you need to be comfortable with the term 'dyslexia' and help your child get comfortable with it, too. But wait, maybe you've heard someone at your child's school talking about a 'specific learning disability (SpLD)', so which term – dyslexia or SpLD – should you be psyching up for? Probably both of them! Don't worry too much about the distinction, but be aware that different local education authorities use different terminology to mean the same thing. Dyslexia is one type of SpLD, but local education authorities (LAs) tend to avoid using the term 'dyslexia'.

If your child attends an independent school, you as a parent – or the school – can still make a request to the LA for assessment, and the resulting proce-dure's exactly the same as for a child in the state sector. Go to Chapter 8 for more information on this process.

Deciding When to Get a Diagnosis

A great reason for having your child diagnosed is to find out exactly what's going wrong for him, especially if other people tell you he's doing okay and you suspect he's really not! But that's just part of the reason. Here are a whole group of reasons to head purposefully towards someone with letters after her name and assessment tools in front of her:

- ✔ You find out whether your child has dyslexia.

- ✔ You find out whether he has other problems, like attention-deficit hyperactivity disorder (ADHD) or dysgraphia (difficulty with writing).

- ✔ You get a baseline from which to gauge your child's progress.

- ✔ If your child qualifies as having an SpLD he gets additional help, and if he meets the criteria set down by the LA he also receives a Statement of Special Educational Needs. (See Chapter 8 for more.)

- ✔ Test results help your child's teacher understand his difficulties and make accommodations for him.

- ✔ You get insight into the best help you can give your child at home.

When your child struggles with reading, you hear a lot of 'wait awhile' advice. You're told things like your child isn't 'developmentally ready' to read yet or 'he'll grow out of it' or 'plenty of children start reading late'.

Most children start to read between the ages of 5 and 7 and make their quickest progress at this time. This time period is a window of opportunity in your child's reading development, so if you see that this window isn't opening up for him, act quickly. He needs extra help right now. Trust your instincts. If you think your child's falling behind, he most probably is, even if teachers tell you he's doing fine. Don't let bad (albeit well-intentioned) advice delay or sidetrack you. Research shows clearly and unequivocally that for struggling kids the 'wait awhile' idea's just plain wrong.

Up to age 10, your child with dyslexia can still make great progress if he gets good help. After age 10, things get harder. He needs more help more often, and you must be sure that whoever helps him (that person can be you) is homing in on his weak skills. We talk about the essential skills people with dyslexia lack in Chapters 3, 4 and 5.

You're never too late to find out whether your child has dyslexia (or whether you do). In fact, the older you get, the easier the testing process becomes. Older children and adults are experienced and articulate. They can demonstrate their dyslexia by giving a complete verbal account of their difficulties. In some cases, a psychologist may need to give them only one or two formal tests. See Chapter 18 for specific info on testing adults for dyslexia.

Examining Different Kinds of Tests

Names, names, names. When your child's assessed for dyslexia, you may hear so many fancy test names that pretty soon you're screaming for mercy. And figuring out exactly what each test measures can be an uphill slog too.

In this section we make things easy for you. We classify tests according to what they measure and give you a smattering of those scary, long-winded titles.

Adults are better able to describe their difficulties to a psychologist than children are, so adult testing for dyslexia usually entails a bit of talking. An adult may take a test, such as the Wechsler Adult Intelligence Scale (WAIS)-Revised, as a measure of his general ability. In addition, he gives a full personal account of his school life and literacy skills and takes reading and writing tests similar to the ones that we list here (only they're adjusted for adults). The battery of different tests takes between two and two-and-a-half hours. They fall into the areas of ability (verbal and non-verbal), attainment (reading and spelling) and diagnostic (test of phonological awareness).

Looking at language tests for pre-school children

Do you know that your GP can refer your child to a speech and language therapist long before he starts school? Well, that's true and worth looking into If you're the least bit concerned about your child at any age from 3 or 4 years old (see Chapter 4 to find out more about signs to watch for in your pre-school child).

Call your LA and keep the number handy. The LA is responsible for any testing you may need in future. Additional options for testing include independent speech and language therapists. Try the Association of Speech and Language Therapists in Independent Practice (ASLTIP) at Coleheath Bottom, Speen, Princes Risborough, Buckinghamshire HP27 0SZ; 01494 488306; www.asltip.co.uk or www.helpwithtalking.com.

You can also get great advice from ICAN, the national charity for children with speech and language impairments, at 4 Dyers Building, London, EC1N 2QP; 0870 010 4066; www.ican.org.uk.

When your child's in school, the local educational authority is responsible for testing him for learning disabilities and for meeting the cost of doing so. If you want a second opinion, you can ask a specialist for a private assessment. (Leave around six months between assessments so that you don't invalidate the tests.) Dyslexia Action (www.dyslexiaaction.org.uk) or Helen Arkell

Centres (www.arkellcentre.org.uk) can help you book private assessments. Private assessment generally costs £400 to £450, depending on your area, but some psychologists charge up to £1000.

Pre-school language tests give your child the opportunity to listen and talk, look and talk and chat generally about things. You can be fairly sure that at some point the assessor will show your child pictures and ask questions such as 'What is this?', 'What's happening?' and 'How is this different?'

Speech difficulties are not the same as dyslexia and can't result in your child getting dyslexia (because dyslexia exists from birth). But untreated speech difficulties can make dyslexia worse and, even if your child doesn't have dyslexia, can lead to reading difficulties further down the line.

Making sense of vision and hearing tests

If you're worried that your child rubs his eyes all the time or seems to respond to you only when you ask him something for the third or fourth time, head straight to your doctor for vision and hearing tests. Don't be afraid to get a second opinion either.

Early testing is best. Your child will be invited to receive routine vision and hearing tests from birth, but if you suspect a problem at any time, see your doctor.

The symptoms in the following list are all possible signs of a vision problem:

- ✔ Head tilting
- ✔ Squinting
- ✔ Rubbing eyes frequently
- ✔ Holding books at an unusual angle or distance
- ✔ Headaches
- ✔ Dizziness
- ✔ Tiredness

Following are some possible signs of a hearing problem:

- ✔ A lot of ear infections
- ✔ Excessive shouting and talking loudly
- ✔ Not answering you
- ✔ Mishearing words
- ✔ Frequently asking you to repeat yourself

According to the American Academy of Allergy, Asthma & Immunology (www. aaaai.org/patients/publicedmat/tips/recurrentinfections. stm), your child is having too many infections if he gets more than four per year.

Ear infections come in two types: outer and middle ear. Outer ear infections are most often caused by swimming, but middle ear infections are linked to all sorts of factors, such as having had a respiratory tract infection or having been exposed to secondary smoking. For plenty of good information on ear infections and speech delays, check out NHS Direct at www.nhsdirect. nhs.uk.

Routine hearing tests detect whether your child's hearing's within the normal range of volume (loudness) and pitch (high and low sounds).

Routine eye tests at school, and free eye tests available for children through the NHS, detect obvious visible defects in your child's eyes (such as cataracts, squints or crossed eyes), whether your child can follow movement in his field of vision (up, down and side to side) and whether your child is short- or long-sighted. Secondary-school-age children may also be tested for colour blindness.

You need to know that vision and hearing tests may not tell you about visual and auditory 'discrimination' (or 'perception' or 'awareness'). You may hear these terms in a dyslexia assessment, and they have nothing to do with whether your child *receives* visual and sound information. The terms refer to how your child *processes* (or doesn't process) information.

In dyslexia assessment, *visual discrimination* is your child's ability to tell the difference between different letters and different orientations of a letter. *Auditory discrimination* is the ability to identify different sounds in words; the term's often used synonymously with *phonological* (or *phonemic*) *awareness*.

If vision and hearing tests don't tell you anything about dyslexia, why have them done? To rule out vision and hearing problems that look like dyslexia or to correct these problems so they don't make your child's dyslexia worse. (If you treat vision and hearing issues and your child *still* struggles with reading and writing, he may be dyslexic.)

Surveying early screening tests

Schools typically test, or *screen*, children for reading problems halfway through Reception or in Year 1. A 5-year-old child can be tested for being 'at risk' of dyslexia even though he can't yet read because he should still have pre-reading skills. He should be able to do the following:

✔ Name the letters, such as *ay*, *bee*, *see*.

✔ Tell you the letter sounds – 'a' (like in *apple*), 'buh' and 'cuh'.

✔ Play with letter sounds, such as words with similar letters (*bat*, *ball*, *bench*) or rhyming words (*cat*, *hat*, *mat*).

If your child can't do these things (whether or not a test picks that up), he needs extra practice, and you may want more testing. To find out exactly how to give your child extra practice, flip to Chapter 12.

Understanding IQ tests

An IQ (Intelligence Quotient) test measures your child's aptitude or what he's capable of. (Psychologists don't always say that IQ tests measure 'aptitude'. They may use the words 'potential' or 'ability'.) Two tests pretty much dominate the field:

✔ Wechsler Intelligence Score for Children IV (WISC IV)

✔ British Ability Scales (BAS)

Your child must be at least 6 years old to take the WISC IV, but children as young as 2 years 6 months old can take the BAS. Both tests measure a whole load of things, like long-term memory (What day comes after Thursday?), practical knowledge (What should you do when you cut yourself?) and visual discrimination (Which pictures look the same?).

Comprehensive IQ tests like the WISC IV and BAS are typically part of the battery of tests psychologists use to determine whether your child has dyslexia or any other learning disability. Only psychologists can administer them (in other words, they're closed tests and aren't open to being sold or administered by anyone). Their results provide measures of many sub-skills, such as spatial awareness.

IQ tests have been around for a long time because psychologists have considered them to be among the most reliable tests of human ability. Theoretically, your child's IQ score should stay pretty much the same regardless of what kind of day he's having. Even if he's nervous, hot, hungry, sick or upset, his IQ score shouldn't change all that much.

Some parents find that their child's test results are *very* different, depending on factors such as who gives the test. When their child feels uncomfortable he scores lower than when he likes the test administrator and feels relaxed.

LAs once used a discrepancy model in their IQ testing, but they've largely abandoned this model now. Many independent psychologists do rely on this to prove dyslexia, however. So what's IQ discrepancy all about? If your child's IQ is average or above but his performance on language and other performance tests is below average, he has an *IQ discrepancy*. Ask what model the assessor uses.

As a rule of thumb, if a psychologist finds that your child is performing at a level about four years below his actual age and he has a normal IQ, his results indicate that he needs a Statement of Special Educational Needs (see Chapter 12); the psychologist must also look more closely at your child's tests and identify his disability. But be aware: many LA psychologists don't carry out a bank of tests but instead just observe your child in the classroom. Unless your child has a behavioural difficulty as well, the psychologist's much less likely to see any problems. If the assessment is just based on behaviour and doesn't give you answers to the problem, then ask for a cognitive assessment of the child.

If your child's very bright, he may still be performing at an average level. The school and LA may well be unwilling to give him additional help. However, your child's still not reaching his true potential and can benefit from help. In addition, he may still need special access arrangements for exams, such as extra time.

For the time being, in most areas the IQ test remains key in the test battery used to identify an SpLD (we talk about the battery later in this chapter). If your child scores much lower in tests of skills (like reading, writing and spelling) than he does on a test of his IQ, this result shows that his performance is lower than you may expect from his aptitude (his IQ). He officially has an SpLD.

A psychologist may also find a discrepancy *within* the IQ test, because the IQ test has several parts that measure aspects like verbal IQ and performance IQ.

Picking out performance tests

An IQ test (covered in the previous section) measures your child's aptitude – what he's capable of regardless of how he performs. Other tests are designed to measure your child's performance. You may want to grab yourself a coffee and a snack, because a lot of performance tests are out there! For the purposes of this section, we divide the tests into four simple groups:

- ✔ General skills
- ✔ Auditory and visual motor skills
- ✔ Phonological skills
- ✔ Oral reading

These tests are part of the battery for assessing dyslexia. Because dyslexia's mostly about reading problems, your child can't really get tested before about age 6, but after he's in Year 1 (or above) and reading just isn't happening for him, you can have him tested.

Testing for general skills

Many performance tests give you the big picture of how your child's doing. They measure things like reading, maths, writing and general knowledge. The test administrator looks particularly for a gap between your child's written and oral skills, because people with dyslexia are typically bright and knowledgeable in most oral tasks but weak at reading and writing tasks (which seem simple to other people).

A couple of the popular tests of general skills are the:

✔ Wide Range Intelligence Test (WRIT)

✔ Wide-Range Achievement Test (WRAT-4)

Testing for auditory and visual motor skills

A test battery for dyslexia typically includes at least one test of auditory skills and one test of visual motor skills. Here are some you may hear about:

✔ **Test of Auditory Perceptual Skills (TAPS):** Does your child mishear directions, say the wrong word ('steps' instead of 'ladder') or leave words out of his speech altogether? If so, a psychologist may use this test to measure his *auditory perceptual skills* or how he processes the information he hears (*auditory* means hearing).

✔ **Test of Auditory Analysis Skill (TAAS):** In this test, your child is asked to repeat a word then repeat it again with part of the word missing. For example:

> Assessor: 'Say "steamboat"'
>
> Child: 'Steamboat'
>
> Assessor: 'Now say steamboat without saying "steam"'
>
> Child: 'Boat'

The test becomes progressively more difficult and requires the ability to delete syllables and then phonemes and then to split and delete parts of blends, for example saying meat without the "m" sound. A child of 8 years is expected to make no errors on this test.

✔ **Bender–Gestalt Test for Young Children:** This is a test of *visual-motor integration,* or how well your child draws what he sees. If your child has a lot of trouble with this kind of task, he may have, or be at risk of having, an SpLD.

✔ **Beery Developmental Test of Visual-Motor Integration:** This test measures visual-motor integration too. Your psychologist may choose either the Bender–Gestalt or the Beery depending on her familiarity with either test and what your LA requires.

Testing for phonological skills

Whether the teacher gives your child a five-minute test or the psychologist puts him through five hours of testing, someone looks at your child's phonological skills. That's because dyslexia's thought to be a phonologically based condition. A person with dyslexia's problem isn't that he can't see or hear letters and words; it's that he can't easily *process*, in his brain, the letter/sound/word information (the phonological stuff) that he hears and sees. A child may be bright and be able to tell you about complex things, but has trouble identifying letters (and some numbers), reading, spelling words and sometimes recalling (from his head) the word he wants to use when he's talking. (See Chapter 2.)

You really need to understand what these tests *do* rather than what names they go by. In plain terms, they ask your child the following kinds of things:

✔ Can you tell me the name of this picture?

✔ Can you point to the word that names this picture?

✔ If you take *p* off *pat* and put *c* there instead, what do you get?

✔ Can you write *stamp*? Can you read these funny sounds: *isk*, *eemp*, *thalep*?

Many tests of phonological skills don't have 'phon' in their names so you have to figure out for yourself that they're testing phonological skills! The followings tests *do* have 'phon' in their names, so you can easily see what they're all about:

✔ Comprehensive Test of Phonological Processing in Reading (CTOPP)

✔ Phonological Awareness Test (PAT)

✔ Togesen–Bryant Test of Phonological Awareness (TOPA)

✔ Hatcher Test of Phonological Abilities

Testing oral reading

A dyslexia assessment can test every kind of language and problem-solving skill you can think of – as well as maths and reasoning.

The Gray Oral Reading Test is one last test you're really likely to hear about. It's been around a long time. Psychologists like to listen to your child read because when he hates doing it, is slow and makes a lot of mistakes, that's a good sign he has dyslexia. The Gray Test measures the number and types of mistake your child makes with oral reading.

Charging up for a test battery

When you look into the possibility of having your child tested for dyslexia, you find people talking about a *battery* of tests or a *test battery*. What they mean is a whole load of tests, both IQ and performance, that measure a whole load of skills.

The school, or more specifically the LA, puts your child through a battery of tests to decide whether he has a specific learning disability (SpLD). To have this testing done, your school must make a formal request. The LA is legally obliged to reply to your request (within a set time – usually six weeks) and test your child, as long as he's clearly struggling in class. If testing reveals that your child qualifies as having an SpLD, he may be given a Statement of Special Educational Needs. Read more about Statements in Chapter 8.

If your child's class teacher has concerns, she generally takes them to the SENCO (Special Educational Needs Coordinator), who may well carry out some additional tests and advise a Statutory Assessment by a psychologist. If your child's teacher or SENCO is unwilling to carry out testing, you can facilitate the process yourself and ask for a Parental Statutory Assessment without the school being involved.

Choosing Your Test Administrator Wisely

You can have your child tested for dyslexia by the LA's educational psychologist (who works for your LA) or by an outside, independent educational psychologist (whom you pay). Or you can do both. In the next sections, we walk you through your options.

Selecting a specialist within your child's LA

The courteous thing to do when you want your child to be assessed in school is to see your child's teacher before you see anyone else. Besides, if you skip her in the chain of command, doing so can come back to haunt you. You want your child's teacher on board from the outset so she knows you're concerned and ready to push your child's case. Hopefully, she agrees that the SENCO should look at your child. Better still, she may preempt you and ask for your consent to refer your child to the SENCO.

In either case, you give your consent, the request for further assessment goes to the LA and the LA's psychologist has your child take a battery of tests. Only the psychologist is qualified to administer the IQ test, which is classified as 'closed'. Many other tests are 'open' to specialist teachers, though the psychologist's interpretation of test results is key to the decision your LA makes. The LA must send you the results and its proposed response within 12 weeks of beginning the assessment.

What are the pros of this option? If your child's tested in school, the tests are free. You have fewer bureaucratic steps to take. You know that the LA accepts the assessment results, the teacher's already in the loop and your child gets additional help, no questions asked (if test results show he meets the criteria for a Statement of SEN).

On the con side, you get no choice of who carries out the tests, you can't choose the venue and you get no voice about the testing day. Also, the psychologist's sure to be very busy, so you may wonder later (particularly if you're sceptical about the test results) whether she did a thorough job.

Investigating independent testers outside your LA

Plenty of people can test your child, but typically only a psychologist can give you test results that the LA accepts – and even that's rare when an independent tester's involved. In addition, insurance companies may pay for the cost of testing when it's given by a psychologist and involves other co-existing conditions such as dyspraxia.

Other practitioners, who usually call themselves 'specialist teachers' or 'assessors', can give you an assessment that helps you (or them) design a practical programme for your child. If your child has severe difficulties they may refer you to a psychologist because a psychologist can carry out a more detailed assessment.

The title of 'specialist' implies that the practitioner has more qualifications than a tutor. It may even mean that the person's qualified (usually with a postgraduate Diploma or Certificate in Dyslexia) to provide you with a diagnosis of dyslexia. You want to check this out by asking the assessor about her qualifications. You can always confirm these with the BDA (British Dyslexia Association) if in doubt.

Only some practitioners use the term 'dyslexia', so if you want to hear about dyslexia in a diagnosis, make sure you find out whether a practitioner's looking for it *before* you hire her. If she doesn't specifically look for dyslexia, find someone who does. Ideally, try to use someone who'll look further for what are called *co-morbid conditions* (such as dyspraxia, dyscalculia or ADD/ADHD). The psychologist can make appropriate recommendations and referrals in the assessment report.

What are the pros of using an independent tester? Why do people pay for independent testing (the cost of which can run from hundreds into thousands of pounds)? Here are five good reasons to opt for independence:

- ✔ The LA isn't prepared to test your child. The LA's not heartless but feels that your child definitely doesn't qualify for extra help and the money needed to test him should go to children with greater difficulties.

- ✔ The LA says it's prepared to test your child, but you don't want to wait (usually for up to six weeks but perhaps longer if holidays fall during that period).

- ✔ The LA's already tested your child, but you're not in full agreement with the results. You want a second opinion. Beware: a good psychologist shouldn't re-test with the same bank of tests within six months, and test results aren't considered valid within the same six-month window.

- ✔ Your child's problems embarrass him. He doesn't want any kind of special education and accepts only the most low-key help. You want to protect his self-esteem (he has a hard enough time anyway). You can afford to pay for private services, so you decide to get private specialist teachers to assess and tutor your child.

- ✔ You place importance on having control over who gives the test as well as when and where the tests are given. You want confidentiality, too (you may not want the school to know the test results).

What's the downside of independent testing? You pay for it. If you want your child's school to know the results (which is advisable but still your choice), you must make a time to see the teacher and then explain the situation. In that case, you have a lot of photocopying and distributing of information to do.

For a list of independent educational psychologists, go to the British Psychological Society. Otherwise contact Dyslexia Action (01784 222300) or if you're in the Surrey area try the Helen Arkell Centre (01252 792400), which has a list of psychologists able to carry out private assessment. PATOSS, the Professional Association of Teachers of Special Needs, `www.patoss-dyslexia.org.uk`, can give you a list of teachers in your area who may be able to carry out additional testing and give advice. To find parents, specialist teachers and dyslexia groups who can advise you, check out Appendix B at the back of this book.

Chapter 18 has the details of getting an assessment when you're an adult. The Am I Dyslexic? online test (`www.amidyslexic.com`) is a relatively cheap way of finding out if you have a specific learning difficulty. For some adults, online testing provides enough information and a full psychological assessment is costly and unnecessary. If you're unemployed, the Disability Education Adviser at your Job Centre may be able to recommend assessment and pay for it.

Do-it-yourself testing

If you want to test your child yourself (or test yourself!), you can find worthwhile tests online. Simply locate the test or tests, create a relaxed atmosphere, behave like a detached but kindly administrator and see what results you can turn up.

Following are some places to start your search for free online tests:

✔ www.dyslexia-test.com (worldwide tests that purport to measure dyslexia)

✔ www.dyslexiacentre.co.uk

✔ www.bda-dyslexia.org.uk

You can also purchase the Dyslexia Screener on CD (published by DI Trading). Go to www.dyslexiaaction.org.uk for this screener and an extensive catalogue of 'open' tests you can buy.

Anyone can use these tests (no matter where you live), but they're obviously not the same as personal face-to-face tests. And remember: do-it-yourself tests are only screening tools; think of them as a starting point.

Preparing Your Child (and Yourself) for Testing

Before the LA assesses your child, give your child's SENCO any paperwork you've saved, like paediatric reports, vision and hearing test results, a list of things you've observed your child struggling with and any other relevant information, such as details of other family members who are dyslexic. She can give the paperwork to the LA psychologist, or alternatively you can deliver the information to your LA yourself. If you're having tests done by someone outside the school system, give her all the same information and your child's school reports, too.

Giving the test administrator the information you have well before the test makes good sense. She needs time to look it over so she can use it as another piece in her complete diagnosis.

This checklist gives you the material you need to gather together to make a portfolio for your child:

✔ A brief account of when your child started to walk and talk and of any difficulties there were with the birth

✔ A brief account of warning signs you've seen (see Chapters 3, 4 and 5 for more about general and specific symptoms)

✔ A brief account of things your child's teachers have said about him and the kinds of reading instruction they've given him

✔ Medical information (especially about eyes and ears)

✔ Formal tests and reports from school

✔ Samples of his writing and spelling

✔ Samples of books (or lists of books) he reads

✔ Lists of words that are hard for him to read and write

Tests are scary for most people, but for someone with dyslexia, who's used to low scores and embarrassment, they can be much worse. Remember to tell your child that he's being tested so he can do better and not feel so bad in class. Tell him that no right or wrong answers exist and that the assessment may highlight some things he's very good at, as well as not so good at.

One aspect of testing you may want to mentally prepare yourself for is the parent questionnaire. Before your child's tested, a teacher or psychologist may ask you to fill out a questionnaire, which you may not like doing. The questions include things like these:

✔ Was your child delivered normally?

✔ Did your child reach normal developmental milestones on time?

✔ Is your child often sick?

✔ Does your child have friends?

✔ Has anyone in your family had reading problems?

✔ Do you read to your child at home?

You may feel like you're on trial, so remind yourself that these tests aren't designed purely to make you squirm – even if you feel that way. The psychologist actually uses this information to get a clear picture of factors (like frequent school absences) that may have contributed to your child's reading failure. Fill out the answers, relax and roll with the punches. You're getting a reminder of how your child feels about being tested and how you need to tell him he's not on trial, not stupid and not being graded.

Receiving Test Results and Putting Them to Work

By now you have a good idea of the tests and assessors who are available and which, if any, you need. But are you reminding yourself that, most of all, test results have to work *for* your child? Knowing that your child is dyslexic or trusting the school to take things from there isn't enough; you must steer or dictate what happens next. If your child gets extra help in school, you need to check that the help's working. If your child isn't making progress, you need to pinpoint why and try something else.

You also need to follow up to see whether your child still gets the same amount of help in the months following testing. Your child may let slip that he doesn't see Mrs Brown (the LSA) three times a week any more but only once, so you need to keep regular tabs on the help he's supposed to be getting. If your child goes to a tutor instead of receiving in-school help, you still need to be watchful because you can't assume that professionals have everything all sewn up.

Dyslexia's an ongoing condition. Your role as supporter and advocate is ongoing too. Your job is to constantly match tasks to your child rather than have people force tasks on him. Not everything works for your child, so you both need to get good at mixing and matching. Your child has individual needs, and you know them better than anyone else. But you also need to help your child do more for himself. The older he gets, the more he needs to speak up for himself and let teachers know exactly what kinds of activities and aids help him perform on an equal footing with other students.

In the following sections, we tell you the terms you often hear in test results and how to proceed with your child's education, whether or not he qualifies for special education.

Breaking down the terminology in test results

When the test administrator explains your child's test results to you, you're bound to hear some terminology you may not be familiar with. Here's advance warning of the meaning of some of the common phrases:

- ✔ **Age:** A test age of 7.2 means your child performed like an average child aged 7 years and 2 months.

- ✔ **Rapid naming:** Can your child pull sound information (like names of things and parts of words) from his mind? This is an auditory processing skill, which is often measured by asking a child to name pictures quickly. If your child can't quickly name common objects, like a toothbrush, vase and curtains, his auditory processing skills are weak.

- ✔ **Auditory memory:** Can your child keep bits of sound information in his mind for a short time? This is auditory memory, which is often measured by asking a child to remember a few words over a few minutes. If your child can't recall a sequence of numbers correctly after being told (and asked to remember) them, and reverse the sequence of numbers as part of the test, he has weak auditory memory.

✔ **Percentile ranking:** If your child gets a percentile ranking of 14, he's 14th from the bottom of 100 average children. In other words, 86 out of 100 children have done better than him.

✔ **Phonemic skills:** This has to do with *phonemes*, or the smallest chunks of sound inside words (like c-a-t and sh-ou-t). Your child's grasp of phonemes is tested when he's asked what sounds he hears inside words.

✔ **Phonological skills:** This refers to general sound, letter and word skills, such as being able to rhyme and name letters. If your child can distinguish different sounds inside words and words that sound alike, he has good phonological skills.

✔ **Standardised:** A standardised test has been given to hundreds of children, so the test administrator has a normal bell curve of scores on which to plot your child's score. She knows how children in general perform on this test and how your child scores relative to the general population the test is for.

Finding out that your child has an SpLD

If your child's results in the tests that indicate dyslexia show that he's performing far below the level you expect of him, he's diagnosed as having an SpLD (specific learning disability) and should get additional help.

You may be told that your child has a 'learning disability', a 'specific learning disability' or a 'specific language disability'. The terms 'specific learning disability' and 'specific language disability' are really just ways of saying your child probably has dyslexia. Other learning disabilities exist, but dyslexia's the most common.

Other learning disabilities include *dysgraphia* (difficulty with writing), *dyscalculia* (difficulty with maths) and *dyspraxia* (difficulty with motor skills). Dyslexia, dyspraxia, ADD/ADHD and Asperger Syndrome are all on the same spectrum and co-morbidity, when a child has two or more SpLDs, often exists.

The following sections give you the details on working with an officially recognised SpLD child at school and at home.

Seeing SpLD at work in class

You're probably wondering what happens when the paperwork's filed away and your child gets into class as a newly assessed child with an SpLD. Specifically, your child's teachers must accommodate his needs in class and document exactly how they do that in his Statement of Special Educational Needs (SEN), a written and working document specifically about him. You attend review meetings to assess how well things are working, but you need to keep in touch with the teacher and the SENCO because the meetings typically happen only once a year.

The SENCO is usually the individual who's ultimately responsible for setting up your child's Statement of SEN and seeing that everyone follows through. She gives your child what you may think of as remedial instruction, usually in her room with just a few other students, depending on the provisions in the Statement.

Watch your child's reading and writing. If he's not making progress, meet his SENCO and request some practical changes, like having enlarged print for your child or allowing him extra time to finish assignments. Bring up your concerns at your review meeting – and keep doing that! Go to Chapter 8 for complete details on the review.

The SENCO is hopefully a nice, approachable person who has many strategies at her fingertips to help your child. If you're lucky, she may also be trained in a reading programme. These programmes are structured, phonological and sequential – just right for a struggling child. Here are some popular programmes designed especially to move readers forward (see Chapter 7 for details):

- **Lindamood–Bell:** Of the several Lindamood–Bell programmes, the Lindamood Intensive Phonological Sequencing, called LIPS for short, is the most common. In a LIPS programme, children become aware of the actions their mouths make when they say different sounds.

- **Orton–Gillingham (O–G):** This programme's probably the most common of all. It's been around a long time, and most other programmes describe themselves as being influenced by O–G.

- **Hickey Multisensory Language Course:** This was developed by Kathleen Hickey, who travelled from the UK to the US in the 1930s to see the Orton–Gillingham methods in practice and to train on alphabetic phonics. When she came back to Britain, she became the first Director of Studies at the Dyslexia Institute in 1972.

- **Dyslexia Institute Literacy Programme (DILP):** This is a structured, cumulative and multisensory reading and spelling programme delivered by teachers who have undertaken a postgraduate training course.

Now when a teacher asks you 'Has your child done Hickey?' you know what she's talking about! These programmes are often named after the people who wrote them (that's why they have unusual names).

Responding to an SpLD at home

After you know that your child has an SpLD, don't think that you're not qualified to help him. No matter what terminology you use, the same basic truth holds: your child struggles in class and needs as much love, support and assurance as you can give him because he's having a tough time. Imagine how he must feel if he's constantly lagging behind classmates and trying to hold his own. Imagine the kind of teasing he puts up with. You're his greatest ally in feeling good about himself, so gear up for the ride! You can help him out with schoolwork too of course, and be every bit as good at helping him as the professionals (after you know how).

To look deeper into helping your child out emotionally, flip to Chapter 15; for help with at-home activities, check out Chapters 11 to 14. Organisations such as Dyslexia Action (www.dyslexiaaction.org.uk) regularly run reasonably priced courses to inform parents about dyslexia and how to help their children at home. Some take place over several weeks, while others run for half a day. Dyslexia Action doesn't need to teach your child for you to attend these courses. The BDA (www.bdadyslexia.org.uk) also has local help groups for parents.

Discovering that your child isn't recognised as having an SpLD

LAs have a limited amount of money to go around, so not everyone can get additional specialist help. Even when your teachers see your child struggling and you're certain he needs more help, chances are your child doesn't qualify as having an SpLD. About five children in each class (or about 20 per cent) struggle with reading, but only the children who are the worst out of 100 (on the first percentile for reading and spelling) or just above, are entitled to a Statement of Special Educational Needs. Test results separate children eligible for additional help in the form of an SSEN from those who aren't eligible.

What can you do when the LA tells you that your child's test results (whether they're from an LA psychologist or an independent tester) don't qualify him for additional support or a Statement? You can take the following steps:

- ✔ Formally appeal against the decision
- ✔ Dispute the test scores and get private testing done
- ✔ See what the school can provide without a Statement
- ✔ Get help from the school by being friendly
- ✔ Get independent tutoring
- ✔ Tutor your child yourself
- ✔ Home-school your child

The following sections discuss the details of these options.

Disputing the LA's decision

If you disagree with the LA's decision, don't give up! You can appeal against the decision. To fight your case, find someone (who talks in down-to-earth terms) to tell you about your rights. Luckily, we've tracked down great help for you so you can save a bundle of time and energy. Interested? Check out Appendix B for more information.

When you contact someone for help, be selective about what you say and stay focused. Offload and grumble to other parents who've been through the same things as you, but with a professional, be professional. Jot down a list of questions you want answers to and stick to your point. After someone tells you your rights and how to proceed, you can find an independent tester (we talk about independent testers earlier in this chapter). If the independent tester confirms the LA's results, you probably want to end your search. If the independent tester disagrees with the LA's results, you can take your new information back to the LA. Hopefully you reach a resolution at appeal, but if not, you may be looking at legal proceedings at the High Court. In either case, you can find people to help you by checking out Appendix B at the back of this book. Some solicitors and organisations like the British Dyslexia Association (BDA) know about this kind of thing as well.

Even if you can't secure a Statement for your child, he can still be on the Register of Special Needs at the school and receive an Individual Education Plan (IEP) if they're at School Action, which is the first stage of intervention (see Chapters 8 and 10 for the lowdown here). Doing so ensures that your child still receives some help.

Securing help from school by being friendly

When you worry about your child, your whole world seems darker. You may find yourself being angry all day, sleepless half the night and not in the best state to say productive things to teachers. Try to have an 'I'm reasonable and caring' image up-front even when you have dark thoughts whirling around behind. Try to believe that teachers really *do* want to help your child, and if they don't seem that way, they're probably overworked or really *do* think your child can catch up. Whatever the reasons, the important thing for you to do is to focus on your child's practical needs.

The best way to make things easier for your child in class is to help the teacher to help him. Suggest (politely and reasonably) practical things to help your child. Thank the teacher for any effort she makes for you and offer to help in any way you can.

Be calm, helpful and friendly to your child's teacher. Let her know that you aren't criticising her and you respect her competence, but you need help in making things easier for your child. Convey the belief that if you both work as a team on your child's behalf, he can succeed in class. We talk about building a good relationship with the teacher and asking her to make classroom accommodations in Chapter 10.

When teachers often see your face in school and know you help out with the Parent–Teacher Association, the Christmas fair, in the second-hand uniform shop or at other school events, your child registers higher in their consciousness. They're more likely to talk about him and think of him when new resources are available.

You may find after-hours school clubs to help your child too. Ask about homework clubs, volunteer tutoring and social or athletic groups that can boost your child's self-esteem. Also try to befriend people who always know what's going on in school. Networking and keeping in the loop can make a big difference to your child. See Chapter 9 for more details on these options.

Finding independent tutoring

If your child's struggling in class, you may decide to have him privately tutored regardless of whether he gets extra help in school. When you look for a tutor or learning centre, consider the following:

- ✔ The cost of the lessons
- ✔ The distance you have to travel
- ✔ The tutor's qualifications and experience
- ✔ Whether the tutor gives structured, phonological and sequential instruction (remember those buzzwords?)
- ✔ Whether you can sell the idea to your child

Check out Chapter 9 for more about finding and using a tutor.

Tutoring your child yourself

No matter what happens in school or with an outside tutor, you can help your child at home. Don't think that because you're not a dyslexia-trained teacher you can't be effective. Of course the term 'dyslexia' brings up scary-sounding things like multisensory teaching and phonological skills, but these terms are really just fancy words for stuff that doesn't need to be difficult. Some children don't like being formally tutored by their parents but you can help your child in a fun way (just as much as a teacher or tutor can) and save yourself a lot of money and commuting time.

To get the naked, practical strategies that successful teachers of people with dyslexia use, flip to Chapters 11 to 14.

Home schooling

Home schooling's getting more and more popular and may be an option you want to know about. If you home-school, you get to monitor your child's performance closely and adapt lessons to suit his strengths, and you don't get the usual homework strife. The drawback's that your child's social life takes a massive cut. In Chapter 7, we tell you why parents choose to home-school, what they teach and how successful they are. A good website if you're considering home schooling is www.homeeducators.co.uk.

Looking at Your Options When You Decide Not to Test

Should you ever do without testing altogether? Most people get tests done because they want to know exactly what's wrong and how to move forward. They want a starting point as a way to gauge progress. Sometimes, parents decide to start tuition to see if it improves the problem before they make the decision to go for formal assessments. Others may consider all the factors (the SpLD label, the likelihood of not getting specialist individual help and their child's anxiety) and decide to do without testing and move straight to tutoring, asking for small accommodations in class and helping more at home.

You should skip testing only when your child's problems seem mild (see Chapter 3 for a list of general symptoms) and after you've had a discussion with your child's teacher. Overall, the solution for diagnosing dyslexia is indeed testing, so if you have any doubts about what to do, have your child tested.

This list gives you reasons why no testing at all may be an option for you:

- ✔ You can't afford it. If this is the case, don't think that your child's disadvantaged. Big, comprehensive tests are good, but so are small, quick tests. Sure, you get all the bells and whistles with a test battery, but the bottom line is that you need to know what practical instruction your child needs. A good teacher can tell this from quick, inexpensive commercial tests she has in class or from tests she devises herself. This kind of test, which measures only your child's skills without comparing them against other children's scores, is called a *criterion-referenced test*. If you want to try one out yourself, flip to Appendix A.

- ✔ You have a great relationship with your child's teacher and know that she goes the extra mile for your child even though he's not formally identified as having an SpLD. You pretty much know that your child can't qualify for additional specialist help anyway because you see other kids in class struggling just as much as your child and have talked the situation over with teachers and parents who've been in the same boat.

If your child's struggling in school, the teacher sees his difficulties and probably does her best to help your child in class, regardless of whether test results boost your case.

✔ You know a good tutor and believe that your child can make progress with her. She may give your child a quick, useful assessment so you save the stress of two to five hours of testing (which says the same things but in fancier words!), save money and sidestep the SpLD label in school.

✔ You read this book, check out the websites listed at the back and join your local branch of BDA. You know your child has weak phonological skills, you know he needs a lot of practice with sounding out and you're helping him yourself or getting a tutor. You don't feel you need to fork out a few hundred pounds for someone else to tell you what you already figured out for yourself. Great, what are you waiting for?

If you have tried all of the above and you still need more help, you can always go for assessment later on and all of the things you have done will add ammunition to your case. It doesn't have to be a final decision.

In case you think that doing without testing sounds overconfident, we should tell you that we talk to plenty of parents who manage to identify and treat their child's problems by themselves. They network, work with their child each night, monitor his progress and see him move into higher reading groups in class and score better marks! In fact, two parents Katrina knows took the do-it-yourself approach and are now training to be special education teachers.

Part III
Exploring Your Options for Schools and Programmes

'Somehow, I don't think this school is going to be a great help to our George & his dyslexia.'

In this part . . .

Of course you want the best school, the best teacher and, naturally, the best reading programme for your child. But in the real world, how much choice do you really get? Does every alternative school cost a fortune? Is your child's school already using the best reading programme (for children with dyslexia)? Can a Statement of Special Educational Needs really make that much difference to your child's chances in school? This part's crammed with the answers to all these practical questions – and a lot more besides.

Chapter 7

Choosing the Best School for Your Child

In This Chapter

▶ Considering general features to help you decide on a school
▶ Knowing what traditional state schools provide
▶ Introducing yourself to staff members
▶ Checking out alternative forms of schooling

Your child needs extra help in class, and naturally you want her educated in a place where she gets a lot of it. You have some important decisions to make when selecting her school.

If your local state school has a great Special Educational Needs Coordinator (or SENCO) who uses a good programme with your child and sees her every morning for an hour, you're on to a great thing! Assuming that you see your child making steady progress and know that she's happy, this is the ideal scenario. And some children are this lucky.

But sometimes your child gets hardly any time with the SENCO or LSA (learning support assistant), and neither you nor your child likes him anyway. Then you have to take a look at the big picture. Maybe your child's generally happy in school, so a good choice for you is to send her to a private specialist for the help she misses out on at school. On the other hand, if your child is unhappy at school and if you've heard of a great school especially for children with dyslexia, you may want to put up with the initial stress of changing schools for the long-term benefits.

In this chapter, we give you a list of features to consider as you decide on a school for your child. We also describe the features and staff members of traditional state schools and explain the alternative schooling options your child has.

Questioning the Kind of School Your Child Needs

Your child needs a lot of support to overcome her dyslexia. She needs to mix with people who understand her and don't bring her down. Maybe she has special talents to nurture, too. Here are some of the questions you need to ask when you make the crucially important decision about which school to send your child to:

- Can I see a copy of the latest OFSTED report?

- How many children are in a class? If my child needs additional support how many children would there be in a group?

- What kind of support can my child get with reading and learning? What programmes does the school use?

- Do the teachers seem happy and sensitive to all the children's needs?

- Does the school use a reading programme like Reading Recovery (see 'Focusing on school programmes', later in this chapter)?

- How much group work do students do?

- Are there withdrawal sessions or in-class support?

- How much homework may my child get?

- Can my child use a computer for most of her assignments?

- What resources does the school have for special needs? Are the learning support assistants trained in SpLDs?

- Does my child's prospective teacher use a classroom buddy system?

- Does the school have a homework club?

- How often can I see my child's teacher to discuss progress?

- What extra-curricular activities does the school provide?

- Does my child have friends at the local state school?

- How much are parents involved in the school?

- Does the school have a tutoring programme?

- Is there any flexibility with the choice of foreign language? (Children with dyslexia often find languages such as French harder than Spanish.)

- Does the school encourage parents to help in class and feel free to drop in any time?

- Does my local state school have a trained SENCO?

- Does my local school look well equipped with things such as new books, computers and interactive whiteboards?

✔ Do the teachers at the local school seem happy and friendly to the children? Do the children look happy and friendly?

✔ Is the head teacher at my local school approachable?

✔ What provision is made for parents to discuss progress and/or problems with the relevant staff?

✔ Does the local school welcome parent visits?

✔ When are reports sent out?

✔ Does the school have a dedicated Learning Support Unit to help those children with specific learning difficulties? (Learning Support Units are in separate, well-resourced areas and the children are withdrawn from class for additional support.)

✔ Do I have special requirements, like wanting a Catholic education for my child or advanced instruction in violin?

✔ What are the fees for private schools and can I afford them? Are any scholarships or bursaries available?

✔ Can I afford to send my child to a private tutor or specialist dyslexia teacher (to augment her education)? What are the costs likely to be?

Decisions, decisions: Do you have a choice of state schools?

Your house sits within a designated local education authority (LA). Within that LA, one primary school is closer to you than the rest, making it your 'local' school. However, admission to primary and secondary schools isn't automatic as all schools have admissions criteria that determine who gains a place if the school receives more applications than it has places available.

Parents have a right to express a preference in a *maintained school*, which include grant-maintained schools and schools funded by the LA. Maintained schools have to provide for children with SEN, including dyslexia, and must also have a Special Educational Needs Policy that they can use to inform parents. LAs and school governors have a duty to comply with parents' preferences, and in expressing a preference a parent doesn't need to choose a school in a particular LA. Sending a child across a LA boundary is possible.

On a proposed Statement of Special Educational Needs, Part 4 is left blank for parents to state their choice of school for their child. Part 4 of the final Statement must state the name of a school, which may not be the same as the parent's choice. Sometimes the final Statement gives alternative arrangements for education other than in a school placement.

The rules are that a school must admit your child unless doing so would make it difficult for them to teach their classes effectively or make efficient use of their resources. If you apply for your child to attend a selective school, they can refuse to admit her if her ability or aptitude

(continued)

(continued)

make her unsuitable. Also, in certain cases – most often with church schools – a school can refuse your child if she doesn't have a religious background.

Schools that aren't full have a duty to admit all the children whose parents want them to attend there. However, some schools are more attractive than others to parents, and popular schools attract applications for children to attend there, often getting oversubscribed as a result. To deal with this, schools have admissions policies that explain their criteria for offering places. Typical criteria give preference to children who live nearby and any who have older brothers or sisters at the school.

If the school you applied to doesn't admit your child, remember that you do have the right to appeal against the decision. Your local dyslexia association can help you with information about the appeals process, as can the `www.direct.gov.uk` website, but you should initially receive details in the letter sent out informing you that the school has refused a place for your child.

If the school you applied to does admit your child, be on the ball when the SENCO tells you (informally if your child doesn't have a Statement, or formally during a review meeting if she does) what kind of help your child is entitled to get at school, and how it'll be provided, so that you can ask for changes or additions and then monitor how the help pans out in practice. (In Chapter 10, we talk more about the kinds of help and accommodations your child can get in class.) And from the outset, be prepared to go to school often, if need be, to push your child's case.

After you prioritise your questions, you and your child need to visit the school of your choice on a normal working day, in the hope that it offers at least a number of the things you want. Many schools provide Open Days so that you can visit in advance of applying to the school. When you get there, go through your questions, try to see classes in progress, visit the Learning Support Unit and go to inspect the places that are important to your child socially, like the atmosphere in the playground and dining hall. Through this mix of academic and social information, you get a feel of what the school is like and can do for your child with dyslexia. Often, after taking into consideration all these points about a school, you just rely on your own gut feelings!

The question of whether your child gets additional support with a Statement of Special Educational Needs, which we discuss in Chapter 8, doesn't only apply to state schools. Although rare, children in private schools can fulfil the required criteria set down by the Local Authority and have a Statement of SEN issued.

Looking at What the State Sector Offers

Your local state school has to account for the way it spends its money and show that it makes appropriate provision for children with disabilities. In the following sections, we lead you through the assessments, special instruction and other services to watch out for and, if they're missing, inquire about.

Supplying assessment services

After your child's school decides that your child needs to see an educational psychologist with a view to being granted a Statement, the head will make a formal request for an assessment from the local education authority (LA) and you get an answer within a set time (usually six weeks). An educational psychologist from the LA then visits the school and hopefully runs your child through a complete battery of cognitive, diagnostic and attainment tests. If he finds that she's performing at a level that falls into the criteria the LA has set, your child is *statemented*. This isn't as easy as it sounds as your child generally needs to be the worst performing child out of a hundred, or just slightly better. If she is the second-worst child out of a hundred she is unlikely to fall into the criteria for a Statement. See Chapter 6 for full details of testing.

At this point, you may hear about your child's 'learning disability' or 'specific learning disability' rather than her 'dyslexia'. Dyslexia's a specific kind of learning disability, but teachers don't often use the word (because they don't feel qualified to do so). Your Local Authority psychologist may not use it either, simply because his mandate is to deal with 'learning disabilities'.

Your child may have dyslexia but still not qualify for specialist help. She may be struggling, but not enough (about four years behind) to qualify for a Statement.

Focusing on school programmes

If you're brand new to special educational needs and reading programmes, boy have we got some news for you! At some point during your child's education, you may hear weird terms like 'Alpha to Omega' and 'Toe by Toe'. These are names of popular programmes that both specialists and non-specialists may use. We run through them in this section so that when a teacher tells you that your child gets Alpha to Omega, you can nod sagely and ask, 'Do you prefer it to Toe by Toe?'

Ready? In this section we describe several programmes, any one of which your child may come into contact with at school. A couple of them are straightforward and inexpensive enough that you may consider trying them out at home. (We feature a few of these reading programmes in even more detail in Chapter 20.)

Some of the following programmes are used in schools and may also feature in learning centres. For more about sending your child to a tutor or a learning centre, check out Chapter 9.

✔ **Orton–Gillingham (O–G):** Developed by Samuel Orton and Anna Gillingham in the 1930s, this is the grandfather of multisensory, phonics and research-based programmes. In real English that means that it engages a few of your child's senses while she learns phonics rules and patterns, and it's backed by plenty of research. Everyone knows about O–G – it's the most popular programme of the bunch – and several other programmes are offshoots of it. Teachers and tutors rarely train in O–G techniques in the UK, but you can train in it yourself if you want. For info, visit www.orton-gillingham.org.uk.

✔ **Lindamood–Bell:** These are programmes designed by Ms Lindamood and Ms Bell. The most widely used is Lindamood Intensive Phonological Sequencing – LiPS for short – for the clever reason that the programme makes children become aware of the actions their mouths make when they say different sounds. Programmes are short and intense. In the US, children get one-on-one help for four to six weeks, four hours a day at a Lindamood–Bell centre. For information have a look at www.lindamood bell.com, but remember that the programme's fairly uncommon in the UK.

✔ **DILP (Dyslexia Institute Literacy Programme):** Only trained teachers who've taken the Post Graduate Certificate or Diploma through Dyslexia Action can use DILP. The programme is structured, cumulative and multisensory, and can be taught individually or in pairs. The programme has a letter order that lists the sequence for teaching letter–sound links, from single vowels and consonants to less frequently used letter strings such as -eu and -eigh. Each pupil has her own pack of reading cards. Individual learners accumulate these cards to remind them of the letter–sound links already covered in reading, to act as a memory aid and to develop automaticity. Pupils also have spelling cards, with each card representing one sound, and can add different ways of spelling the sound to it as the learner covers them in the language programme. DILP also offers multisensory strategies for spelling, and reading and spelling practice at each teaching point. The programme organises word lists so that learners can use pattern and analogy to aid reading and spelling. DILP encourages a flowing handwriting style to ensure that recurring letter patterns become automatic, and also encourages *metacognition*, or learning about one's own learning style. DILP helps pupils to become independent learners.

✔ **Units of Sound (Version 4.4):** Children from about age 8 (or younger if they have good keyboard skills) can effectively use this multisensory reading and spelling programme either at home or at school with a learning support assistant. A test places the learner on one of three stages for reading and spelling, and the resource allows her to work independently on the computer. In each stage, the programme builds reading accuracy, vocabulary, spelling, sentence-writing skills, listening skills, visual skills and comprehension. Units of Sound can be networked and is used in many schools with small groups of children. Each of the three stages costs £90; the complete set's available for £250 from DI Trading (`www.dyslexiaaction.org.uk/store`).

✔ **Reading Recovery:** This well-known programme originated in New Zealand and focuses on children in Year 1. It offers an intensive blast of daily instruction for 12 to 20 weeks. It's not a top programme for teaching children with dyslexia because it isn't phonics-based or multisensory, but it does give children individual instruction and a lot of reading at their level and gets good results with most participants. For more information, visit the Institute of Education at the University of London website (`www.ioe.ac.uk`).

The programmes that we list next are smaller, less popular programmes than the ones in the preceding list, but they're still great and plenty of SENCOs and LSAs use them in schools. You don't get the training courses and substantive research that accompany the bigger names, but you can buy what you need quickly and easily, whoever you are. Because the programmes we outline in the following list are also readily available to parents, we also give prices and a quick summary of what you get for your money:

✔ **Alpha to Omega** by Beve Hornby and Frula Shear (Heinemann) costs £11.00 for the student's book. You can buy the whole programme from `www.dyslexiaaction.org.uk/store`.

✔ **Sound Linkage** by Peter Hatcher (Whurr Publishers) costs £52.50 and is available from WH Smith. This book focuses on the sounds of speech and offers ready-made lessons and materials to promote phonological awareness.

✔ **Toe by Toe** by Keda and Harry Cowling (Keda Publications) is a workbook/manual in one. (Many LSAs in schools as well as parents use Toe by Toe.) For £25, you get a book of exercises and progress charts for tutoring your child for 20 minutes a day. Your child progresses to the next lesson only after passing a mastery test. You can find Toe by Toe at `www.toe-by-toe.co.uk`.

Just because a programme has a good track record doesn't mean that your child succeeds in it. Different children like different methods, so don't think you've come to a dead end if your child hates a programme that everyone else raves about. Try another one. Look for a teacher or tutor who has experience with struggling kids. Even if he doesn't talk about Orton–Gillingham or Lindamood–Bell, he may still do great phonetic and multisensory activities with your child. (See Chapters 12 and 14 for more about these types of activities.) Watch how your child fares. You don't need a PhD in reading programmes to see whether she's getting the hang of sounding out, enjoying the tutoring and becoming a better reader.

Giving help above and beyond the classroom

Schools can do great things for your child with dyslexia outside class. When enthusiastic teachers and parents come up with ideas and give their time, all kinds of things – like homework clubs – can happen.

Here are some of the clubs and activities you may want to ask about in a school:

- ✔ **Buddy system:** Your child can be a younger child's buddy or get taken under an older child's wing herself. Either way, this is great stuff! Schools that put children to work being friends and helpers for other children are great places to be.

- ✔ **Homework club:** If your school runs a homework club, checking it out may be worthwhile. Older children often help out in homework clubs or listen to readers, and if that's the case in your school, you may be able to commandeer a kind, interested one to take special care of your child!

- ✔ **Special responsibilities:** Good teachers know that giving a child special responsibilities, like being lunch monitor, works wonders for her self-confidence. If your child isn't already doing a special job, put in a good word for her.

- ✔ **Speciality one-off programmes:** Sometimes a school offers a short, one-off programme to help children with things like assertiveness or social skills. Keep your ear to the ground so that your child doesn't miss out. If you can't volunteer in school, get friendly with another parent who's always there so that you get to hear what's going on.

- ✔ **Sports and arts:** Yes, these things are pretty obvious, but we feel that we have to mention them quickly anyway. Encourage your child in any non-academic activities she enjoys. She needs many ways to feel happy and successful, because happy children are better equipped to weather the knocks that dyslexia can bring.

- ✔ **Tutoring for your child:** Most schools ask parents to volunteer to listen to kids read. Often they set up programmes in which a parent is trained and regularly works with a child once or twice a week. Look for this kind of programme because after a volunteer parent knows how to help your child, great reading progress can come from this special one-on-one coaching.

- ✔ **Your child tutoring other children:** On the surface, asking a child with dyslexia to tutor another child may seem ridiculous, but it works. As long as the teacher finds something your child can cope with, like marking spellings from an answer sheet, your child can feel useful and important (and who doesn't need that!) and brush up on her own skills in the process.

A responsible position

Recently Tracey's daughter's teacher told her that he wanted to give her child some special responsibilities. 'She'll rise to the occasion,' he said. A few days later, Tracey's child came home from school with this to say: 'Guess what, mum? I'm now officially a very important person. Mr Peterson gave me a truly responsible job. I'm in charge of the class fish for the term, and if I'm really good I'll be promoted to being in charge of the class hamster.'

Tracey's daughter, evidently being tongue-in-cheek, was really telling her that she'd seen right through the plot, but even so, Tracey could

tell her daughter was a little bit proud to be in charge of the fish. She held her position for the term and really did rise to the occasion.

Any reasonable responsibilities that you give your child with dyslexia can make her feel more confident. Even if she grumbles about a job, it still gives her a feeling of independence and being relied on. And children with dyslexia, even more than other children, need to strengthen their people skills and work ethic so that they can outshine the weak spots in their literacy skills.

Providing sensitivity to your child's needs

A couple of years ago Tracey asked her child's teacher if her child could do a slightly different weekly spelling list than the other children. She gave really great reasons and offered to provide the list and come to class each week to help mark it if that helped. The teacher said, 'If I let one child do it differently, they all want to.' (She also spent a lot of time shouting at the children and telling them they were the worst she'd ever taught, but that's a whole other story!)

This teacher was inflexible, which is exactly what you don't want. It shouldn't happen, of course, especially if your child's been officially deemed dyslexic (or learning disabled), but it does. We could start lengthy tirades about the awful things we've seen happen to children with dyslexia, but instead – because doing so's more productive – we're going to tell you about the great things we've seen teachers (who take the trouble to put themselves in your child's shoes) do. In schools and classrooms that are sensitive to a child's extra needs, you see these kinds of things:

✔ **Small group activities:** Your child with dyslexia probably enjoys small group activities because she can talk tasks through with her group and contribute in ways that emphasise her strengths and sidestep her weaknesses (for example, drawing posters or taking photos instead of writing). In a small group, your child may also feel more secure. Fewer eyes are on her than when she has to ask or answer questions in the whole class.

✔ **Partners working together:** As long as both partners get along, partnerships are a perfect fit inside your child with dyslexia's comfort zone. An understanding partner may allow your child to dictate words for her to write, assume responsibility for tasks that take the least writing and develop a friendship in the process.

✔ **Creative projects:** Here's where your child with dyslexia gets to shine. She shows her artistic, dramatic and technological skills and gets better at thinking of ways to apply these skills to other classroom projects too.

✔ **A designated classmate that each student can call on when she needs help:** At one time or another, all children forget what they're supposed to be doing for homework and need to call a friend. You can pretty much expect your child with dyslexia to get stressed about homework often, so a friend on the end of the line (phone or Internet) is a must. Help your child keep and use a reliable contact list.

✔ **Use of computers and digital recorders:** Older children with dyslexia can save themselves a lot of trouble by becoming computer literate and knowing how to use a digital recorder. If you can manage, try to keep abreast of technology or even just keep pace with your child's technological know-how. If not, maybe a friend can help you out.

✔ **Word lists posted on walls:** After you show your child how to sound out the parts of words that sound out easily and highlight other parts, tape those words to a bathroom or other much-viewed wall. If you have a whole list of spellings, try to put them into word families too (like *round*, *sound* and *pound*).

✔ **Classroom help from parents:** When parents help in class, the teacher gets more time with students. Your child with dyslexia benefits, along with everyone else.

✔ **Scheduled time with the teacher for every child:** One-on-one teaching is the most effective teaching your child with dyslexia can get. Scheduled, personal time with the teacher's a definite plus.

✔ **Respectful tone of voice in use by everyone, including the teacher:** Your child with dyslexia has enough to deal with without having to listen to a teacher shout at students or other students shouting at each other (or being rude in other ways). A respectful classroom in which the teacher has kind but firm control is the ideal.

✔ **Full break time for everyone (detentions aren't common):** Your child with dyslexia needs her break time. In a great classroom, the teacher deals with issues like non-completion of assignments in ways that don't deprive children of their wind-down (and eating) time.

Meeting the Staff at School

When we walk into our children's school, it hits us right away – these are really nice places (and we think we're pretty good judges having worked in several schools and sent children to several more)! The secretary's nice, children walk past and say 'Hello' and you don't see a line of miscreants waiting outside the head teacher's office. And when the head appears, he smiles and sometimes stops to chat!

In the following sections, we introduce you to the main people at any given state school. If you get a good feeling after meeting them, you can feel more comfortable about putting your child with dyslexia's education in their hands.

Familiarising yourself with the classroom teacher

Please, please, please, let your child have a good teacher! If your child's ever had a really bad school year, you know (and endless research substantiates it) that the teacher's the single most important factor in your child's success in class. In the following sections, we explain the qualities of a good teacher for a child with dyslexia and show you how to improve your chances of getting your child happily paired with one. (For complete details on working productively with teachers, see Chapter 10.)

Sizing up qualities in a good teacher

A good teacher for your child with dyslexia sets up his classroom in the ways we talk about earlier in the chapter: he fits small group activities into his programmes, matches up buddies, encourages creativity and maintains a warm but disciplined atmosphere in his dyslexia-friendly classroom. He has some special skills too because your child has a few special needs. Specifically, he's:

- ✔ **Approachable:** Your child can always go to him after class and ask for extra guidance.

- ✔ **Flexible:** If one strategy doesn't work for your child, he's happy to try another.

- ✔ **Aware:** He understands that when your child can't do things in the same way as other kids, this doesn't mean that she can't do them at all. He shouldn't allow your child to skip tasks; instead, she needs to try out different strategies until she finds her fit.

Requesting a specific teacher for your child

Teachers get together at the start (or end) of the school year to decide which child goes with which teacher. The head teacher oversees the process, but the teacher your child just left probably wields most power. Cultivating a friendship with your child's teacher so that you can get preferential treatment may sound mercenary, but of course, that's exactly how the world works. Dyslexia can be taxing enough (for your entire family) without finding out that your child gets the super-uninspiring, no-control teacher from hell.

The fact that you don't get to choose your child's teacher hardly seems fair, does it? Because that's the case, however, here are some things you can do to raise your odds of getting a good teacher:

- ✔ Be friendly with your child's current teacher so that you can brazenly ask him (if you dare) to allocate your child to a specific teacher the following year. Tracey was once at a school where parents were quietly and dutifully filling out their information forms when a parent marched straight into the classroom and said, 'Judy, Oliver hates Mrs Young, so you have to put him with Mr Knight.' And yes, the next year Oliver was in Mr Knight's class!

- ✔ If your child's on School Action or School Action Plus, talk to her SENCO. Tell the SENCO which classroom teacher you want for your child so that he can add her comments to the selection process. (See the following section for more about SENCOs.)

- ✔ Talk to the teacher you want your child to have. He may remember you and ask if he can add your child to his list (as long as no one else has other plans).

- ✔ When the new school year begins, if you don't like your child's teacher, go to the head teacher right away. If you present a good case, he may put your child into another class, but if you wait longer than about three weeks, he's likely to tell you that you're too late.

   Both parents should see the head teacher, but make sure that you present a united front. Be calm, clear and tactful. Specify what's going wrong in concrete terms, but avoid personally criticising the teacher ('Ellie is unhappy' rather than 'Mrs Smith is awful'). Be firm and persistent.

- ✔ If your child hates going to school and you don't know whether to complain or sit a bad year out, remember that she can fall seriously behind in the early years. Write down all the incidents and comments your child tells you about, and date each one. Take this record with you to the head, if you have no luck with the class teacher or SENCO, and ask, on the basis of your child's stress or academic failure, for a change of class. Take someone (preferably someone who's good at negotiating) with you if you need to.

   No luck? Ask to see the governor responsible for special needs – every school has someone with that responsibility. Again, keep documenting what you're concerned about (for example low grades, punishments or

snide comments). If you feel that the school, not just the class, is causing your child to fail or be miserable, and your record of events shows
it, you may even (after a lot of fighting) get your LA to agree to move
your child to another school within the area. If all else fails and you're
prepared to take extreme measures, you may need to move to a different
area so that you can send your child to a school you've researched and
love the look of.

If the preceding sounds like we're scaremongering by telling you to march
boldly into school with your issues, that's because we hear from a lot of parents whose children are struggling in class. They're not sure whether their
problems are big enough to warrant serious complaint. They're not sure
whether they should keep quiet because the school on the whole is nice, their
child has friends and so on. Here's what we think is the deciding factor: your
child's reading problems don't get better by themselves. Without intervention,
they get worse. If your child doesn't get good intervention or she gets great
help with the resource teacher but she's so unhappy in her classroom that
she can't learn, speak up. Now. Trust your own judgement and don't wait for
someone to give you the okay. And if your child's seriously unhappy (she
cries most days, has bad dreams or has started wetting the bed), you're not
over-reacting by wanting to change a class or even school. In fact, you should
be making doing so a priority.

Acquainting yourself with the SENCO

A typical school has a SENCO teacher who's responsible for keeping your
child's Individual Education Plan (IEP) running smoothly and productively.
Typically, your child works with a learning support assistant (LSA) to get
extra help in a small group (either in class or outside) or, if she's lucky, has
one-to-one tutoring with the SENCO. Your school decides exactly what your
child gets, however, and budget and staffing influence that. (See Chapter 8 for
complete IEP details.)

SENCO teachers do great work, but just like in any other job, you get good
and not-so-good ones (and even with a great SENCO, he and your child may
not click). When Katrina took her Postgraduate Certificate in Education in
1993 to qualify as a secondary teacher, she received little more than half a
day's training on how to teach children with Specific Learning Difficulties.
No wonder so many teachers are in the dark about dyslexia! At the moment
the SENCO doesn't have to have specialist qualifications on top of his Initial
Teacher Training. The government is now trying to ensure that all SENCOs
are trained to Master's Level, but we've met many parents who have far more
knowledge of dyslexia than the SENCO in their child's school.

If your SENCO runs a special dyslexia treatment programme, like the Dyslexia
Institute's Literacy Programme or the Orton–Gillingham programme, you're
likely to be pleased with what you see. (We cover Orton–Gillingham and other

dyslexia treatment programmes in 'Focusing on school programmes', earlier in this chapter.) But does a good programme always equal good results? No. The teacher factor's still crucial. Your child gains much more from a teacher she likes than from one she doesn't like, so ideally you want a good teacher (see 'Sizing up qualities in a good teacher', earlier in this chapter) who uses a good programme.

Ah, but maybe even that isn't strictly true. Plenty of great SENCO teachers use their own eclectic mix of strategies rather than a commercial programme. They (as well as the programme users) understand how important phonetic understanding is for your child, and they're great at livening up the work too. Teachers are under pressure to train in new programmes, but you still can't beat experience, empathy and an open, lively mind. You should be able to spot these qualities simply by talking to the SENCO and checking out his room. (See 'Providing sensitivity to your child's needs', earlier in this chapter.)

SENCOs and LSAs deliver additional help to children who are entitled to it. The SENCO or Gifted and Talented Coordinator will also have a programme for gifted children. Your child with dyslexia may well fall into that category and need enrichment activities to ensure that she doesn't get bored.

Checking out school specialists

An LA-employed psychologist assesses your child for dyslexia, or a Specific Learning Disability (SpLD), and she may meet a few other specialists too. He's qualified to diagnose your child and is the only person who can administer some of the tests your child takes as part of the whole battery of tests for SpLD. You can get the specifics on assessment in Chapter 6. If your child needs other services that regular school staff don't provide, like speech or physical therapy, and these needs are part of her Statement, the LA district provides them too. Your child visits a specialist, or the specialist comes to school to visit her. We tell you all the ins and outs of Statements in Chapter 8.

Paying special attention to the support staff

Here's a thought: you probably have almost as much contact with the school secretary as you do with your child's teacher. You speak to the secretary any time you make an appointment to see the class teacher or SENCO, or when your child forgets her lunch, stays home sick or has an outside appointment. If you're nice to the secretary, your life runs more smoothly.

Sounds easy, doesn't it? We're (fairly) honest people, however, so we feel compelled to warn you that you may encounter an officious school secretary or two. Of course, we speak only from our own encounters, but some of them haven't been pretty. We've grovelled shamelessly to many a secretary for things as trivial as use of the school phone (and only for the briefest of local calls too). All we can say is that when you deal with the school secretary, you're in the presence of real power – so tread warily!

Oh, don't forget to befriend the caretaker too. He can let your child in the classroom after hours when no one else can, and you can bet your life you're going to need that some time when your child swears someone took her homework (due tomorrow) from her bag and put it right back in her desk.

Taking note of the head teacher

In a small primary school you may have a lot of contact with the head teacher, especially if he has an interest in children with special needs. If your child is of secondary age then you may deal with heads of departments or the head of year. But often you deal almost exclusively with your child's teachers, and in fact you may hope for that, because meetings with the head teacher may mean you have a problem that you haven't been able to resolve at the lower ranks.

Meeting the head teacher and getting on friendly terms with him is easy when your child's in a small primary school. When your child goes to a secondary school, however, contact can be much harder. The head teacher's harder to track down and has all the responsibility of being at the helm of a big organisation. Even if you schedule a meeting with him, he may not remember you a few weeks later.

Realistically, you can count on not having much to do with the head of a big school unless you have serious complaints. Even then, the head's near the end of the line of people you need to contact (the classroom teacher, SENCO and deputy head come earlier in the line). Jot down some contact details about him and file them away safely, just in case.

Getting the Full Story about Alternative Schooling

If you think that your child may not get all the help she needs in your local state school or you have other reasons for wanting to keep your child out of the state sector, you have a few options. You can choose from schools that operate by their own unique set of beliefs, schools that meet your religious needs and schools that cater specifically to children with dyslexia. In the following sections, we give you a quick tour of all the choices available to you as a parent.

Finding out about special schools

Special schools make educational provisions for children with Statements of Special Educational Needs whose needs are not being met within mainstream schools. You can find more information about special schools in the UK on the website www.specialneedsuk.org.

Choosing a private school

If you choose to send your child to a private school, check out the same kinds of things that you look for in a state school (see 'Questioning the Kind of School Your Child Needs', earlier in this chapter, for a list of considerations).

Just like in any school, you find good and not-so-good teachers, so take extra care to talk at length to your child's prospective teacher. Is he easy to talk to, and does he seem flexible and accommodating?

Private schools often have smaller classes and can provide better help for your child with dyslexia. You have to ask a private school what kind of help it can give your child. Some have dedicated units for dyslexia, but some try to avoid being seen as a school that has many children with special needs and may not be interested in your child. If you have a psychological assessment (see Chapter 6), provide the school with a copy in advance so that it can decide whether it can address your child's needs fully. Consider all the same questions that you would ask of a state school when considering which is the best school for your child (see the section 'Questioning the Kind of School Your Child Needs' at the beginning of this chapter for a list of questions).

Examining Montessori schools

Montessori schools began in the early 1900s with Maria Montessori, an Italian physician and educator. Now you can find Montessori schools all over the world – and not just for small children. Key features of Montessori include the following:

✔ Classes have 20 to 30 students and two or three teachers.

✔ Students in the classes are of mixed ages and start at age 2.

✔ The alphabet and sounds are introduced at age 2 with materials like letter blocks and sandpaper cutouts.

✔ All children get to do a lot of hands-on activities. Children help themselves to specially designed materials from low shelves.

✔ Teachers watch your child and give her new materials when she looks ready.

✔ Teachers introduce your child to specific stimuli (like dance and music) when they think she's at the most receptive age for them.

✔ Your child works as an individual and starts doing group work only in high school.

✔ Classes are quiet, clean and orderly, with an emphasis on self-care and responsibility.

Can your child with dyslexia thrive in a Montessori school? Maybe. Montessori schools introduce your child to phonetics at an early age (before difficulties set in) and use multisensory and non-competitive strategies, and that's all great. The downside is that your child may not master reading early on and then she may need specialised tutoring (even though you're already paying extra for Montessori!).

If you like the look of a Montessori school near you, do your homework. What exactly can the school do for your child to help her with her special needs? For the fine details on Montessori, check out the website www.montessori. org.uk.

Walking the Steiner (or Waldorf) path

Back in 1919, Dr Rudolph Steiner, an Austrian, started a school that was funded by a Mr Waldorf. Now there are more than 600 independent, private Steiner (sometimes called Steiner–Waldorf) schools in more than 32 countries. Steiner schools aim to educate the whole child, 'head, heart and hands', without competitive grading and with protection from the harmful influences of broader society. Steiner schools have these key features:

✔ Letters are only introduced in Year 2, and children learn to read from their own writing.

✔ In Years 1 to 8, your child keeps the same 'main lesson' teacher.

✔ All subjects for younger students are introduced through artistic media.

✔ All children learn to play the recorder and to knit.

✔ All children learn a stringed instrument from Year 3 on.

✔ Children don't use textbooks until Year 5. All children have main lesson books, which are workbooks that they fill in during the course of the year.

✔ At primary level, teachers don't grade children but write a detailed evaluation at the end of each school year.

✔ Young children are discouraged from using electronic media, particularly television.

Is Steiner right for your child with dyslexia? Hmm, maybe not. Your child gets plenty of loving care at a Steiner school but is taught to read and write later than other children of the same age in her school career. Also, while teachers can give her extra help, they may not have the time or expertise to give as much of it (or the right kind) as she needs.

If you like the sound of Steiner, you need to carefully check what happens if your child struggles with reading and writing. For all the ins and outs of Steiner–Waldorf, check out www.steinerwaldorf.org.uk.

Deciding on a school for your child with dyslexia

Many private schools cater specifically for children with dyslexia. Some of them are boarding schools. They all have websites and brochures that you can browse through after you recover from the shock of how much you pay! The big advantage of these schools is that your child is surrounded by students just like her and the teachers are focused on teaching her in a dyslexia-friendly way. The factors that may put you off are financial and geographic. You have to pay for these schools, and you may have to travel a long way to take your child there each day (unless your child boards, which has its own drawbacks). In addition, even before you get into those issues, you have research to do. Every school is different, so you have to research and get a feel for each one individually. For a list of schools in your area, download the CReSTeD booklet, which is a register of independent and local authority schools that cater for those with SpLD, from www.crested.org.uk.

Thinking about home schooling

Home schooling may be an option that you don't want to dismiss out of hand. These days, you can find many places to turn to for help with planning curricula. In addition, home schooling may be cheaper for you than private schooling or tutoring. Here are a few things to ponder:

✔ Home schooling your child with dyslexia can work out cheaper than sending her to private school, and you don't have to travel long distances.

✔ Plenty of home-schooling curricula, online courses and support groups are available all over the place (for example, www.education-otherwise.co.uk and www.oxfordhomeschooling.co.uk are worth looking at). Parents of children with dyslexia often say that being able to pick and choose from curricula is the biggest benefit of home schooling. They can find materials that suit their children instead of trying to push them through the one-size-fits-all state system.

✔ Home schooling allows you to respond to your child with dyslexia's academic needs but also to protect her emotional health (if she gets teased or feels depressed at school). Be aware, though, of the social implications of withdrawing her from the school's social life. Many parents and children compensate for this by socialising with other home-schooled families.

✔ Although taking a child out of school isn't illegal, strong legal implications exist and the parent has to prove that they're going to provide alternative education that is acceptable under the law.

✔ If ready to return, you can always send your child with dyslexia back into the state or private sector.

Must a home-schooling parent have vast reserves of patience and calm? Not necessarily. Home-schooling parents say that as long as you're reasonably level headed and can get along with your child without too many showdowns, you may be pleasantly surprised by how stress free home schooling becomes after you know the ropes. And of course, you can make your own discoveries about flexible, fun lessons and teaching your child phonics through multisensory techniques.

If you're considering home schooling your child with dyslexia, you need to check out a range of websites and books. In fact, all that research can get overwhelming, so here are just four websites that get our 'informative but simple' award:

✔ For an informative and interesting look at home schooling, have a look at www.bbc.co.uk/schools/parents/life/you_and_school/helping_at_home/.

✔ Education Otherwise gives legal information, tips and helpful frequently asked questions (FAQs) about home schooling. Go to www.education-otherwise.org.uk.

At www.homeschool.co.uk, which is a site for Christian Home Education, you get straightforward general information that includes a page about phonics home-teaching packages.

✔ Ever thought about part-time home schooling? Flexible schooling's a fairly new concept that can work well for some children and is becoming a more popular option for parents. One boy I know well successfully attends his school for a part of the week and spends the rest of the week with a specialist tutor who gives him individual tuition at her home. Have a look at www.home-education.org.uk.

If you decide to take the home-schooling plunge or are just working with your child after school, you need materials. In the next sections, we give you suggestions for sets of readers (reading and writing), workbooks and other bits and pieces that are super-handy to have alongside your abacus and cane!

Reading textbooks

With so many children's reading books to choose from, what kinds of texts should your child with dyslexia use? For all-by-herself reading, your child needs attractive books with well-spaced text spread comfortably throughout the pages. Most words should sound out regularly, and if new and tricky words, like *enough* and *who*, are given in a separate list, your child can look at that before she launches off. And so that your child can read several books before you have to search all over again, you may want to focus most of your book search on series. In the next list, we describe book series that you can be sure satisfy all or most of the good-reading-books-for-people-with-dyslexia characteristics.

- **Oxford Reading Tree:** This is a reading scheme for 3 to 11-year-olds and is probably the most popular reading programme in the UK, used in more than 18,000 primary schools. The idea of a tree represents the structure of the reading scheme, which aims to make reading a fun experience. Find more information and a parents' guide at www.oup.com/oxed/info/parents.

- **Ladybird Books:** Generations of children (Katrina included!) have been bought up on these iconic books. Ladybird publishes a wide range of books in its 'Learn to Read' series. The 'Key Words' books utilise the 100 words that researchers McNally and Murray found as 'key words to literacy'. Focusing on key words helps readers with dyslexia recognise a bank of high-frequency words. The books are £1.99 each and graded in four levels, with six stories at each level. Each story is a manageable length for a beginning reader and is filled with colourful illustrations. Repetition of words and phrases helps to reinforce new vocabulary. Titles include *Snow White and the Seven Dwarves* and *The Three Little Pigs*. Go to www.ladybird.co.uk for more information.

- **Dandelion Readers:** Dandelion Readers introduce phonics concepts sequentially in a structured way, which enables children to build up confidence from the very beginning. Each series comprises ten books and is complemented by reading and writing worksheets. Each ten-book set is £20. Get more information from www.phonicbooks.co.uk.

- **Dr Seuss:** The easiest books in this classic series are *Hop on Pop*, *Cat in the Hat* and *Green Eggs and Ham*. Check out the word families at the back of *Hop on Pop*. Published by Random House, the books are available at most good bookshops.

- **Barrington Stoke Books:** Barrington Stoke specialises in books for reluctant readers aged 8 to 16. Readers need to have a minimum reading age of 8 or more years. The books have been developed in consultation with specialists and readers with dyslexia to produce a visually attractive format that encourages unconfident readers. Barrington Stoke also produces an excellent pack for parents. All the books are £4.50. Find more information at www.barringtonstoke.co.uk.

For more help picking books, download the Waterstone's Guide to Books for Young Dyslexic Readers from www.dyslexiaaction.org.uk (go to the 'Parents' link). This guide is filled with excellent suggestions for readers up to the age of 13 (and beyond). In addition to providing the age of the child who may enjoy the book, the guide also gives the reading age of the book. For example, *The Secret Seven* by Enid Blyton appeals to a child aged 8 to 11 but has a reading age of 9.3. Some branches of Waterstone's bookshop may have copies of the booklet as well.

Workbooks

Having a few workbooks that your child can write in is a handy starting point for home schooling. But a lot of workbooks that look nice on the outside and purport to be straightforward turn out to be confusing for your child to follow. You need books with simple instructions and a sequential progression of phonics activities. Here are the ones we like:

- **Spelling Made Easy** by Violet Brand is a series of workbooks and textbooks that teach spelling in a structured and multisensory way. The books revolve around the story of Sam and his friends and retail at around £7. Buy books at www.betterbooks.com (which is an excellent source of SEN books and resources) or look for copies on www.amazon.co.uk (which is a good starting point for all books – especially if you're stocking up!).

- **Reading Made Easy** by Kathleen Paterson is a reading scheme with a clear, logical and well-structured phonics approach. Books cost £4 and workbooks £16 from Better Books (see the preceding bullet).

- **Explode the Code** by Nancy Hall and Rena Price is a set of books that promote reading and spelling skills. Visit www.explodethecode.com.

- **Toe by Toe** by Keda and Harry Cowling is a series we mention in the earlier section, 'Focusing on school programmes', but it's very popular for home use as well. The workbook/manual contains exercises and progress charts. You tutor your child for 20 minutes a day, and she progresses to the next lesson only after passing a mastery test. The books are available at www.toe-by-toe.co.uk for £25.

Extra materials

Some teaching tools and extra bits and pieces are especially handy for teaching letter sounds and spellings to children with dyslexia. In the following list, we give you inexpensive, portable items that are worth having around:

- **Letters:** Look for a set of wooden or magnetic letters, both upper- and lowercase, to do all sorts of phonics work and early word building. Wooden letters have the benefit that you can colour in the vowels with a felt-tip pen to aid recognition. Buy them from school stationery shops or online at DI Trading (www.dyslexiaaction.org.uk/store).

✔ **Book-sized whiteboards:** Children like writing on whiteboards. Buy two, and you can write words and play word games together. Look in school and office stationery shops.

✔ **Flashcards:** Flashcards can help your child practise phonics rules and patterns she's already grasped. Look for packs of 100 cards with clearly printed words that you can group into families. Buy them from school stationery shops or online at DI Trading (as above).

Here are some other places to start looking for books, toys, guidelines and more:

✔ **Charts and graphs:** Help your child with dyslexia represent her ideas pictorially rather than in writing by downloading, for free, pie charts, bar graphs and other diagrams at `www.edhelper.com/teachers/ graphic_organizers.htm`. It's an American site but is well worth a look.

✔ **Note taking:** Check out this site that gives useful tips about note taking and note making: `www.academictips.org/acad/literature/ notetaking.html`. Many UK universities have excellent study skills links as well.

✔ **Puzzles and toys:** At `www.ldalearning.com`, you get lots of resources and games targeted for children with special needs.

✔ **Reviews:** For recommendations on new products, surf `www.parenting. com` (under Software of the Year). For software and book reviews, go to `www.familyfun.go.com`.

✔ **Speed Reading:** If you can, try to get a copy of *Speed Reading* (David & Charles) by Tony Buzan on `www.amazon.co.uk`; it has some excellent ideas. If that doesn't work for you, software such as Speedreader X or Rocket Reader are both good for children. Have a look at `www. speedreaderx.com` and `www.rocketreader.com`.

✔ **Spelling rules:** At `www.usingenglish.com/weblog/archives/ 000021.html` and `www.alt-usage-english.org/I_before_E.html` you can find a discussion about the efficacy of the '*i* before *e*' rule.

Chapter 8

Getting a Statement of Special Educational Needs

*F*or some parents, getting your child a Statement of Special Educational Needs (SEN) is the equivalent of finding the Holy Grail. The process is long, arduous and filled with frustration at every turn. For the few who reach this goal, a Statement of SEN can mean that your child is educated at the schools of your choice. For those parents whose children are turned down, dealing with disappointment can be very upsetting.

Exactly what a Statement of Special Educational Needs means and provides for children – particularly children with dyslexia – is the focus of this chapter. We show you all the hoops you need to be ready to jump through in the process of petitioning for and getting a Statement. We also explain what you can expect from your local authority in fulfilling its duty of care for a child with special educational needs.

Pursuing a Statement: Following the Code of Practice

According to the Code of Practice (see the sidebar 'Getting your copy of the Code'), children have special educational needs if they have learning difficulties that call for special educational provisions to be made for them. These learning difficulties must make learning harder for them than most children of the same age. These children may need extra or different help from what other children, who are the same age, receive.

The Code of Practice recognises the needs of children with specific learning difficulties such as dyslexia as well as:

- ✔ Physical or sensory difficulties
- ✔ Emotional and behavioural difficulties
- ✔ Social and relational difficulties
- ✔ Speech- and language-based difficulties

The Code states that any child with SEN should have his needs met and that the views of the child and his parents should be taken into account at all times.

Provision for a child with SEN can often happen within normal mainstream education. However, the child may require the services of some outside specialists, including an occupational therapist, speech and language therapist or advisory teacher.

At each stage of the process of getting a Statement of SEN for your child, you, as a parent, are entitled to be involved. The following sections take you through the various steps you're likely to experience in the journey.

Speaking with the class teacher

The place to begin if you have any concerns about your child's educational progress is your child's teacher or special educational needs coordinator (SENCO). Chapter 3 covers symptoms of dyslexia that can help you determine if arranging a meeting with them is appropriate.

Don't bypass your child's class teacher unless you really can't work things out with her. Your child's class teacher can be your best resource in pursuing a Statement of SEN. If you get this person on your side, you may get outstanding help and service – and potentially cut through weeks of red tape.

The main focus of your meeting with the class teacher should be to tell her what you've noticed about your child that makes you think he has dyslexia and to explain your concerns. The best way to do this is to make a list of specific things you've noticed. This would include typical dyslexic errors such as erratic spelling or writing letters the wrong way round, or may be to do with behaviour, such as not being able to concentrate or organise himself.

After you've pointed out your concerns, then you could ask the teacher the specific questions in the next section. Alternatively, you could just ask for an overview of your child's progress to see if it meets National Curriculum targets and to see how well he's doing in comparison to his peers.

See Chapter 10 for additional information on working with teachers.

Getting your copy of the Code

The Code of Practice (1994, revised 2002) clearly sets out the processes and procedures that organisations, such as your child's school or the local education authority (LA), need to follow.

Free copies of the Code of Practice are available from the DfES Publications Centre on 0845 6022260 or from its website (`www.dfes.gov.gsi.uk/sen`). The free SEN Toolkit, which is available from this website, is also worth reading and includes a copy of the Code of Practice. Alternatively you can download the Code from `www.dyslexia-parent.com`.

Planning your questions

When speaking to your child's class teacher, plan to ask the following questions:

- ✔ How is my child performing in each subject? Are some subjects better than others? Does he participate in class or is he very quiet and unwilling to answer questions?

- ✔ How is my child doing with essential classroom skills such as concentrating, completing tasks, following instructions and organising assignments? If you're told that he is consistently day dreaming and not keeping up with the pace of the lessons, you might have cause for concern.

- ✔ Is my child meeting the appropriate National Curriculum level for his age? If you're told that he is much better at science and maths than English, again your child might have possible problems.

Making lists

Making lists of specific observations about your child's educational strengths and challenges is important. You don't want to forget important topics amid the talk and general activity.

As soon as you schedule a meeting, start making a list of things you want to discuss (in addition to the general questions in the preceding section, 'Planning your questions'). Topics to bring up include:

- ✔ **Specific things you observe in your child's schoolwork.** Share your thoughts on how your child seems to be performing. For example, you can point out how well your child seems to be doing on a new reading programme – or that he doesn't seem to be benefiting from a programme at all.

- ✔ **Your child's strengths and weaknesses.** You may want to mention your child's out-of-school successes and challenges, particularly if these may affect what your child does in class and his own view of his strengths and weaknesses. This type of information is especially useful if your child is always obliging and seemingly happy in school, but complains about schoolwork immediately after stepping through the door at home.

✔ **What you expect your child to learn this year, especially in reading and writing.** Be as specific as you can. For example, pinpoint your child's reading speed, comprehension or instant recognition of sight words. Chapters 12 and 13 cover these language-based topics in greater detail.

✔ **What you envisage your child doing in the future.** If your child is hoping to go into further education, his teachers need to know before he makes GCSE subject choices, as colleges often prefer some subjects over others or require your child to have studied certain subjects.

✔ **Strategies that have helped your child.** Point out techniques and tools that seem educationally beneficial to your child, such as phonics (for more go to Chapter 12) and strategies for remembering sight words (take a look at Chapter 11).

Organising documents

In addition to making a list of questions and of topics to address, call the school before the meeting and ask whether a draft of the school's proposed Individual Education Plan (IEP) is available (find out more about IEPs in the section 'School Action' later in this chapter). Ask for a copy and find out whether you can share, in advance, your reactions and a list of the issues you want to raise. For example, sometimes the IEP is very generic and not specific enough to your child's needs. The school should always take into account your comments and input. The Code of Practice clearly regards parents as partners who have an active and valued role in the education process.

Photocopy all essential educational documents (like test results from a private tutor) that you want everyone at the meeting to see. Put them in a folder and take it with you to the meeting.

If your meeting is to determine whether your child is eligible for a request for formal assessment, ask that you have results from any screening the school has conducted in hand *before* the meeting. You can better prepare yourself for the meeting and avoid being surprised by complex documents. And to make sure you understand what you're looking at, ask a professional or knowledgeable friend to help you interpret these assessments, if necessary.

No matter what you ask for or discuss at any point during the process, take notes about your conversations and date them. Use a notebook, binder or folder to organise a record of all phone calls, emails and copies of documents.

Don't let answers like 'We don't have the resources', 'He's going to grow out of it in time' or the ever-popular 'He's not the worst in the class' put you off. Be persistent. Your child is one of many, and your advocacy is the only way to push his case to the fore. Keep your goals in mind and remember that your child needs your support. He can't get help without you – and every extra day your child waits is a day to fall farther behind. The important thing to remember is that your child can learn but needs to have a different approach. Your local dyslexia association is a place to meet other parents of children with dyslexia who should be able to help you with some ideas. To see you getting stressed about his learning won't help your child. Remain calm and let him see that you believe he can do it – it's just a matter of finding the best way for him.

Involving the SENCO

The special educational needs coordinator, or SENCO, in a school is pivotal. Often someone takes on this role in addition to another high-profile position such as the deputy head or head in a primary school. In some secondary schools, the SENCO is also a head of department, which must be a difficult combination of responsibilities. We've also come across two learning support assistants who hold the position of SENCO.

While SENCO training courses are available, many SENCOs have not had any training in special needs (although the government is trying to rectify this situation). Many parents who research their child's dyslexia in depth don't realise that they often have more knowledge than the SENCO.

Although the SENCO is a busy person with many responsibilities, remember that your child matters most to you. Remain calm and firm with the SENCO, but try not to be confrontational. Ultimately, even a busy SENCO has the child's best interests at heart and has a duty to meet his needs.

Do not let a SENCO overwhelm or intimidate you. Most are trying to do an exceedingly difficult job with minimum resources.

The key responsibilities of the SENCO may include:

- ✔ Overseeing the day-to-day operation of the school's SEN policy.
- ✔ Coordinating the provision and records of children with special educational needs.
- ✔ Liaising with and advising fellow teachers and managing learning support assistants.
- ✔ Liaising with parents and external agencies such as occupational therapists or speech and language therapists.
- ✔ Contributing to in-service training days where the SENCO may hold a session on creating a dyslexia-friendly classroom, for example.

Sometimes it may well be imperative to meet with the SENCO straight away rather than wait for a referral from your child's class teacher. Ask whether your child can go onto the Register of Special Needs at the school and be put on School Action or School Action Plus (see the sections 'School Action' and

'School Action Plus' later in this chapter for details). The SENCO in a primary school may well be a class teacher or the deputy head and meeting with both at the same time may be possible.

The SENCO can recommend a variety of responses to your child's educational needs. The following sections cover the most common responses.

School Action

The SENCO may decide that School Action can meet the only additional help your child needs, for example with small group teaching. School Action is the first step and is defined as 'intervention that is additional to and different from that provided as part of the school's normal differentiated curriculum and strategies'. For some children it may provide enough additional support, such as small group work with a learning support assistant.

Triggers for School Action include the class teacher's or SENCO's concern about a child making little or no progress when teaching approaches are targeted to an area of weakness.

When the school recommends School Action, it then needs to draw up an *Individual Education Plan*, or IEP, for your child. The SENCO is responsible for devising and monitoring the IEP.

Your child's IEP should describe:

- ✔ What type of specific special help your child is being given
- ✔ How often your child receives help
- ✔ Who specifically provides help
- ✔ What the targets for your child are (for example, that he will be able to put out the wooden alphabet accurately by a specific time)
- ✔ How and when your child's progress is monitored
- ✔ What help you as a parent can give your child at home

Targets listed in your child's IEP need to be SMART – that is, Specific, Measurable, Achievable, Realistic and Time-related. We've seen many IEPs where the targets are anything but! Indeed, some IEPs look as if they are churned out by the dozen and apply to *any* child. So make sure your child's IEP is personal to his very *individual* needs. For example, 'Alex needs to be able to read more fluently' is a meaningless IEP target, but 'Alex needs to know how to read 90 per cent of the Key Stage 1 high frequency words by the end of the summer term' is SMART.

Additionally, the IEP should include information about:

✔ Teaching strategies, such as multisensory teaching, used to improve these skills

✔ The provision the school is to put in place, such as one to one or small group support or using a learning assistant

✔ When the IEP is to be reviewed (ideally twice a year)

✔ A description of a success or exit strategy

✔ Outcomes, such as your child being able to correctly spell the days of the week by a set period of time (to be recorded by the SENCO when the IEP is reviewed)

The IEP may include targets for key areas other than literacy, such as maths, communication, behaviour and social skills. If you're unhappy with or confused by anything that appears in your child's IEP, talk to the class teacher, SENCO or head teacher.

Teachers and specialists who know each other and talk the same jargon can be intimidating. Keep in mind, though, that your knowledge of your child's needs is greater than theirs, and you have every right to make sure that your child's needs are met. If anyone uses any term that you don't understand, ask for an explanation. Be firm and persuasive but not confrontational.

School Action Plus

School Action Plus is the next stage on from School Action (see the preceding section, 'School Action'.) The triggers for School Action Plus according to the Code of Practice can be that despite receiving an IEP and/or concentrated support under School Action, your child continues to make little or no progress.

Finding support

Organisations such as Parent Partnership, the BDA and SENDiST can provide advice and support when you're working to get your child's special educational needs addressed. Parent Partnership services can help minimise difficulties between you and your child's teacher or SENCO – difficulties that can escalate into disagreements. These organisations are neutral and don't 'take sides' or fight for your child. Instead, they can help you make informed decisions.

Look for contact information for Parent Partnership groups in your local area in the Department of Children, Schools and Families booklet *Special Educational Needs: A Guide for Parents,* which you can download from their website (www.dcsf.gov.uk).

You can also access informal disagreement resolution services through your LA. The website www.direct.gov.uk/en/parents contains links to individual LAs.

The SENCO and class teacher, along with external specialists such as the occupational therapist or speech and language therapist, then consider new and appropriate targets for the IEP as well as additional support for your child, including specialist teaching or additional occupational or speech and language therapy. The school can access further funding at this point to pay for additional support. I've seen some children with the appropriate support achieve more at School Action Plus than with a Statement of SEN.

Statutory assessment

If, despite assistance under School Action and School Action Plus, your child is still demonstrating cause for serious concern, the head teacher may request a *statutory assessment*.

When putting forward a request for a statutory assessment, the school needs to provide written evidence about how it has addressed your child's needs through School Action and School Action Plus. This evidence typically includes copies of IEPs, records of review meetings and any professional involvement, National Curriculum levels and attainments in literacy and mathematics.

The views of parents and the child are part of the statutory assessment and are extremely relevant in the request.

Request for a statutory assessment

Under the Education Act (1994), the local education authority (LA) must notify parents in writing of the school's intention to make a statutory assessment. This notification document includes:

- ✔ **An outline of specific procedures the school plans to follow in drawing up a statutory assessment statement.**

- ✔ **An explanation of the stages and timing of the process.** The period between receipt of request and issue of a statutory assessment statement should be no longer than 26 weeks.

- ✔ **The name of the case officer assigned to the request.**

- ✔ **A deadline for parental response.** Parents have 28 days to respond and provide additional evidence.

- ✔ **Details about the local Parent Partnership service or 'befrienders' from the BDA.** See the sidebar 'Finding support' for more information.

A child's school or a parent can make a request for an assessment. Many parents don't realise that they can bypass the school completely and take matters into their own hands under Section 328 or 329 of the Education Act 1996. The LA must comply with such a request for assessment within six months of the date of the request and inform the child's head teacher that the parents have made this request.

The parent of a child who's home schooled can apply for a statutory assessment. And if a child attends a private school, a parental or school request for a statutory assessment is still possible. The same procedures apply and the factors that the LA considers are the same as if the child were in state school.

The LA must, using all the evidence available, decide within six weeks whether it should carry out the assessment. If the LA decides not to carry out the assessment, it must write to the school and the parents with the reasons as to why an assessment is not taking place. Parents may appeal against this decision and are given advice on how to do so appropriately.

The assessment

While a private psychological assessment includes the battery of tests we describe in Chapter 6, the LA assessment is not under any obligation to go into such detail. In fact, many LA psychologists make a classroom observation as part of the assessment, which is only productive if your child has behavioural difficulties.

The kinds of tests that assessors use can vary but they generally include ability, diagnostic and attainment tests which can take between two and two and a half hours. Testing takes place in a quiet room so that your child isn't disturbed. You're entitled to be with your child during this or any other assessment or examination.

After your LA has carried out the assessment, it has 12 weeks in which to inform parents whether it's going to issue a Statement of SEN. Be aware, though, that an assessment doesn't always lead to a Statement of SEN.

Exploring a Statement of Special Educational Needs

According to the Code of Practice, the Statement of SEN has six parts:

- ✔ Part 1 gives general information about your child, such as your child's date of birth, name and address, religion and home language.
- ✔ Part 2 describes your child's needs following the assessment.
- ✔ Part 3 describes all the special help to be given for your child's needs.
- ✔ Part 4 gives the type and name of the school your child should attend.
- ✔ Part 5 describes any non-educational needs your child has. Social Services or the Health Authority determine these.
- ✔ Part 6 describes how your child may get help to meet these non-educational needs.

Your LA sends you a draft Statement before writing a final Statement. The draft Statement is complete except for Part 4, which is left blank because you have 15 days during which to respond about the kind of educational provision you want for your child. You can also ask for a meeting and can have an additional 15 days after that to ask for more meetings if necessary.

Within 8 weeks of the draft Statement, the LA must finalise the Statement and say specifically what SEN provision is needed and send you the completed copy with the name of the school filled in.

Receiving a note in lieu

You may receive a *note in lieu* from the LA at this stage, rather than a draft Statement. A note in lieu is not a legally binding document. It describes a child's special educational needs, explains why it has not issued a Statement after a statutory assessment and makes recommendations about what help, if any, the child should receive.

Receiving a note in lieu can be very disappointing for parents. You can appeal against this decision at an SEN Tribunal. (See the following section, 'Disagreeing with the Statement'.) You can find assistance for the Tribunal from voluntary organisations such as Parent Partnership (see the sidebar 'Finding support'), which can give you unbiased help, or a befriender from the British Dyslexia Association. Befrienders are trained volunteers who help parents to deal with the local authorities.

Disagreeing with the Statement

If you disagree with any of the contents of a Statement when you receive it, you need to speak to the named case officer. Sometimes Statements are not specific enough or do not specify the kind of support your child needs – for example, a trained specialist teacher, who can make an enormous difference.

You also have the right to appeal to the Special Educational Needs and Disability Tribunal or SENDiST regarding Parts 2, 3 and 4 of the Statement. In fact, you can appeal if you're trying to sort out any disagreements with the LA. SENDiST has a helpline and a very clear website (www.sendist.gov.uk) outlining procedures for parents to follow. The organisation is independent of central and local government agencies and covers England and Wales only. It can make decisions on the grounds of discriminatory actions and LA decisions. The idea of going to appeal can seem very intimidating but many people will give you help and advice and make the process seem less stressful.

If you disagree with the SENDiST's decision, you have 28 days to appeal in the High Court, if you believe your decision involves an error of law. At this point many parents employ legal representation and expert witnesses, such as an independent psychologist who has carried out an assessment report.

Many processes associated with appeals and Tribunals are scheduled to be revised after 3 November 2008. See the sidebar 'Tribunal changes' for more information.

Don't let the thought of going to appeal or even to the High Court intimidate you – these actions are often the only way to gain a successful outcome. You can't receive legal aid for a SENDiST, but organisations such as the Independent Panel for Special Educational Advice (ISPEA) offer free representation as well as free legal advice. Its website www.ipsea.org.uk gives further information about the law regarding special educational needs, as well as case studies and model letters.

Tribunal changes

After 3 November 2008, the SEN Tribunal procedure features some important changes. Subject to Parliamentary approval, the SEN Tribunal plan is a two-tier system:

✔ **The First Tier Tribunal** hears all SENDiST appeals against LAs in England. SENDiST is part of the provisionally entitled Health, Education and Social Care Chamber, or HESC, with the Care Standards Tribunal (CST) and the Mental Health Review Tribunal (MHRT). HESC is headed by an appointed Chamber President and each Chamber has its own unified rules, which are intended to be simple, flexible and easy to understand.

✔ **The Upper Tribunal** hears appeals by individuals wishing to challenge a decision who believe that their rulings involve an error of law. Appeals move from First Tier to Upper Tribunals instead of going to the High Court.

The changes to SENDiST also allow LAs to have unlimited witnesses to support their cases, while parents can only call on one or two people. Changes may lead to a Tribunal lasting for two to three weeks (as opposed to one or two days). Many organisations and parent groups feel that the new system seems to favour the local authorities by abolishing a restriction on witnesses and by getting rid of the substantial written element of the case.

And one of the biggest issues is that children can be summonsed to appear, which can be a very stressful experience.

Obviously, the new system is going to generate contention. Visit www.sendist.gov.uk for up-to-date information about the changes and the implications for parents.

The Advisory Centre for Education (www.ace-ed.org.uk) is another good source of information. You can even text the organisation on ASKACE 66808. Follow the instructions for it to send you booklets, tips and answers to your questions.

You're likely to feel worn out by pushing your child's case or having to listen to hours of edu-babble as part of the appeal process. You may tire of justifying your every request and having to listen like a hawk to every detail in order to make sure you're getting your child the best deal possible. But keep your child's needs in mind at all times – the effort will be worth it in the end if you get your child the help he needs.

Surrounding yourself with supportive people

At every stage of the appeal process, make sure that you have the support you need – or that you know where to find it. See the sidebar 'Finding support' for more ideas.

If you don't have a partner, bring a knowledgeable friend to all meetings. Let the school know in advance whom you're bringing. You're likely to feel better with someone you know and trust at your side. Choose a person who listens carefully and makes notes, activities that can make quite an impression. As a bonus, you have a witness and notes to refer to if you need to contest anything later.

Another way to keep a careful record of your meetings is to tape-record them. Always ask in advance whether you can do this.

Contact the British Dyslexia Association for details of your nearest chapter. Many areas have thriving associations where you can meet people who are all going through the same things as you!

Contact the BDA at:

> Unit 8, Bracknell Beeches,
> Old Bracknell Lane, Bracknell, RG12 7BW.

The BDA also has a helpline at 0845 251 9002 and a website at `www.bdadyslexia.org.uk`.

Living with an SEN Statement

Congratulations! Your child has an SEN Statement that meets his needs. So what's next? This section covers the ongoing activities of helping your child get the most from a Statement.

Considering the cons of a Statement

The pros of a Statement are self-evident to a lot of people, especially if you want to get special education for your child but don't qualify for a Statement. However, some parents believe Statements have disadvantages, including:

✔ Being labelled a child with SEN may have a stigma attached to it.

✔ Going through an appeal can be a harrowing experience for all concerned.

✔ The SENCO may have a general education degree, but may not have any specialist training.

We're not going to whitewash over these concerns because they're entirely valid. The stigma issue can be particularly worrying for older students. Children who get extra help do suffer name-calling from other children and do feel different because they know they're on the special needs table. However, they must prepare for those challenges and work to deal with them.

Children need help to understand what their Statement means. The more they understand about their own learning and how and why it may be different from other children's learning, the better equipped they are to cope. Stress to your child that all children learn differently and that the fact that he learns differently doesn't mean there's anything wrong with him as a person. Point out his strengths and talents as well – we all have things we can do well and things we find harder. This will give him the confidence to deal with the behaviour of other children towards him.

Hopefully your child can become more comfortable with having a learning disability by identifying the issue in primary school and continuing to deal with it in later years. If your child can't bear to be a child with SEN, try to find a compromise – like reducing, but not eliminating, hours away from regular class – before withdrawing him from the additional help. Few parents want to give away this help.

Attending annual reviews

The school must review your child's Statement annually in order to check his progress and make sure that the Statement continues to meet his needs. To do this the school must invite everyone involved in the child's support to the review meetings.

Typically, the school invites you to send in your views on your child's progress and to come into the school for a review meeting of written reports from the parents and from the child. Consider having your partner, an independent adult or a friend attend at least part of the meeting with you.

After the meeting the school sends you a copy of the report, and the head teacher sends a report to the LA recommending any agreed changes to the Statement by the end of 10 working days or by the end of term, whichever is sooner. Your local authority may then amend the Statement.

Surveying the services your child receives with a Statement

The SENCO at school probably has the most to do with implementing what's written in the Statement (and with luck this person is specially trained). Your child sees the SENCO and her learning support assistant (LSA) to get the special education your child is entitled to.

With the SENCO or learning assistant, your child gets tailor-made extra help. Examples include working with a special reading programme like Units of Sound (flip back to Chapter 7) or reading books with limited vocabulary.

While your child's Statement makes provision for payment for an LSA, that assistant may share time with other children without a Statement, which means your child may not get the one-to-one help he needs.

Your child may go to a *Learning Support Unit*, a quiet, supportive place, to work with the SENCO. The Unit is often equipped with computers and materials that your child can access. Your child can also read books of an appropriate level for him in the resource room, so other children can't tease him.

Because the SENCO (or LSA who is helping your child) sees fewer children than mainstream classroom teachers do, you should be able to contact her more easily and expect a good knowledge of your child. The SENCO can ask other teachers to make allowances for your child, such as designating a buddy to read especially hard text out loud or allowing extra time to finish assignments.

Teachers who are experienced in working with children with special needs have special ways of presenting new information to the class, too. They talk in short, clear terms and change from one topic to another by saying transitional sentences like 'Now I'm going to talk about *ch* words. After that, you can write some of your own *ch* words.' They write key words on the board alongside lengthier text. They establish helpful routines, like having sheets that summarise topics, and make diagrams available for kids to take home. Part IV explores these and other useful techniques.

If your child's school is experienced at teaching students with dyslexia, contact the British Dyslexia Association via its website www.bdadyslexia.com and request or download a Dyslexia Friendly Schools Pack, which has ideas for a whole-school approach to dyslexia.

Knowing your rights – and your child's

Things that sound great on paper don't always come out that way in practice. In real life, your child's teacher has a lot of things to do and a lot of other children to take care of. Your school's budget is stretched. The staff at your child's school may not be specially trained to help your child. Even if all parties are doing their best, you may feel short-changed by how your child's Statement translates into practice.

We've come across children with Statements who've made negative progress and others who've done well on School Action. Your child's success really depends on the execution of the provision.

If you get a Statement and still aren't happy – or don't receive a Statement – you and your child still have options. We discuss possible ways to get your child help at home or privately in Chapter 9.

Chapter 9

Securing Help without a Statement

In This Chapter

▶ Tapping into school resources

▶ Choosing private tutors, learning centres and more

▶ Helping your child at home

A *Statement of Special Educational Needs* (SEN) is a written working plan of exactly how special education is delivered to an eligible child. The hard truth about Statements is that not every child gets one. More importantly, not every child who seems to be in need of one gets one. In this chapter, we tell you which direction to go when *your* child goes without. We cover resources in and out of school and methods that you can use to support your child at home.

If your child doesn't qualify for a Statement, she may still be eligible for extra help at School Action or School Action Plus. In this chapter we talk about getting help without a Statement, but if you go to Chapter 8, you can revisit the main points about both.

Making the Most of Choices in School

If your child struggles in school and you think or know she has dyslexia, even though she doesn't qualify for a Statement, you have options. You can ease her progress through school in a few ways, including the following in-school choices:

✔ Be nice to your child's teacher and keep in contact with him. Without badgering him, thank him for any extra help he gives your child, and when your child can use a bit more, tell him. A teacher can do small things that make a big difference to your child's happiness and success.

✔ When your child can't do her homework or classroom assignments, pinpoint where the problem lies. Think of practical ways to help and propose them (respectfully) to the teacher. He's going to be more amenable to your practical suggestions than to your vague complaints.

✔ Regular parents' evenings come round only two or three times a year. Don't be afraid to ask for additional meetings with staff. As long as you have useful information to share with the teacher or legitimate concerns, you can both benefit by touching base a few times each term.

✔ Keep your eyes and ears open for special extra-curricular programmes in school. Let the teacher know that you want your child to be considered for breakfast clubs and social or sporting clubs that can help her feel confident.

You can read more about extra-curricular school programmes in Chapter 7. In Chapter 10, we give you the nitty-gritty on working with your child's teacher.

Looking for Help Outside School

You've probably used private services for your child with dyslexia or at least considered using them. Your child may have seen a specialist optometrist to see whether she has Irlen syndrome (also known as *scotopic sensitivity* or *visual stress*; you can read more about this in Chapter 4), you may have paid for an assessment (see Chapter 6 for details) and maybe you've tried a tutor – or two. Getting outside help can take a weight off your shoulders, put the spark back in your child's eye and give your child's teacher something to smile about. It can also make a sizeable hole in your wallet and leave you feeling despondent.

In the next sections, we outline the kinds of private help you can get so that you have an idea of what's what before you shop around.

By the way, be prepared to shop around because dyslexia isn't a condition for which one size fits all. You need to match your child to a specialist that she clicks with, a programme that makes sense to her and a schedule that she can follow without getting overwhelmed or overtired. And you need a Plan B in case, even after all your careful planning, your choices don't work out.

Checking out specialist dyslexia therapies

Some dyslexia programmes address what they see as the underlying cause of dyslexia rather than the symptomatic reading and writing problems. Such programmes, which tend to originate in the US, include:

- ✔ **All Kinds of Minds:** Your child is shown how to use her best learning style (because being pushed into using her weakest learning styles is the real problem).

- ✔ **Fast For Word:** Your child gets better listening and quick response skills (because these attention and response difficulties are the real concern).

- ✔ **Processing and Cognitive Enhancement (PACE):** This programme runs your child through brain exercises (because her problem's underdeveloped specific brain skills).

You can go straight to Chapter 20 to read more about these and other specialist dyslexia therapies, but upfront you may want to know the price range you can expect and the broad pros and cons:

- ✔ Prices for assessment in a specialist therapy centre typically run into the hundreds or thousands of pounds, if you can even find a centre near you in the UK.

- ✔ The good thing about some of these programmes is that they're usually short (lasting a few weeks) and intensive (a few hours each week), so that you get to see whether your child improves relatively soon.

- ✔ The weakness of these programmes is that you can expect your child to need, in addition, at least some specialist reading and writing instruction.

As a parent you need to be aware that you're going to need to be involved in some way with helping your child, no matter what external help is required. Some of the suggestions we give can involve a significant financial outlay while others are free. Whatever method you choose, however, you can be sure that working with your child will be a positive and hopefully fun experience that can only improve her confidence and self esteem.

Considering dyslexia centres

A local dyslexia centre can be an attractive option for augmenting your child's education in school. So that you can get a general idea of how they operate, this section summarises what happens at Dyslexia Action, an organisation with 26 centres spread across Britain in locations such as London, Cardiff, Coventry, York and Bristol.

Dyslexia Action provides a structured, cumulative and multisensory phonics-based reading and spelling programme. The programme also helps with related problems, like poor working memory, phonemic awareness, visual perception and visual motor integration.

Your child begins the programme by having a full psychological assessment to establish whether she has dyslexia (for approximately £450, depending on the area). A teacher planning interview (around £70) follows, during which your child takes some additional diagnostic tests including a Woodcock Reading Mastery test and a single word spelling test. Results of the evaluation determine your child's personalised teaching plan. Teaching can commence without a full psychological assessment or if one was carried out elsewhere. If no cognitive testing has been done, a student planning interview (for around £90) is carried out instead of a teacher planning interview, with the addition of a WRIT (Wide Range Intelligence Test). This test establishes verbal and non-verbal ability levels.

After assessment and testing are complete, you receive a copy of a teaching agreement that contains details of your child's specific programme. This plan can contain, for example, the Dyslexia Institute Literacy Programme at the Standard, Accelerated or Simplified level or Units of Sound at Stage 1, 2 or 3. (See Chapter 7 for more on these programmes.)

Your child receives a 90-minute weekly session with specialist teachers with a Postgraduate Certificate or Diploma in Dyslexia and Literacy (or the equivalent). Sessions cost around £50 each, depending on the area. Some bursaries are available, and the organisation makes every effort to help families who can't afford lessons. Lessons are taught in pairs with a child of similar age and ability. Sessions are followed up with reading packs that parents are trained to do with their child at home on a regular basis. Parents receive two reports on their child's progress per year and another assessment every six months. An annual meeting with your child's teacher occurs in the spring term to discuss her progress.

You can find out more at www.dyslexiaaction.org.uk, which gives details for finding your local centre or by calling the head office on 01784 222 300.

Dyslexia Action also provides services to adults with dyslexia.

If you live in the Bristol area, try the Bristol Dyslexia Centre (www.dyslexia centre.co.uk), which offers assessments, tuition and resources. Similarly in the Surrey area, The Helen Arkell Centre (www.arkellcentre.org.uk) offers tutoring, training and assessments.

You can also use a search engine like Google or Yahoo! to find local dyslexia centres offering tuition. Just type 'dyslexia tuition' or 'dyslexia teaching', along with the name of your town, and see what pops up! If the number of results you get is too dizzying for you, try the BDA website (www.bdadyslexia.org.uk) for a list of local associations and the PATOSS website (www.patoss-dyslexia.org.uk) which provides help and advice about local services. Checking these out and getting involved can help parents to find out what is locally available. Also remember to talk to other parents for word-of-mouth recommendations about local providers.

Paying an individual tutor

In an ideal world, your local dyslexia association recommends a tutor who's sensitive, fun and qualified to the hilt to teach her the latest dyslexia-busting methods. Your child visits the tutor for a few idyllic sessions and emerges a fluent and error-free reader and writer. That's the ideal world.

In the real world, you may have a hard time finding a tutor, let alone someone who's experienced with dyslexia. And even if you do find a tutor who looks good on paper, you can't be sure your child clicks with her.

So is searching for a tutor worth the effort? To help you answer that question, here are the potential benefits that tutoring can have for your child:

✔ Tutoring gives your child more personal attention than she can possibly receive in class (as one of 30 or so children).

✔ Tutoring can provide your child with challenges to keep her excited about learning and extra support to strengthen her weak areas.

✔ Tutoring takes the pressure off parents. Even if you have a perfect relationship with your child, you probably (like most parents) have trouble helping her (especially in her teen years) with homework.

✔ Tutoring can help your child feel privileged.

Does using a tutor have disadvantages? The term 'disadvantages' is probably a bit harsh, but here are a few things at least to watch out for:

✔ Your child may describe her tutoring as 'good', which is an adequate explanation to her but not much help to you. You may want to schedule meetings with her classroom teacher so that you can see whether the tutoring is in fact making any difference in class. See Chapter 10 for more details about having a conference with your child's teacher.

✔ Naturally you want good value from tutoring, but you need to be clear about what counts as good value. Improved grades in class are obvious indications of success, but your child's improved confidence and better attitude in school count too and can be a far more important factor.

✔ Tutoring that isn't enjoyable may do more harm than good, especially to little children. You want your primary school child to develop a positive attitude towards school (after all, she's going to be there a long time), so if you have to drag her to tutoring, look for another tutor. The same thing applies to older children, of course, but they're a bit better at letting you know how they're feeling (and putting up a fight!).

✔ Paying for tutoring and getting your child there each week can be hard enough. You don't want to end up paying cancellation fees too. Check out a tutor's cancellation policy before you start marking your child's tutoring sessions on the calendar.

We can't take you to a load of tutors and point out the ones who may be right for your child, but we can tell you what to look for and where to start your search. You need a tutor who:

✔ Is nice! You may think that it's not important that your child's tutor's nice, but if you've ever had to drag your child to tutoring or had to listen to her whine and grumble every time she goes, you appreciate why nice is relevant. Especially if you want your child to go the distance (months or years) with a tutor, nice is something you should look out for.

✔ Strikes a chord with your child. Your child should relate to the tutor and want to please him. As a result of this relationship, she tries hard and gets better marks for her work.

✔ Is a trained and experienced reading teacher or special education teacher with experience in teaching reading. A tutor with a teaching degree and at least three years' teaching experience is a great start.

✔ Can tell you about her phonics-based and multisensory teaching methods. *Phonics* is the teaching method in which students are shown how to match letters (and clusters of letters) to speech sounds (see Chapter 12). In multisensory activities, your child uses a few of her senses at the same (or roughly the same) time (see Chapter 14).

✔ Is able to measure reading and spelling scores in tests and show you your child's progress after a few weeks of tutoring. But remember: even with experienced and effective tutors, your child may take months, rather than weeks, to make progress. You should, however, be able to enjoy seeing your child becoming a happier and more confident learner within weeks, provided that she starts to have success with tasks at which she previously failed.

✔ Is within your price range. Tutoring can range in cost from about £25 per hour for a college student (not the best option for your child with dyslexia unless perhaps the student is training in a reading programme like DILP and/or is dyslexic and full of handy strategies) to about £40 per hour for an experienced specialist teacher.

✔ Has a quiet room where your child can work uninterrupted for his lesson and a good number of quality resources to work with.

PATOSS, the Professional Association of Specialist Teachers, suggests the following when considering tutors:

✔ Ask for a copy of the teacher's CV and check they he has a DfES (Department for Education and Skills) number that indicates he's a qualified teacher.

✔ Check that he has experience teaching children with dyslexia as well as credentials such as:

- An SpLD (specific learning difficulties) qualification, such as a Post Graduate Certificate or Diploma in Dyslexia. A trained teacher isn't the same as a trained specialist who understands your child's very specific needs and can plan a programme around them.

- AMBDA (Associate Member of the British Dyslexia Association) status. This is seen as the 'gold standard' among teachers of SpLD.

- A Practising Certificate, which indicates that he is committed to professional development in the field of assessment.

✔ Ask the teacher if he has any personal liability insurance and whether the CRB (Criminal Records Bureau) has checked whether he has a criminal record.

For further advice and specific questions to ask prospective tutors go to `www.patoss-dyslexia.org`. The website also features a register of specialist teachers in your area and an excellent (and free) test that you can administer to gauge handwriting speed.

Tutoring's a great option for adults too. Tutors are often happy to work with adults and your local dyslexia association can help you find specialist tutors who work with and often run free courses for adults. Your local library is a good place to search for free or low-cost adult literacy programmes such as those offered through Learndirect but these programmes aren't taught by dyslexia specialists.

Opting for a general learning centre

A general learning centre may offer you more flexibility than an individual tutor. For example, you may be able to take your child to a centre at different times, including weekends. In addition, your child may enjoy seeing different tutors, and especially if your child gets small group tutoring rather than one-on-one, you may end up paying less. That's the good news.

The bad news is that tutors in centres aren't usually qualified in special needs. They don't have training in remedial reading techniques, like Reading Recovery, and they may not know much about dyslexia.

If your child's dyslexia is mild, if she hates the idea of visiting a tutor but thinks a centre's cool or if you have a friend whose child with dyslexia did well at your local centre, a centre may still suit your needs. In Appendix B we give you contact details for the big learning centres that operate in most towns, and in the following sections you get a quick summary of how they operate. Each centre's different, though, so you probably want to use the details we give here as a guide for asking the right questions (including info on updated prices).

When someone tells you that your child gets individual instruction, check what this means. Centres that give small group instruction may still call it 'individualised' because, as they explain, each child follows her individualised programme even though she's part of a small group. Another piece of terminology that may catch you out is 'certified'. Instructors can be certified teachers and/or certified in the methods of the centre (which means that they're not necessarily qualified to be classroom teachers).

Kumon Maths and Reading Centres

Toru Kumon, a parent and teacher, started Kumon Maths and Reading Centres more than 50 years ago in Japan. More than 1,000 centres service students in North America and 43 other countries. Kumon is for any child from pre-school to secondary school age who needs tutoring in reading and maths.

At Kumon Maths and Reading Centres, your child learns by working through sequential worksheets that instructors administer and mark. Your child must complete her worksheets, have them marked by the teacher and complete any corrections before she leaves (in 45 minutes), so that she gets immediate feedback.

Students typically attend Kumon twice a week all year round and do brief daily assignments (about 15 minutes) on the other five days. Pre-school children attend at fixed times, but other students can show up at any time during open hours.

Kumon offers two incentive programmes to your child. In the Kumon Cosmic Club, your child earns points redeemable for prizes. The Advanced Student Honour Roll recognises older children performing above their year-group level.

Tuition at a Kumon centre costs £50 per month per subject, with an initial registration fee of £25. You get a small discount on the cost of having your child tutored in a second subject (either reading or maths), and everyone gets an initial assessment at no extra cost.

Find more information and a centre near you by visiting www.kumon.co.uk or calling 0800 854 714.

Kip McGrath Centres

Kip McGrath is a family-run company with more than 30 years' experience and numerous centres throughout the UK. The centres tutor children ages 6 to 16 in maths, reading, spelling and English.

While Kip McGrath Centres don't profess to be specialists able to teach children with dyslexia, they do cater to the needs of anyone seeking some extra help. Their aim is to motivate children to succeed by encouraging each child to work at her own pace and providing an environment where learning's fun. Each lesson is 80 minutes, and children follow an individual scheme of work within a small class of a maximum of five children. Children can have an individualised programme that addresses both maths and English in each lesson. The initial assessment is free and lessons cost £25 each, with children generally attending on a weekly basis. For further information, visit www.kipmcgrath.co.uk or phone 01452 382 282.

Explore Learning Centres

Explore Learning Centres have sprung up recently in supermarkets (such as Sainsbury's) as a way of giving your child extra tuition in English and maths while you shop. The company also offers stand-alone centres.

The centres address the needs of children aged 5 to 14 and offer a free trial session. Membership costs between £80 and £98 per month and entitles your child to a maximum of two visits per week. Sibling discounts are available. The centres are OFSTED inspected (OFSTED is the official body for inspecting schools) and they take childcare vouchers. You may be eligible to qualify for help under the Tax Credit scheme, and a scholarship programme is available for low-income participants.

Most Explore Learning Centres are located in the south-east or London, but you can find them elsewhere in Britain, too. Find locations near you and book a free trial lesson by searching online at www.explorelearning.co.uk.

Giving Academic Support at Home

Your child may act as if she hears about half of what you say and goes along with about a tenth of that, but without realising it, she absorbs your habits and beliefs. If she's having a hard time in school, you can help her. In the next sections, we focus on home-based ways to help your child with dyslexia.

You may want to go all out with your support at home and decide to home-school your child. For full details on this education option, see Chapter 7.

Letting your child take the lead with homework

When your child with dyslexia struggles with homework, you can easily get into the habit of doing things for her. You see her working hard to keep up with classmates and you want to help. Be careful. Do what's best for your child by giving her practical help that leads gradually to her helping herself, such as the following:

✔ Type her projects for her, but also see that she starts training on a typing programme so that she's able to type more and more work for herself.

✔ Dictate spellings to her, but ask her to proofread her answers before you check them.

✔ Discuss books with her, but encourage her to ask relevant questions for herself.

Any time you help your child, think about how you can take a supporting rather than a leading role. Your child must develop independence from you – and besides, work that she can call her own is always more important to her than work that someone else did.

The older your child gets, the more self-reliant she must be. Right from the beginning of school, help her get to know her strengths and weaknesses. Help her make good choices (like using *mind maps* for taking notes; Chapter 20 has more information about these) and ask for help when she needs it. She may need to find ways around her difficulties all her life, so right now's the time to prepare her and give her the confidence to do so.

Setting up homework management methods

All children do better homework when they establish an effective homework routine. This is doubly true for a child with dyslexia because she has disadvantages to contend with. Not only are reading and writing hard for your child with dyslexia, she also may have trouble focusing on homework and remembering precisely what she's supposed to be doing. Help her manage the homework monster by trying out these strategies. (If you're already on top of them, give yourself a hearty slap on the back for being a smarty-pants.)

✔ **Getting set:** In the first week of a new school year, some schools send your child home with a homework survival list. You're supposed to buy everything on the list, so that when your child announces that she must make a mobile using different colours of craft paper, some string and several sticks, right now, you at least have everything but the sticks. Have your child's survival kit (of craft paper, glue, tape, pens, a ruler, an eraser, a hole puncher, a stapler, scissors, string and anything else you think of) at the ready. Then you're one step ahead of the homework monster (and he's pretty fast). If your child's school doesn't do this, talk to the teacher to find out what your child will be doing, how you can help and to ask what you need to provide.

✔ **Planning:** A daily planner's part of your child's school equipment. Often you buy a planner directly from the school so that every child has the same one. The planner's really a diary in which your child's supposed to jot all homework reminders and which you, the parent, sign each day to verify that she did indeed complete all the day's homework.

The reality about the planner that your child with dyslexia has is that she may write illegibly in it and you may hastily sign it in the morning, worrying more about whether you get peanut butter on it than whether it's actually working. Unless you schedule time for looking *properly* at your child's planner each day, doing so can feel like a daily burden. Help your child understand that short, legible notes are best and that each piece of homework gets checked off *after* she's done it. Try to muster up nice feelings about the planner so that it really *is* a link between you and the teacher and a gauge of how well your child's keeping abreast of her daily obligations.

✔ **Prioritising:** Some assignments are more important than others. Your child with dyslexia can easily become absorbed in her lizard poster when she should in fact be doing her fractions. Help her put first things first and establish the habit of referring to her planner every single day. Which things must she do immediately and which can wait? Does your child need special supplies (like modelling clay) within the next few days?

✔ **Setting time limits:** Your child with dyslexia may take longer with her assignments than you think she needs to. She may spend a long time fussing and complaining. Setting a time limit for each homework subject can help. If your child has 45 minutes per subject homework per night, stick to that and don't be tempted to let her exceed that limit. If you link rewards (like TV viewing time) to your child completing a subject in, say, 30 minutes, the system may work even better. Parents who enforce limits and carry through, even though they feel like army sergeants during the first few days, may find that this strategy ends up imposing relative calm on a previously homework-shocked household. However, for this to work, you have to know what length of time is realistic for your child. This could be a counter-productive measure if the child feels pressurised to do things too fast. Pressure of time usually makes dyslexia symptoms worse.

✔ **Studying from a guide:** A study guide, such as the Letts guides, is an at-a-glance summary of the main points of a topic or, as in algebra, the techniques. If your child has trouble figuring out the key concepts in a subject (and for that matter, you do too), you may find that a study guide helps you sort the wood from the trees.

✔ **Using hand-held devices:** Spell checkers/dictionaries and reading pens are ultra-simple-to-use gadgets that can make your child's homework go infinitely smoother. A simple spell checker looks a bit like a calculator. Your child types in her word, probably spelled phonetically, and sees the correct spelling displayed on the screen. For a bit more, you can buy a spell checker that displays *and* speaks the words. A reading pen performs the same functions as a displaying/speaking spell checker, only your child just has to run the reading pen over a word (or sentence) to get it displayed and read out to her. To view these nifty hand-held devices, have a look at www.dyslexic.com. See 'Using technology', later in this chapter, for more.

✔ **Using software and online materials:** Your child with dyslexia can do her homework much more easily if she has access to a comprehensive encyclopaedia. You can install an encyclopaedia on her computer or sign up for online use. One popular encyclopaedia available in both of those options is Encarta. To buy the CD-ROM or DVD (Windows), go to www.amazon.co.uk. To subscribe for online use, go to www.encarta. msn.co.uk.

For software in special subjects, like foreign languages, search the software category at an online store like www.amazon.co.uk using words like 'children', 'learn' and 'French'. The BBC Learning website (www. bbc.co.uk/learning) is also a good place to start.

✔ **Replacing lost items:** At some point your child's going to lose something that she vows she can't live without. 'I can't do my homework without it. I've looked everywhere. I'm going to fail,' she sobs. Do you punish her? If she loses a book, do you zip to an online bookshop and buy her another? Do you make her buy another from her own money?

The point we're making here is that you probably need to decide, in advance, on a strategy before you become exasperated and your child's homework (which she can't do without her book) mounts up. Having a wall chart or white board can help with this problem. Get the child to write what she needs for the week and/or the next day on this to enable her to prepare in advance. You need to do this for or with a younger child.

Using technology

Children who adeptly cruise the Internet and tap confidently on a keyboard have a big advantage over those who don't. You're hard pressed to find a child who's completely in the dark in these areas, but still, the more knowledge the better. You may find running to your 10 year old every few minutes for help navigating the web a bit humiliating, but in the big picture, the benefits are worthwhile (easy for us to say, huh?).

We don't delve into the benefits of the Internet in the following sections (all that pretty much speaks for itself), but we do look at the simpler forms of technology (like word processors) that you may not be making full use of for homework, and the alternative kinds of technology (like speech-recognition software) that you may have only heard of. Chapter 20 has more info on some of these tools.

All the gadgets in the following sections can, of course, be useful for adults with dyslexia too.

Word- processing programs

Basic word-processing know-how's pretty much a necessity for anyone who has to write stuff. But word processing can be especially beneficial for a child with dyslexia who types her homework because:

- ✔ Her work looks legible.

- ✔ She can enlarge her letters and choose a clear font so that she can more easily read what she writes.

- ✔ She can easily change the background colour and highlight words which may help her to read them more easily.

- ✔ Showing her how to cut and paste can make her feel in control if she knows that she can move information around easily.

- ✔ Typing can be easier on her hands than writing.

- ✔ Writing's quicker for her, especially if she practises keyboard skills.

- ✔ She learns a skill and keeps abreast of current trends (not many children use pen and paper for coursework these days, and after about Year 10 many teachers specify that assignments *must* be typed).

As soon as your child lays her fingers on the keyboard of her computer, have her use the spell check and thesaurus functions in whatever word-processing program you use. The spell check can iron out a lot of her spelling mistakes, and the thesaurus can turn her little words into the bigger ones she knows but can't pull out of her brain. To help further, you can even buy keyboards adapted for children.

The read-back feature that you can get on most computers these days is a great tool for people with dyslexia too. When the computer reads back items your child's typed, she can hear the words she's written and any mistakes she's made. Your child should also get comfortable with the cut and paste features so she can jot down her first draft of an assignment, run the spell check and thesaurus over it and then give it a final clean-up by rearranging the words if she wants.

You may not even realise (most people don't) that you have the text-to-voice function on your computer. Go to your help menu to find it. You get a mechanical-sounding read-back of what you type, but it's still worth having. To buy text-to-voice software to install on your computer, check out Dragon Naturally Speaking Software at www.dyslexic.com.

If you're really savvy with computers, or have a friend who is, you can search the Internet and find free downloadable text-to-voice programs, including those that read Internet pages out loud to you.

The following websites are full of info on software that can improve your child's word processing:

- ✔ For software to help your child get quicker at keyboarding, look at English Type Junior and Senior, for sale from DI Trading (`www.dyslexia action.org.uk/store`).

- ✔ For reviews from parents of children with dyslexia of software that helps with spelling, go to `www.dyslexia-parent.com/software.html`.

- ✔ See a review of the award-winning 'Read and Write' program (and useful links) at `www.dyslexia-parent.com/mag31.html`.

- ✔ For links and advice on technology for children, check out `www. education-world.com`.

Pocket spell checkers

Pocket spell checkers are widely available. Take a look at `www.dyslexic. com` for a selection. These nifty little gadgets are inexpensive and, according to many students with dyslexia, particularly useful. Things to look for when buying for young children are the size of the screen and of the buttons.

Digital recorders and recorded books

A digital recorder is a great investment for all kids, but especially for older kids. Your child can use it to record lessons (ask the teacher's permission first) so that she can listen to them later and fill in any gaps in her notes or understanding.

And don't forget the benefits of having your child listen to recordings of books either. If your child's panicking because she has to read *Charlotte's Web* in a week, or write a report on a book that has more than 300 pages, no problem. Get the book on tape, CD or as a download digital audio file. Libraries stock these, too. If you're really on the ball, get, in advance, a list of all the other books her class is using over the year or term so you can order your recorded books early and avoid the wait.

Here are two options for recorded books:

- ✔ **Listening Books.** You can join Listening Books for as little as £20 per year. Its lending library has more than 500 titles in subjects ranging from literature and history to maths and the sciences, at all levels. Chances are if the book's in your child's curriculum, it's in the library. Anyone with a documented disability (in other words, your child's dyslexia assessment results) is eligible, and funding's available if you're unable to pay the full membership fee. For more, visit `www.listening-books.org.uk`.

> ✔ **Calibre Audio Library.** This lending option features more than 8,000 audio books for all tastes – fiction and non-fiction – with more than 1,400 books for children and young people all read by leading actors. Postage is free and you don't pay fines for late returns. Membership is free if you have a disability such as dyslexia. Find more at www.calibre.org.uk.

Photocopying and print-recognition software

People who have dyslexia read things over and over. When everyone else reads a passage once and gets the drift, someone with dyslexia needs to read and re-read before she gets it. Distinguishing key concepts from secondary concepts is hard for someone with dyslexia, so she needs to mull over the text and use a highlighter pen on it. Talking to her afterwards about what she has read may also help.

Get comfortable with photocopiers and scanners so that you can ask your child's teacher if you can sometimes photocopy his notes, or pages from books he refers to, for you and your child to read later on. Then, when your child has an important report to do, you get a better understanding of what's required and can be a bigger help to your child. Your child gets the opportunity to re-visit material that may have escaped her in class.

Fancy print-recognition (or optical character recognition) software lets your child scan pages into her word processor so that she can alter and add to the text. This process may sound puzzling for technology scaredy-cats, but if you or someone in your family's good with computers you may want to include print recognition among your dyslexia-busting arsenal. This kind of technology can save a lot of tears when your child wants to do something like scan her handwritten project into a Word document instead of re-writing it.

Check out www.dyslexic.com for software such as Text Help Read and Write Gold. This is a wonderful resource for older children and adults with dyslexia who find reading large amounts of text difficult. You can scan in any printed material and then have the computer read it aloud. For more details see Chapter 18.

Speech-recognition software

Speech-recognition software (also called speech-to-text software) lets you talk into your computer and have your words appear on the screen. In the last five years the technology's come a long way, correctly hearing your speech and saying things back to you in a fairly normal-sounding voice. Older students typically use speech-to-text software when they do reports and other lengthy written assignments. Here's how it works:

1. **Buy the software (called names like Dragon Naturally Speaking, Kurzweil and Via Voice) and install it on your computer.**

2. **Train your computer to recognise your child's voice by having her talk to it for many hours.**

   In the training process, the computer says words back to her so that it can verify her words.

   The training takes a long time, and the playback sounds weird because the computer doesn't use the same inflections that she uses in regular speech. After she gets all this under her belt, however, you're set to go.

3. **Read out what she wants to write.**

   The computer types it for her.

4. **Paste it into a Word document for final editing.**

   Hey presto! She has a piece of written work anyone would be proud of.

And here are the benefits of voice-recognition software:

- ✔ All those words she could never get down on paper are at last there to show the world that she's clever after all!

- ✔ The vocabulary she has in her head now shows up in her reports, and she gets better marks.

- ✔ She has the confidence to do things she's never done before – like send a note to someone she likes!

- ✔ She may get the feeling that her reading's improving.

- ✔ She has the confidence to go on with her education now that she can write well.

Speech-recognition technology overwhelms some people, so it's not the answer for everyone. But for those who use it, it's liberating. The software's an equaliser and people rely on it. And therein lies the cause of some controversy. Special education teachers are catching on to this technology, but some classroom teachers can be less enthusiastic. Their concern is that this software prevents kids from learning for themselves, but so far, research shows the opposite. Children who use speech-recognition technology seem to be making gains in reading and spelling, and when you think about what's happening, you can see why. Multisensory techniques (see, hear, say and do) work, and that's what this software gives you. Say a word, then see it on the screen and then change the text (type, cut and paste) if you want. (Check out Chapter 14 for more about multisensory methods.)

Steering clear of a maths meltdown

Dyslexia's primarily a language disability, but it can have an impact on your child's performance in maths. She may have trouble remembering sequences of numbers, like multiplication tables, and what specialised words like 'product' and 'reciprocal' mean. In addition, she may confuse written symbols, such as the division and multiplication symbols, and struggle with wordy maths problems. And she may have these problems even when she's a whizz with harder mathematical processes and concepts.

In the following sections, we cover easy methods for helping your child with dyslexia with maths at home.

Introducing simple maths concepts

If maths is a struggle for your younger child, here are a few simple things you can do at home to help:

- ✔ Use beans, counters or coins to help your child see the four functions (adding, subtracting, multiplying and dividing) in action.

- ✔ Bring fractions to life by cutting up cake, bread or fruit.

- ✔ Demonstrate how your child can work out the area of your floor. Do the same thing with a tabletop and count the individual squares to check that the formula (length × width = area) really works. Demonstrating how to measure her hand and seeing how tall she is are other good ideas.

- ✔ Help your child see small angles by having her open a door and tell you when she's made a right angle or a bigger or smaller angle.

- ✔ Explain place value with pennies and pounds (because ten 10p coins equal a pound and children are familiar with these small coins).

- ✔ Help your child to keep a note of what she spends.

Tackling word problems

Maths word problems can give anyone trouble, so in this section we give you handy tips that your child with dyslexia's bound to find useful either for herself or when she helps friends with *their* maths!

- ✔ **Read the question at least twice.** This advice is important for any child but especially for your child with dyslexia. She needs to identify not only which words are key but that she has read the question correctly in the first place.

- ✔ **Highlight key words.** For example, in a problem like 'David has discovered a number pattern that starts with 1, 4, 9, 16, 25. What are the next three numbers in this pattern?' the key words are 'pattern' and 'next three numbers'.

- ✔ **Draw a table.** This method's good for questions like 'Ashley saved £2 on Tuesday. Each day after that, she saved twice as much as she saved the day before. If she keeps doing this, how much does she save on Friday? How much does she save in total?' The following table shows how to get the answer.

Day	Amount Saved
Tuesday	£2
Wednesday	£4
Thursday	£8
Friday	£16
TOTAL	£30

- **Work backwards.** This technique is for problems like 'Beth walked from Pangbourne to Reading. It took her 1 hour and 25 minutes to walk from Pangbourne to Tilehurst. Then it took 25 minutes to walk from Tilehurst to Reading. She arrived in Reading at 2.45 p.m. At what time did she leave Pangbourne?' Your child first has to establish what she needs to find out (what time it was when Beth left) and then that the way to do the problem is to subtract times backwards from the time she arrived. Subtract 25 minutes from 2.45 (giving you 2.20) and then 1 hour and 25 minutes from that (giving you a leaving time of 12.55 p.m.).

- **Guess and then verify.** This works for a problem like 'Rebecca and Rachel sold 12 raffle tickets in total. Rebecca sold 2 more tickets than Rachel. How many tickets did each girl sell?' Your child must find two numbers that add up to make 12, with a difference of 2 between them. Guesses: 8 and 4; 9 and 3; 7 and 5 (bravo!).

The Dyslexia Action store (www.dyslexiaaction.org.uk/store) sells games and resources for helping your child with maths, and Dyslexia Action also run courses for parents who want to help their children with maths at home.

Chapter 10

Working Productively with Your Child's Teacher

• •

In This Chapter

▶ Getting ready for a formal meeting

▶ Ensuring a successful meeting

▶ Accommodating your child's needs

▶ Dealing with grades, tests and rote learning

• •

Your child's teacher is your greatest ally in helping your child handle dyslexia. Being in a partnership with your child's teacher is better than being at odds with her. Here's why:

✔ When you have a friendly relationship with your child's teacher, she's more likely to stay after class to quickly make sure your child knows what the homework is, jot you a note to let you know the tricky parts of the homework and regularly touch base with you by phone or email.

✔ When the teacher's comfortable with you, she can call you or leave a note in your child's diary so you get quick information. Otherwise, she may communicate with you via the school secretary and formal notes.

✔ When your child's teacher knows you don't question her judgement, she tries out different strategies with your child to make tasks easier for him.

✔ When you're on friendly terms with the teacher, she's likely to tell you about new books or programmes she hears about.

And that's just the beginning! In this chapter, we tell you how to conduct successful meetings with your child's teacher, plan effective accommodations and help your child avoid classroom pitfalls.

With the right instruction and accommodations (more help with this in the section 'Coming Up with Easy Accommodations', later in this chapter), children with dyslexia get better at reading (even becoming keen readers) and have pretty much the same experiences at school as anyone else. So let your child know that!

Requesting and Preparing for a Formal Meeting

On paper, establishing a harmonious relationship with your child's teacher sounds easy. And in many cases it is. But when your child struggles in class, tells you how miserable he is and cries a lot, you may feel that the teacher isn't doing enough to help or isn't doing the right kinds of things to help.

Even if you're calm and composed, and even if your child is generally happy and keeping up in class, you need to schedule a meeting with your child's teacher. Talking for a few hasty minutes after class or even writing notes or emails to the teacher isn't the same as getting scheduled, uninterrupted, personal time with her. The following sections give you the lowdown on successfully setting up and getting ready for a formal meeting.

Don't use going to someone more senior than the teacher as your first response. Have a discussion with the teacher initially, because she may understandably feel slighted if you bypass her, and you may never make up that lost ground. If she doesn't respond to your requests for a meeting, is rude to you or acts problematically in any other way, then you can justifiably approach the head teacher.

Asking the teacher to meet

Ask your child's teacher to meet you before or after school for about half an hour to discuss your child's progress. Ask her in person or via a note, an email or a phone call. If possible, both parents (or guardians) should attend.

Parents are usually allotted one or two parent/teacher meetings a year at the time that reports are given out. You can have a meeting at other times too, so don't be afraid to ask. Remember, though, the teacher has a life and may not be happy staying after school to talk to you about trivial things. If Johnny always loses his school-to-home notes or doesn't want to sit next to Jane, you can probably work out things via notes. Formal meetings are for bigger issues.

Assembling important information

What exactly do you want to happen as a result of the meeting? What points do you especially want to make? Do you already have practical ideas that you think may help your child keep up in class? You need to jot all this info down so you don't get sidetracked and waste any of your time with the teacher.

Keep a paper trail of everything you ask for or tell the teacher about, because you never know when you may need this record. Mistakes happen and details get forgotten. If they do, your notes allow you to remind teachers what you explained or planned and bring your discussions quickly back on track.

How does your paper trail relate to a meeting? Before you meet with the teacher, jot down suggestions you have for dealing with general issues and get to the nitty-gritty of specific problems too. For example, if your child's unhappy, how exactly do you know? If his homework plunges him into despair, which particular assignments cause him the most grief? If a book is beyond him, what's its title and how much time does he have to read it? Jot down the details, including dates and conversations, so the teacher knows you're a person she can work with. If your child's going through weeks or months of being upset, jot down specific incidents and the dates they happened.

If you present this information to the teacher in an I-care way (rather than an I-blame-you way), you increase your chances of getting a great response from her. Who doesn't want to join forces with a reasonable, organised and caring parent (that's you, by the way!)?

You may want to share your sketched-out plan with the teacher before your meeting, perhaps by sending an email or letter. By having a rough idea of the issues that parents want to address, teachers can reflect on them in advance and not feel like they're on the spot during the meeting. Teachers can also bring along work samples, future assignments, current grades and so on if they know these items may be helpful to you at the meeting.

Determining whether to bring your child

Before the meeting, you need to decide whether you want your child to come too, bearing in mind his age and awareness of his problems. You could also ask the teacher for her opinion as to the advisability of including your child at this early stage. You might consider waiting until after the initial meeting and having a follow-up meeting with your child at a later date to be a better move. If you think he can benefit from attending, you need to invite him to come and tell him what may happen, what kinds of things he may want to talk about and how he should also jot down key points so the meeting stays succinct and on track. Whether you do or don't invite your child, let the teacher know your decision in advance.

Advantages of having your child attend the meeting include the following:

✔ He gets practice at speaking up for himself.

✔ He finds out what happens during formal meetings so he's prepared to take a more active role in them as he gets older. His attendance can be useful if he needs to make an input into his IEP at a later stage, for example. (For more on IEPs, take a look at Chapter 8.)

✔ He's heard immediately and, likewise, gets immediate feedback.

Possible disadvantages are that your child may have no interest in attending (he's a child and he wants to play or hang out), and he may find it hard to talk openly to teachers. He may prefer that you relay his thoughts because he can tell them to you without feeling shy or disrespectful. The other risk is that it reinforces to the child that he's struggling and has problems, and this may affect his confidence and self esteem. Sensitivity is crucial.

Keeping a Meeting on Track and Following Up Smartly

You don't get a whole lot of time in a meeting with your child's teacher, so you want to be sure you make all your points, send out 'I'm competent, concerned and very easy to work with' kinds of vibes and pin down specific outcomes you expect to see as a result of the meeting. We walk you through all these topics and more in the following sections. For examples of accommodations that teachers can use in response to your child's issues, see the section 'Coming Up with Easy Accommodations', later in this chapter.

Creating a positive mood

So how exactly do you project an I-care and I'm-competent tone during the meeting with your child's teacher? The trick is to be concise and positive. (That's why you write a list of points to cover – see the section 'Assembling important information', earlier in this chapter, for details.) You want to focus on practical solutions, not blame, and your comments must tell the teacher that you're willing to collaborate and accept her professional judgement.

Your opening remarks should be positive and open. Say something supportive to the teacher, like 'I'm so glad to have this chance to talk to you', and then quickly ask for her impressions of (and concerns about) your child's schoolwork and behaviour. You need to hear from her early on for two reasons:

✔ Then she feels more at ease. Like everyone else, the teacher likes to talk about things she's knowledgeable about, and she likes to be listened to. When you give her this opportunity, she feels she's on safe and familiar ground.

✔ You get a chance to check out the territory. You find out what the teacher believes about your child, and you can adjust your own remarks accordingly. For example, suppose that your child cries about his schoolwork most nights and says he's miserable in class, but the teacher seems to have no idea about his feelings. You can say something like 'Johnny may be giving you the impression that everything's OK' rather than 'I'm sure you know that Johnny's only barely coping'.

Remember to show your appreciation of the good things, big *and* little, that the teacher does for your child. The first rule for positive and effective work relations is to home in on a person's contributions so that she's motivated to make more.

Emphasising your child's needs

The way to make sure that you avoid blaming the teacher for your child's difficulties and instead form an alliance with her is to focus on your child's needs (not what the teacher may or may not have done). If you talk in terms of your child's needs, you pinpoint *his* problems – not the teacher's – and set the stage for planning practical steps that address them.

Describe your child's problems in terms of his own learning style and personality traits rather than focusing on the teacher's actions. Lay out your points, making sure that your tone stays solutions based. To see exactly what we're talking about, check out Table 10-1.

Table 10-1	Telling the Teacher about Your Child
It's Better to Say	*Rather Than*
Johnny doesn't want to go to school in the morning and feels that he's hardly managing to keep up in class.	You make him unhappy.
He spends at least three hours on homework every night and it really worries me.	You give him too much homework.
I'm wondering what kinds of strategies I can use to help Johnny finish his work without missing out on break time.	You keep him in at break time.

(continued)

Table 10-1 *(continued)*

It's Better to Say	Rather Than
Johnny's book seems to be frustrating. There are so many words in it that he can't figure out and he feels overwhelmed.	You give him books that are way too hard for him.
How can I make the spelling list easier for Johnny? He tries so hard, but the copying activity, in its present form, really doesn't help him remember.	You give him spelling words that are way beyond his ability.

Pushing your points firmly

In real life your conference doesn't stick to a point-by-point format. You may want to disagree with the teacher. You may feel that she isn't doing anything to adjust classroom requirements to meet your child's needs. You may feel like you're not really being heard.

One strategy that can help is to re-visit your list of main points. Stay calm, keep your voice at a normal tone and repeat the points that you think are key. As you make those points, have the following goals in the back of your mind:

✔ Focus on your child, not the teacher

✔ Seek specific solutions, not blame

✔ Make suggestions, not demands

✔ Project an all-round air of collaboration, not confrontation

In Table 10-2, we give a few examples of how a teacher may respond to your concerns and how you can stick to your points in reply.

Table 10-2	Clarifying Your Main Points
What Your Child's Teacher May Say	How You Can Press Your Point
Our reading programme is excellent.	I'm sure the programme is great, but it isn't meeting Johnny's needs.
All children must do homework.	With some minor accommodations, Johnny can be much more successful with homework.
All assignments must be handed in on time.	Advance notification of the term's assignments may be a great help to Johnny.

What Your Child's Teacher May Say	How You Can Press Your Point
Every child must give class presentations.	Because Johnny struggles with the written component of the presentation, can he make charts or diagrams in place of some of the writing?
Your child must read three books each month.	Johnny has to read a book several times in order to understand it, so can we get the book list early on so we can order the books on tape too?
Your child is discourteous and disruptive.	Johnny's frustration comes out this way.

All teachers want to have good communication with parents and are keen to offer advice about resources and strategies that might help at home. They have large classes and generally receive gratefully any help that you offer as a parent. Think of this as a two-way street – if your child improves at home he'll improve at school, and vice versa.

Adhering to the teacher's goals

When you speak with your child's teacher about solutions to problems, respect the fact that she's in charge of the class. Keep her goals in mind so that you're more likely to come to an agreement in which the goals that both of you have are maintained. Also remember that your child is one of many in her class. Acknowledging that fact helps the teacher to know you understand her situation and makes her more inclined to understand yours.

Your child's teacher may have plenty of good ideas for helping your child keep up with assignments and improve his language skills. If so, help her by monitoring your child's behaviour at home and augmenting anything done in class. During your conference, you may want to offer the following:

- Working through a phonics programme with your child at home, under the teacher's guidance (see Chapter 12 for more about phonics).

- Doing guided reading with your child at home, under the teacher's guidance (see Chapter 13 for time-tested reading strategies).

- Practising spelling strategies that the teacher recommends. For example, using plastic letters to spell the word and then muddling them up and asking your child to put them in the right order is fun and can be done before asking the child to write the word.

- Making copies of the teacher's notes or texts so your child is prepared for forthcoming projects or can re-visit information that he got in class.

✔ Making a calendar with your child so he can see how long he has until the next deadline can be fun, and can help your child understand the need to start on it early.

✔ Getting book lists from the teacher so you can reserve books on tape at your library or from programmes that offer books for the blind and people with dyslexia (check this out in Appendix B).

Stay in the teacher's good books by remembering that she's in charge. Ask for her help. Say that you may have forgotten this or misunderstood that. You may feel like you're eating a generous serving of humble pie, but that approach is easier than getting into a confrontation (by lashing out with statements like 'You didn't give me this or properly explain that'). Don't be eager to second-guess every move the teacher makes, and don't immediately challenge her professionalism and skills.

Your child needs to use cooperative and constructive words with his teacher too. Teachers, like everyone else, prefer to deal with polite rather than impolite people. By talking the right talk, your child practises the important life skill of showing respect for authority. Help him use terms like 'It's better for me if' and 'I like to' rather than 'No' and 'I won't'.

Taking action after a meeting

Immediately after a meeting, update your paper trail with the details of what was said and promised. If you're good with computers, you may want to start a chart or database with headings that note dates, attendees, points discussed, goals and follow-up activities (see Figure 10-1). Record everyone's contact details on your chart and (in note form) all the important things that were said. Determine the dates when you're to re-assess your child's progress, and have some idea of behaviours or scores you're looking for to show whether your child is making headway. Make a plan for what you're going to do to help your child and start to think of things you can do at home to help him (www.dyslexia-parent.com has lots of good ideas). If your child has an Individualised Education Programme (IEP), these details are included on it (I talk about IEPs in Chapter 8).

Coming Up with Easy Accommodations

By using the word 'accommodations' while working with your child's teacher, you sound informed. The word appears in laws that relate to children with dyslexia (see Chapter 8 for details), and accommodations are what teachers and professionals talk about.

Date	Attendees	Points Discussed	Goals	Follow-up
10/4	T. Wood	TW asked for next term's book list.	Get the booklist.	Call LC on 14/10 to check that goals are being reached.
	R. Richards	TW asked about a homework buddy.	Ask LC and Jason to choose a homework buddy.	
	L. Conley	LC said Jason needs to speak up.	Coach Jason to approach LC after class and explain what he needs.	

Figure 10-1:
Keep track of your conference notes with a handy chart.

Contact info for R. Richards: (01771) 123456, extension 31; rrichards@meadowlea-school.com

Contact info for L. Conley: (01771) 654321, extension 12; lconley@meadowlea-school.com

What precisely are *accommodations?* They're the big or small changes you make to your child's environment and to the tasks he does that enable him to perform better. When you and your child's teacher home in on his specific difficulties, you can probably think of dozens of accommodations. For some initial inspiration, take a look at the following sections.

Understanding oral instructions clearly

Your child with dyslexia may have trouble understanding oral instructions because he can't keep a firm hold on sequences of information. He may forget parts of the sequences, moving for example from step one straight to step four, or he may muddle up the order of the steps. The following accommodations can help your child:

✔ Let the teacher know that your child sometimes struggles with lists of verbal instructions and ask her to speak clearly and in small bites of information to him. Also let her know that your child may sometimes ask her to reiterate things. The teacher may have a preference about whether she wants your child to do this in class or after class.

✔ Help your child have the confidence to speak up for himself, perhaps by role-playing an actual conversation at home. Your child may be nervous about asking for help even though to you the request seems simple. Or he may want to ask and ask, so you can show him how to behave courteously and appropriately. Be sensitive and give your child time to develop these skills, starting with simple requests.

✔ Have the teacher find your child a buddy he can chat with to clarify what the teacher said.

✔ Encourage your child to makes notes and lists. At home, help your child improve his note-taking skills. We talk about this in detail in Chapter 16.

✔ Ask the teacher if she can write all assignments on the board, on a short handout, on the Internet or in Johnny's notebook.

Reading large amounts of text

Reading a lot of text at once usually presents problems for a child with dyslexia because he ends up spending hours and hours on an assignment that's meant to be fairly short. You can do your part to help:

✔ When the teacher assigns books to read, borrow books on tape for your child. He can listen to the text on tape while following the written version.

✔ Read through homework text with him a few times (see Chapter 13 for tips on reading with your child effectively). Think of ways he can approach the homework and make a plan to help him get started.

Comprehending text

A child with dyslexia's text comprehension may not be strong because he loses the flow and gist of what he's reading when he takes a long time figuring words out. You can accommodate his needs in the following ways:

✔ Encourage your child to draw story maps and mind maps, highlight key words in the text and talk the text over with other students (maybe a buddy). (A *story map* is a pictorial depiction of events in a story, and a *mind map* is like a story map, only it depicts whatever you're learning with bubbles and connecting lines.)

✔ Ask your child to tell you in his own words about what he's just read, perhaps after every paragraph, for example.

> ✔ Help your child at home by starting to draw story maps and mind maps for assigned books and going over text with him until he understands key concepts and sequences of events. Later, your child can draw them himself as this helps to reinforce the information in his mind. This then helps to transfer information from his short-term memory into his long-term memory where it will remain.

Writing large amounts of text

Writing can give a child with dyslexia trouble because he really has to think about most of the words he's jotting down. He can find it hard to know what to say and to put his thoughts in logical order. The following suggestions can help your child with writing:

✔ Encourage your child to learn to plan work first. Children with dyslexia often have excellent ideas in their heads but find it difficult to put these ideas onto paper. Mind mapping can help to 'unlock' these ideas.

✔ See that your child learns to touch type. *Touch typing* is the art of typing without looking at the keyboard, and your child needs to get at least to the stage where he uses all his fingers on the keyboard and checks on them only intermittently. Check out www.bbc.co.uk/schools/typing for an excellent free online typing programme.

✔ Type for your child while he dictates homework assignments to you.

✔ If your computer doesn't already have it, buy speech-to-text software for your child and help him learn how to use it. He gets to dictate things to his computer and have it appear in a word-processing document, thus saving him the hard work of writing.

As long as your child understands what he's dictating, this software doesn't make him lazy but helps him compete on an even field with classmates. In fact, some researchers say that speech-to-text software actually improves your child's spelling because he's saying the words, then seeing them appear on the screen, so his learning is multisensory. See Chapter 9 for more information.

If you don't have the technology, or if the cost of obtaining it is a problem, then ask your child to tell you what he wants to say while you write it down. Do check with the teacher first that this will be OK, though, because it may not be for formally assessed work.

Copying from the board with ease

A child with dyslexia can have difficulty copying words from the board; by the time he shifts his eyes from the board to the paper, he's forgotten the image he just saw. You can find ways to make copying words easier for your child:

✔ Ask the teacher to make sure that your child sits close to the board.

✔ Ask the teacher to underline key words; your child can copy only these.

✔ See if the teacher can provide a *cloze procedure*, where your child only needs to add in a handful of words to a pre-written sheet with blank spaces where the words should be. This means that if your child is slow at copying, he is able to produce the same amount of work as his classmates.

✔ Make sure your child has a buddy whose notes he can take home to copy (or maybe the teacher can photocopy them).

Spelling successfully

Spelling can be rough for your child because he has trouble matching letters to sounds and may have difficulty placing individual letters the right way too. Consider these ways of accommodating his needs in this area:

✔ Help your child develop his phonemic and phonics skills (word recognition) when he does language homework by showing him word families like *might*, *sight*, *tight*, *slight* and *right*. We talk about this in detail in Chapter 12.

✔ Help your child group spellings he brings home from class into families. (You can find more information about word families and lists of them at www.enchantedlearning.com.)

✔ Help your child sound out parts of his spelling words and highlight (to visually memorise) parts that don't sound out.

✔ Coach your child on the memorising strategy: look, cover, write, check. First he looks at the word, then covers it with his hand or paper or a book, writes it from memory and finally checks what he's written against the original word and makes corrections. Your child with dyslexia usually needs to write a word out several times before it sticks in his visual memory, and even then, he should check that it's still there a few hours later!

✔ Help your child to put each spelling word from a list on a small piece of paper so he can spread and overturn all the words in playing-card fashion. In Chapter 11 we describe how your child can keep ten words in an envelope and play a few games with them each day (for about five minutes) to help him remember them.

Finishing classroom work and homework on time

A child with dyslexia's time-management skills may be weak; he takes longer than other students to complete tasks, and he may be more disorganised than the average child too. Here are ways to help your child finish his work on time:

- ✔ See that your child has a buddy to help him in ways the teacher specifies, like putting away supplies, so that he has fewer things on his plate and can focus on the more important tasks at hand.

- ✔ Help your child keep a calendar or pocket organiser and follow a time line to complete assignments.

- ✔ See that your child uses speech-to-text software, books on tape, a laptop and other time-saving gadgets.

Avoiding Dyslexic Land Mines

For children with dyslexia, some things that typically go on in school are virtual land mines. Children with dyslexia usually dread being graded and taking standardised tests, hate being timed or having to race the clock when they do spellings and can never churn out facts and figures, such as multiplication tables, that other children learn by rote in a few weeks. In the next sections, we give you advice on helping your child skirt around these land mines.

Making the grade

Your child may get Cs, Ds or worse in his school grades no matter how hard he tries because grades primarily reflect his ranking (how he compares to classmates) rather than the effort he makes.

Can anything be done? Absolutely. You can ask for special consideration for your child, and this is where the good relationship you cultivate with the teacher really comes in handy! (See the section 'Keeping a Meeting on Track and Following Up Smartly', earlier in this chapter, for details.) The teacher may allow him to have extra time for completing a task so he isn't disadvantaged by his slow processing. Ask your child's teacher if she's able to tweak her normal grading system to meet your child's extra needs. Most schools do give an effort grade in addition to an achievement grade.

Exactly what kind of tweaking helps? The kind that calls attention to your child's effort. You want your child's grades to reflect his effort and the improvement of his own skills without comparison to anyone else, so that he knows he's getting better. So that everyone knows what counts as effort, you may want to collaborate with the teacher to draw up a list of *identifiers* that influence his grade. For example, you may want the list to indicate when your child accomplishes the following:

✔ Writes more than one page

✔ Answers every question

✔ Uses full stops and capital letters

✔ Writes his name and the date

✔ Starts each line against the margin

✔ Includes diagrams, lists or pictures

The teacher should have plenty of ideas about what to include as grading identifiers, and after the list is drafted, you may want to finalise it with your child. This list is really his because he can look at it and see that any effort he makes really pays off. He should understand how the system works and, as a result, feel motivated. Of course, encouraging comments, stars and smiley faces on his work may count just as much to him too.

Surviving standardised tests

When all the parents in school are talking about achievement tests, and you get a note from the school saying that your child's taking tests for two whole weeks and that only famine, disease or pestilence should keep him from attending school at this important time – the pressure's on! This is the standardised, high-stakes testing that politicians assure parents improves standards in schools.

These tests are 'standardised' because hundreds of children have taken them in order to get a *norm* (what most kids the same age can be expected to score) and a *range* (how far either side of that norm the rest of the kids usually score).

SATs and other important exams

Standardised achievement tests (SATs) begin at the end of Key Stage 1 for children aged 7, with national tests in English and maths. These are marked internally at school by teachers who decide the level the children achieve.

At the end of Key Stage 2 (age 11), children sit national tests in English, maths and science. These are marked externally, and all schools' results are published nationally. SATs results at Key Stage 2, together with teacher assessments, can stream your child's secondary schooling, so these tests are very important for children making the transition from primary school.

In some areas, children aged 10–11 sit the 11-plus for entrance into the grammar school system.

At 14, children sit the Key Stage 3 SATs in English, maths and science. Like Key Stage 2, these are marked externally and all schools' results are published nationally.

Private schools are able to choose whether they want their pupils to sit the SATs. Many do, but the papers are all marked internally by the schools themselves and the results aren't published.

Results of the SATs are reported in the following levels:

- Level W, which means working towards Level 1, very weak
- Level 1 is average for a typical 5 year old
- Level 2 is average for a typical 7 year old
- Level 3 is average for a typical 9 year old
- Level 4 is average for a typical 11 year old
- Level 5 is average for a typical 13 year old
- Level 6 is average for a typical 14 year old
- Level 7 is above average for a typical 14 year old
- Level 8 is only available in maths, and is achieved only by the most able pupils aged 14 years

Additionally you may find bands 'a', 'b' and 'c' given within the preceding levels, which indicate a range within the level. An 'a' band is the highest and 'c' the lowest.

According to www.satsguide.org.uk, if your child is sitting the Year 6 Key Stage 2 SATs and achieves a level 4, well done. A level 5 signals a very able or gifted child, while a level 3 indicates that you and your class teacher should work together to identify what you both can do to give your child extra help and promote confidence and a desire to learn. More information and some practice tests are available on www.direct.gov.uk.

Easing your child's SAT anxieties

Standardised tests, predictably enough, are hard on your child with dyslexia for a few reasons:

- ✔ Your child may have trouble reading the questions.

- ✔ He may take longer than other children to process the information and/or need more time to answer the questions (because he reads more slowly).

- ✔ He may mark the wrong answer boxes in multiple choice tests because he confuses *b* and *d* or forgets which letter he was thinking of.

- ✔ He may be improving in class, but the test results don't show that.

- ✔ He may perform badly on tests because, knowing that he does badly on them, he's understandably nervous.

You (with the help of your child's teacher) can help your child get through these tests and come out unscathed – and even optimistic:

- ✔ If your child has an Individualised Education Programme or IEP (I talk about IEPs in Chapter 8), you need to use it to plan for tests. Decide how your child's teacher can prepare him for tests and what accommodations he can use during the test. Exam accommodations such as having extra time, a reader to read questions out loud to your child or a scribe to write down his answers can make all the difference to his score.

- ✔ Your child with dyslexia needs plenty of practice runs on these tests. Check out good bookshops for Practice Papers for major standardised tests such as SATs and 11-plus examinations. Attack these practice tests in short blasts and offer good things to eat while practising. You want to prepare your child and help him feel less anxious in a test situation, but not to exhaust or terrify him.

- ✔ Tutors can help your child prepare for tests and may offer test-preparation courses specifically for exams like the GCSE. We talk about tutoring in more detail in Chapter 9.

Staying back a year

Generally, keeping children back a year doesn't happen in the state sector, but the decision is more common in private schools where children often skip a year as well. Many parents and teachers believe that retention allows a child to mature and get extra practice in class, but many researchers say that the evidence just doesn't bear this out.

Based on studies of the way in which these children see themselves and perform in class tests, researchers say that children who stay down a year:

- ✔ Feel ashamed or embarrassed in front of other kids because they're bigger and older than their classmates.

- ✔ May feel bored because they're repeating work.

- ✔ Get teased by classmates for being 'stupid'.

- ✔ Feel that their parents forced or misled them into staying back a year.

- ✔ Don't make appreciable headway in the skills they initially lacked and often fall back even further (compared to struggling kids who were not kept back).

- ✔ Are much more likely to drop out of school.

- ✔ Often say that being held back was the worst thing that ever happened to them.

Holding a child back is done with the best intentions, but it can have long-term dangers. These children invariably report that being held back traumatised them, and some researchers link increased rates of substance abuse and depression in adolescence with being held back in earlier years (for details, check out www.schwablearning.org/articles.asp?r-315).

We've seen – and lived through – evidence for and against this system. Katrina's own child was jumped a year at the age of 8, and this change had an enormous impact on him socially and academically, requiring around four years for him to overcome his difficulties. Katrina eventually made the decision to remove her son from his school and put him in the correct year group in a new school.

Staying back a year can work if your child was born in the late summer. Children who are almost a year younger than most of their peers often struggle, and we've seen many such children who do stay behind perform much better.

The best way to address your child's academic problems is to give him individualised instruction in his areas of weakness (if he has an IEP, this instruction is described in it). And if your child has dyslexia, the arguments against being kept behind are especially pertinent. Research shows that a child with dyslexia doesn't catch up to his peers by being given more of the same instruction. He catches up through multisensory instruction that takes him systematically through phonics or other appropriate methods. (I cover phonics in Chapter 12 and multisensory activities in Chapter 14.)

Learning parrot fashion

Rote learning is the process by which your child learns isolated facts (like multiplication tables, dates of events and names of cities) by parroting them out many times. Not many people are great at rote learning because it's hard to remember things without using memory joggers (like rhymes) or attaching meaning to them. But your child with dyslexia may find rote learning even harder because his short-term recall of information is weak even *with* memory joggers (see Chapter 11 for more about these memory tricks). The added challenge of having to recite facts at a fast speed, which happens in most classrooms, can cause major stress.

Strategies that can help your child join in activities like chanting multiplication tables include allowing him to use a calculator or a times square. The teacher, together with your child, should probably explain this accommodation openly to the class first so that other students realise the work isn't being made easier for your child, just accessible.

Smoothly integrating children with disabilities into a classroom requires good communication. When other students can walk a few miles in the shoes of children with disabilities and see that they're not being favoured in class but rather included, integration has every chance of being successful. Anything that helps a child with dyslexia to learn usually helps all children to learn, so many things can be done for the whole class so the child doesn't feel singled out. You need to discuss this with the teacher, who may be very skilled at dealing with individual differences within her class in a sensitive way. Parents too have a role to play in talking to the child about why some things are changed for him and not for others.

Part IV
Taking Part in Your Child's Tuition

'Your qualifications as a teacher are <u>just</u> what we're looking for but I think you'll get on even better with our children if you change your name to Smith, Jones or Brown, Mr Zgorzelkiewiecz.'

In this part . . .

When your child has dyslexia, she struggles with phonics. In this part of the book, you get everything you need to know about phonics, including how to help your child sound out tricky words like *right* and *round*.

But of course, phonics isn't the whole picture. Your child needs to recognise 'sight words', such as *who* and *they*, instantly, and she needs plenty of real reading and multi-sensory activity. And in addition to all of that, her dyslexia makes things, like following sequences of instructions, difficult, so she also needs help there. In this part, we give you practical advice on all these topics.

Chapter 11

Putting Memorising, Visualising and Rhyming to Good Use

*E*verybody uses rhymes and memory joggers now and then. '*I* before *e* except after *c*' is probably etched on millions of minds, and think how handy 'spring forward, fall back' is for helping you set your clock to a new hour twice a year!

When you're dealing with dyslexia, rhyming and visualising can be virtual lifelines. In this chapter, you get the handiest memory joggers of all for helping your child with dyslexia master many words that start off looking pretty formidable.

Just about all the activities we describe in this chapter (especially the ones related to spelling, sight words, sound-alike words and mnemonics) are good for anybody, young or less young. After all, a few extra years don't suddenly make you want to avoid effective learning strategies, even if they *are* more fun than you expect!

One by One: Starting with Single Letters

Remembering 26 of anything can be hard, so you need to give your child with dyslexia a lot of practice with the look and sound of each letter of the alphabet before she can remember all 26 letters in both upper and lower case.

You can run through the 'a is for apple' type of activities and flip through alphabet books with her, and that's good, but an even better approach is to bring each letter alive. Draw sound-associated pictures into them and make some of them into quirky characters. This notion may sound ethereal, so look at our practical examples in the following sections.

If your drawing skills are non-existent then the DIY Readers' Support Pack from DI Trading includes a no-name alphabet for your child with memorable pictures instead of letters. When the no-name alphabet is secure, your child can use the letters of the alphabet in upper and lower case. Have a look at www.dyslexiaaction.org.uk for details of this really useful resource.

Drawing pictures into vowels

Looking at apples, alligators and ants to learn about the letter *a* is a fairly complex business. In fact, the fact that children learn this way at all's amazing because, unless your child already knows the *a* sound of the letter *a*, how does she recall that *apple*, *alligator* and *ant* are all *a* words?

A much easier way for a child with dyslexia to grasp the 26 letter sounds is to get to know just 26 images. Help your child remember the letters by turning them into visual images or models she can feel.

Vowels are especially tricky for your child with dyslexia because each vowel always has at least two sounds, short and long, and can make other sounds too (about 44 of them) when grouped together with other letters. In the following vowel activities, you do away with vowel names altogether and focus wholly on sounds and vowel-specific visual images.

✔ Help your child remember the sound of short *a* by having her draw the letter *a* from an actual apple. She holds the apple on paper, draws around it, and then adds the vertical stick to make *a*. Have her make the *a* (like in *apple*) sound while she's holding and drawing the apple.

✔ Help your child remember the sound of short *e* by having her draw a big *e* and nesting an egg (hard boiled!) in the semicircular part of the letter. Explain that no other letter has that nice shape that fits snugly into that semicircular part, so when she sees the letter *e*, she can think of *egg* (the short *e* sound is like the *e* in *egg*).

✔ Help your child remember *i* for *ink* by having her hold down a pen and draw around it. Have her add the ink blob on top to make *i* and remember *i* is for *ink* (say it out loud).

✔ Help your child remember the sound of short *o* by having her draw an octopus's legs coming off the letter *o*. Tell her that *o* is a round, smooth octopus that has its eight legs tucked under it when you see it as a plain *o*. Remember to say *o* for *octopus*.

✔ Help your child remember *u* with a u-handled umbrella. *U* is for *umbrella*. If you don't have a u-handled umbrella, you can just turn *u* into a nice image. Add arrowheads to the two ends of the *u* (pointing upwards) and tell your child that *u* is for *up*. (She has to say that out loud, of course, to get the full multisensory complement!)

You may already have guessed this, but we're not the first people to think of turning letters into characters. Many early learning and phonics programmes draw characters into letters to help kids remember them. Two programmes well worth looking at are Letterland and Jolly Phonics. Both programmes have books, flashcards, CDs, readers and loads of resources. So if you want to start your child on letter sounds from scratch, check them out at www. letterland.com and www.jollylearning.co.uk or go to Chapter 4, where we tell you more about these products and give some prices.

Knocking b and d into shape

A child with dyslexia typically has trouble facing her letters the right way, and the letters that cause her the most trouble are *b* and *d*. You can help your child get her *b*s and *d*s to behave in two good ways, and they both involve visualising clever images.

Batter up!

If your child's a cricket or rounders nut, you may like this trick. Tell your child to think 'bat and ball' and hear the *b* sound. Now have her draw a standing-up cricket or rounders bat and next to it, on the ground, a ball. You've made the letter *b*, and now you just have to remember that *d* faces the opposite way.

The one problem with the bat and ball image is remembering which side to place the ball. Try telling your child to think of the direction in which you read and write – left to write. You write from left to right, and that's the direction to remember when you draw *first* the bat and next the ball.

Make your bed!

Here's a way to remember *b* and *d* together in one snuggly image. Take a look at Figure 11-1 and then read the instructions that follow:

1. Explain to your child that the bed picture in Figure 11-1 can help her remember which way *b* and *d* face.

2. Draw this simple shape: l__l

   Have your child do the same.

3. Draw a pillow and blanket on top of yours and have your child do the same with her picture.

4. Write the word *bed* in the bed picture, using the sides of the bed as the vertical lines in your *b* and *d*, and sound the word out so that your child hears the *b* and *d* sounds. Have her do the same on her picture.

5. Tell her that when she can't remember *b* ('buh') or *d* ('duh'), she can just make her bed! Be sure that nothing's sticking out – that's the big secret. (If letters face the wrong way, they stick out and someone may trip over them.)

6. Explain that she's making a big bouncy bed as a quick way of remembering the orientation of *b* and *d*.

Figure 11-1: You can help your child remember a cosy image for *b* and *d*.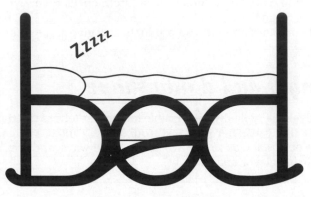

 You can also show your child how to make her bed with her hands. Figure 11-2 demonstrates how. Just have your child touch the tips of her thumb and forefinger together on each hand (making a circle), then point her remaining fingers straight up together (making a *b* shape with the left hand and a *d* shape with the right).

Putting P in its place

 Some kids with dyslexia have trouble distinguishing between the number 9 and the capital letter *P*. Here's a way to iron the confusion out:

1. Ask your child which direction she reads and writes in. Get the answer 'left to right' from her and have her point to the right.

2. Ask her to tell you a name that begins with *P*, like Peter, Paul or Polly.

3. Tell her to draw a face on the circle part of *P*, the nose pointing in the reading and writing direction.

4. Ask your child to add features like hair, a cap and glasses and write the person's name above.

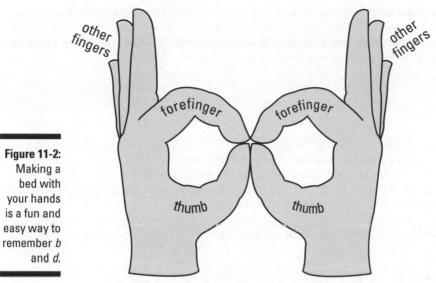

Figure 11-2:
Making a bed with your hands is a fun and easy way to remember *b* and *d*.

5. Tell your child that whenever she's not sure about P, she can draw her character, facing in the reading and writing direction. You can see a sample *P* drawing in Figure 11-3.

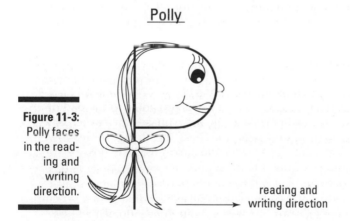

Polly

Figure 11-3:
Polly faces in the reading and writing direction.

reading and writing direction

Letters Joining Forces: Getting on Top of a Few Good Spelling Rules

When letters band together, they can retain their individual sounds but still blend smoothly together, or they can make new sounds that you just have to get to know afresh, like *ch* and *ir*. Luckily, some of the most common letter clusters are governed by nifty and easy-to-remember rules. Kids with dyslexia especially need to have a few rules up their sleeves so they can impose order on letters that otherwise make no sense to them.

In the next sections, we introduce you to blatantly *Bossy e*, friendly vowels that conform to the adage 'opposites attract' and the timeless rhyme '*i* before *e* except after *c*'.

Get full use from the tables we provide in the following sections by having your child go through plenty of re-readings, spot spelling rules and write words out for herself. This kind of repetition and *consolidation* (firming up understanding) is really helpful to children with dyslexia, so to make sure you cover it, have your child do the following:

- ✔ Read all the words, first to last.
- ✔ Read all the words, last to first.
- ✔ Read words in random order as you point to them.
- ✔ Read every second or third or fifth word.
- ✔ Find words as you call them out.
- ✔ Highlight each family (*a-e* words, *e-e* words, *i-e* words, *o-e* words and *u-e* words) in a different colour.
- ✔ Write out words that you dictate.

Blatantly Bossy e

Have you ever noticed the pattern in words like *pin* and *pine*, *hop* and *hope* *mad* and *made*? This simple rule explains it: when you add *e* to the end of small words like *pin*, or to word parts like *lak*, the *e* bosses the earlier vowel into shouting out its name. *Pin* becomes *pine* (hear the change in the vowel sound), *lak* becomes *lake*, and all the while the surreptitiously *Bossy e* stays silent itself.

The *long sound* of a vowel is the same as its name, like in *ay*, *ee*, *eye*, *oh* and *you*. We say that the vowel shouts its name in response to *Bossy e* because that concept tends to be easier for a child to remember than telling her that the vowel makes its long sound.

The *Bossy e* rule helps your child with dyslexia who's mastered the sounds of the alphabet read and write hundreds of words. If you're the creative type and have a younger child who is confident with her sounds, you may prefer the *Magic e* version of the same rule:

Magic e is a special letter. When it sits on the end of a word, it throws its magic dust out. The dust floats over the neighbouring letter but sticks to the vowel. The vowel feels so special that it shouts out its name.

With this rule, you get to grab some glitter or glitter pens (magic dust) and draw posters of *Magic e* doing its thing. This looks cute and helps to plant the rule firmly in your child's mind. Wands and cloaks add even more magic.

Now that you know the rule, you're probably wondering about the hundreds of words that use it. Table 11-1 lists just a few dozen of those *Bossy e* words.

Table 11-1	*Bossy e* Words	
ape	graze	tale
bake	lake	tape
base	lane	wake
blade	late	wave
blame	made	dive
brave	mane	drive
cake	mate	file
came	name	fine
cane	pale	five
cape	pane	hide
case	plate	hike
crate	rake	nine
chase	sale	bone
date	save	broke
fade	scrape	code
fake	shade	cone
flake	shake	hole
flame	shape	home
game	skate	hope
gate	snake	cute
gave	state	fume
grade	stale	mule
grape	take	rule

Your child likes to show off to you. Let her read and write words for you and be appreciative of her effort. Soup up the writing part by providing her with a book-sized whiteboard and coloured markers. Have your own too so you can write her messages or join in the activity with her.

Extroverted and introverted vowels

All vowels can make a *short sound* (like in *apple*, *egg*, *ink*, *octopus* and *up*) or a *long sound* (which is the same as saying the names of the letters). The rule we give you in this section helps your child with dyslexia distinguish which sound (short or long) a vowel's making in a word. Prepare to smile, because this rule's such a cute rhyme that it's easy to remember:

'When two vowels go walking, the first one does the talking.'

How does the rule work? Time and time again, your child sees four particular pairs of vowels side by side in words. They're the friends *ee*, *ea*, *ai* and *oa*, and they're special because when they go walking only the first one does the talking. The second vowel's the quiet type and says nothing. The first vowel's the loud type and it shouts (no surprise) its name.

Your child only has to remember the four pairs of friends (each comprising an extrovert and an introvert), and like with Bossy *e* words, hundreds of new words become clear to her. In Table 11-2, you get plenty to try out. You can add some pictures to the chart if your child finds it too hard. Go through the reading, finding, highlighting and writing activities we give earlier in this chapter, and your child should soon be feeling comfortable with the walking vowels.

Table 11-2	Words with Two Vowels that Go Walking	
bee	bleed	cheer
creek	creep	deep
feel	feet	free
green	jeep	heel
keep	meet	need
see	seed	seen
sleep	speech	speed
steel	steep	sweet
tree	week	bead
beak	bean	beat

cheap	cheat	clear
deal	dream	each
ear	east	eat
fear	feast	hear
heat	meal	mean
meat	neat	reach
read	real	scream
seal	seat	sneak
speak	steal	steam
stream	teach	team
braid	brain	chain
drain	fail	mail
main	pain	rain
sail	tail	train
wait	boast	boat
coat	float	goat
road	roast	soap
throat	toad	toast

The groups your child highlights for this rule are *ee*, *ea*, *ai* and *oa* words (the four most common walking partners). Ask your child which groups are the biggest and smallest so she can see how often *ee* and *ea* crop up.

An old favourite: 'i before e except after c'

Here's the old-timer of spelling rules. Just about everyone's heard of it, including parents and grandparents, and it's handy because it helps your child with dyslexia tame some pretty ferocious spellings, like *receive*, *perceive* and *receipt*, and *neighbour* and *eight* too. Here's the full verse:

> '*i* ("eye") before *e* ("ee") except after *c* ("see") unless you hear "ay" (like in *neighbour* and *weigh*)'

Table 11-3 has some spellings that demonstrate the rule.

In compliance: Most words follow the 'i before e' rule

Words like *believe* and *weigh* follow the 'i before e except after c unless you hear *ay*' rule so nicely that this sidebar may spoil the mood. You see, a lot of words don't follow the rule, leading people to say downright peevish things like: 'Is this rule useful at all?' Well, at the risk of incurring the wrath of those of you who can think of a million words that don't give a hoot about 'i before e', we have to say we remain fans.

And we just happen to have found someone who likes counting words and has investigated just how often, or not, the 'i before e' rule works. At www.usingenglish.com/weblog/archives/000021.html, you can find a discussion about the efficacy of the 'i before e' rule that ends by saying that the rule, when taught properly, works approximately 90 per cent of the time. The 'properly' part means that you should tell your child not just 'i before e except after c unless you hear "ay" (like in

neighbour and *weigh*)'. Your child also needs to know this rule:

'*i* before *e* except after *c* unless you hear "ay" (like in *neighbour* and *weigh*) or when the sound is "ee" (like believe or field) or when *cie* makes a "shuh" sound (like in *ancient, proficient* and *deficient*)'

Phew, have we blinded you with science yet? If not, and you rather enjoy a debate, you can find a nice discussion of the 'this rule is useless' side of the argument, and a whole bunch of rule-breakers (which may in fact work if you follow the 'or when *cie* makes a "shuh" sound' addition to the rule!) at www.alt-usage-english.org/I_before_E.html. You can also try *I Before E (Except After C): Old-School Ways to Remember Stuff* (Michael O'Mara Books), a surprise bestselling book by Judy Parkinson.

Table 11-3	i before e except after c	
believe	ceiling	weight
thief	deceive	veil
niece	perceive	vein
priest	receipt	neighbour
shield	receive	eight
brief		

I Know You! Having Fun with Sight Words

Some words in the English language crop up a lot more often than others. Take the word *they*. You see *they* time and time again, so it's a word your child with dyslexia must get to know early on and thoroughly.

Luckily, a man named Edward W. Dolch counted the frequency of commonly used words back in the 1950s and came up with a list of 220 of the most common words of all. (You may see these words called Murray McNally key words, named after two researchers in the 1950s who found that 100 words make up half of people's verbal output and 300 comprise about three-quarters.) Ever since the 1950s, teachers have used these and similar lists to help children develop 'sight' recognition of the most common words.

You may hear teachers call these words 'most common' words or 'frequently used' words or 'sight' words. We call them 'sight' words because your child needs to have instant (or sight) recognition of them.

If your child has instant recognition of all 220 of the sight words she can be a fluent reader. Without this, she is a stop-start, 'I'll get it in a minute' kind of reader, which is frustrating for her and everyone else. Children with dyslexia obviously find it hard to learn these sight words but using techniques such as mnemonics can help. Make a 'tricky word pack' with these words on one side and a funny mnemonic to help remember the word on the other. We give more information about mnemonics at the end of the chapter. In Table 11-4 we list Mr Dolch's 220 sight words.

Table 11-4				220 Sight Words		
a	call	funny	just	only	small	use
about	came	gave	keep	open	so	very
after	can	get	kind	or	some	walk
again	carry	give	know	our	soon	want
all	clean	go	laugh	out	start	warm
always	cold	goes	let	over	stop	was
am	come	going	light	own	take	wash
an	could	good	like	pick	tell	we
and	cut	got	little	play	ten	well
any	did	green	live	please	thank	went
are	do	grow	long	pretty	that	were
around	does	had	look	pull	the	what
as	don't	has	made	put	their	when
ask	done	have	make	ran	them	where
at	down	he	many	read	then	which
ate	draw	help	may	red	there	white
away	drink	her	me	ride	these	who

(continued)

Table 11-4 (continued)

be	eat	here	much	right	they	why
because	eight	him	must	round	think	will
been	every	his	my	run	this	wish
before	fall	hold	myself	said	those	with
best	far	hot	never	saw	three	work
better	fast	how	new	say	to	would
big	find	hurt	no	see	today	write
black	first	I	not	seven	together	yellow
blue	five	if	now	shall	too	yes
both	fly	in	of	she	try	you
bring	for	into	off	show	two	your
brown	found	is	old	sing	under	
but	four	it	on	sit	up	
buy	from	its	once	six	upon	
by	full	jump	one	sleep	us	

The more practice you give your child with sight words, the better she remembers them, especially if you present them in a fun multisensory way. That said, the following sections are devoted to simple activities, using every-day items from around the home, which you can do with your child to really bring those words home.

Ten at a time

The simplest way for your child to learn to read or write a new word is to read and/or write it plenty of times. Have her do this by running her through these activities using ten sight words at a time:

1. Write a sight word on each of ten pieces of paper. Have your child spread them out face down and then ask her to turn each word over, read it and then, without referring back to it, write it on her piece of paper.

2. Have your child put the ten words into a stack and ask her to turn each one over, read it and then write it down.

3. Holding the words in a fan facing you, ask your child to pick a word, read it and write it down.

4. Holding the ten words in a fan facing you, ask her to select but not look at a word and then take three guesses at which word she's selected.

If she guesses correctly, she reads it and writes it down. If not, it goes back into the fan. Keep going until she's done all ten words.

These activities take only five or ten minutes. Have your child put her ten words into an envelope and do any or all of the activities every day for a week (breakfast or bedtime are great times). By the end of a week, she'll be right at home with the words. If not, pop any words she still struggles with back into the envelope to comprise part of her next ten words.

Use fewer than ten words if you think that works better for your child, but don't use more than ten words. Your child can't remember more than ten, and getting a solid grasp of ten words is better than a tenuous grasp of twenty. Alternatively, you could use a mixture of words that she knows already and new words. That way you can gradually increase the number of new words as she becomes more confident.

Picture this

Children with dyslexia remember graphic images far better than written words, so turning words into images whenever they can (so they remember them better) makes perfect sense. Sight words like *jump*, *walk* and *eat* are ideal for this. Your child can make letters jump out of *jump*, add a pair of feet to the bottom of the *k* in *walk* and put *eat* on a plate.

Grab some marker pens and a snack and settle down with your child for some cartoon fun. If your child's a great artist and you're not, she may especially enjoy sympathising over your indistinct doodles while being a paragon of modesty about her own masterpieces.

Bang!

Here's a noisy game for a few players that provides lots of laughs. Write 32 sight words on individual pieces of paper and write the word 'bang' on 8 pieces of paper. Place all the pieces of paper into a box or a can. Player number one takes a word and reads it out. If she's correct, she keeps the card and play goes to the next player. Players keep taking one card and reading out the word until a player pulls out a 'bang' card. She shouts out 'bang' and puts *all* her cards back. The winner's the person left holding the most cards.

Word roll

For this group game, you need three pieces of coloured paper, a dice and three boxes. Cut each piece of coloured paper into 20 ticket-sized pieces and write a different sight word on each ticket. Put each colour into a separate box. Player number one rolls the dice and takes from any box the number of words that corresponds to the number she rolled. She reads the word, and if she's correct play goes to the next player. If she misreads any word, all her words go back into the box. The winner's the player with the most words when all the boxes are empty.

If your child can't sight read enough words, use pictures on the back of the card to give a clue to start with. Your child needs to feel that she can do it or she'll give up. Make sure she feels success with all of these activities and give her plenty of praise when she wins!

Soup this game up by having number 1 on the dice mean 'miss a turn' and number 6 mean 'you win an extra roll'.

Five up

This is a card game for two or more players. The size of your card deck depends on how many people are playing. For two players, you need a pack of 30 cards comprising 15 pairs of identical sight words.

Deal four cards to each player, face up in a row. Deal five face-up cards in the middle of the table. Place the remainder of the pack face down in the middle of the table. Player number one checks her cards and reads each one aloud against the five centre cards to see if she has a match. If she does, she takes the card or cards that match, keeps her pairs and draws cards to rebuild her hand and the five centre cards. Play moves to the next player and so on until all the cards are paired. The winner's the player with the most pairs.

Bingo

Many children like playing bingo, and prizes like packets of marker pens, chocolate bars or simple stickers with smiley faces can add incentive. You need blank bingo-type cards or sheets of paper divided into 25 squares (5 rows × 5 rows). You also need a list of 100 sight words, scissors, a pen and coins to use as markers.

Write a different arrangement of words from the list of 100 on each bingo card. Have players take a bingo card and a bunch of coins and pick one person to be the caller. The caller cuts up the list of 100 words and puts them into a calling box. She pulls words out of the calling box, one at a time, and calls them out. She jots down each called word too so she can check the winner's words at the end of play. Each player places a coin over any called word she has on her card until someone gets a row of five. That player calls out 'bingo', and if the caller finds the words on the card were indeed all called out, that player wins.

Playing the numbers (and name) game

Children with dyslexia not only have trouble with reading and spelling words, they can have a hard time with numbers and names too. You can help your child remember stuff like who to call and how with a few handy tips:

- Have your child remember phone numbers in chunks of numbers rather than in single numbers. It's easier to remember 782 22 33 240 than 7 8 2 2 2 3 3 2 4 0. Even better, attach meaning to the chunks: '7 ate (munch, munch) 2'; 22 (my aunt's age); 33 (one digit up from 22); 240 ('two was regurgitated, then doubled and then zeroed out!').

- Have your child remember people's names by visualising them in different poses, clothes or whatever, or by remembering who else has that name. Tracey once had to remember the name 'Verpee' and could only do it by starting off with 'verb'. Names like Mr Hill, Mr Mountain and Mr Wood (all topographical) go together nicely, and Tanya can have a tan, Ashley can smoke and Kelly can be smelly!

Have your child help write the 100 words and the bingo cards. Let the players take turns at being caller too, because all this practice with words helps a child with dyslexia memorise them.

Do You See the Sea? Distinguishing between Sound-Alike Words

Plenty of words sound the same but are spelled differently, which may really confuse your child with dyslexia. Sound-alike words are called either 'homonyms' or 'homophones'. You may hear the word 'homographs' too. Here's a quick explanation of all three terms:

- **Homonyms:** A general term for words that are the same in sound but not in spelling (like *son* and *sun*), in spelling but not sound (like *bow* in your hair and *bow* of a ship) or in both spelling *and* sound (like *grave* in a cemetery and *grave* as in serious). Homographs and homophones are subsets of the bigger, general term 'homonyms'.

- **Homophones:** These words sound the same but are spelled differently, such as *you* are nice and the farmer has a *ewe*.

- **Homographs:** Words that are spelled the same but are pronounced differently, like *bow* in your hair and *bow* to the king.

Table 11-5 lists some common pairs of sound-alike words.

Table 11-5	Common Pairs of Sound-Alike Words	
aloud/allowed	pain/pane	son/sun
ate/eight	pair/pear	steal/steel
blue/blew	passed/past	straight/strait
board/bored	patience/patients	symbol/cymbal
break/brake	peace/piece	tail/tale
buy/by	plain/plane	there/they're/their
cereal/serial	principal/principle	threw/through
deer/dear	rain/reign/rein	thrown/throne
for/four	real/reel	tide/tied
groan/grown	rode/road/rowed	to/too/two
hair/hare	sale/sail	wear/where
hear/here	scene/seen	week/weak
hole/whole	scent/sent/cent	whether/weather
knot/not	seam/seem	who's/whose
lead/led	see/sea	witch/which
meet/meat	sew/so/sow	write/right
naval/navel	sight/site/cite	
no/know	some/sum	

How can you help your child read and spell the common pairs of sound-alike words, like *seen* and *scene*, which bother even people without dyslexia? You can do the following:

- ✔ Help her put words in 'families'. A family's a set of words with the same ending, like in *light, bright, tight, sight* and *might*. Your child remembers one written pattern and, from it, generates a whole host of words. Any time you see a family, show it to your child so you give her a quick hoist up the spelling ladder.

- ✔ Be sure she understands what each word in a pair means and, if appropriate, which word's more common. Pairs of words in which one word of the pair's much more commonly used than the other include *seem* and *seam; where* and *wear;* and *not* and *knot*. When your child learns the common spelling first, she at least knows which situations it doesn't apply to. To find the more unusual spelling after that, she can try a few drafts of possible spellings to see which one looks right.

- ✔ Help your child mark parts of words that don't sound out, or sound out in unusual ways, so she learns them by their visual appearance.

Coloured highlighter pens are good for this, but circling or underlining the letters works too. The words to have your child mark are words like *break* (the *ea* is unexpected), *allowed* (two *l*s and the *ow* spelling) and *scene* (pronounce it to help remember its spelling). Mark away! Encourage your child to mark any word in any way that helps her remember the look of it.

✔ Look for words within words. For example, a good way to remember the difference between *there* and *their* is that *there* is a place and has the word *here* in it. The same applies to *where*. Also, a great way to remember the correct spelling of the word *separate* is to know that there is *a rat* in sep**arat**e.

Searching for a great book of word lists? *The Reading Teacher's Book of Lists*, by Edward Fry (published by Jossey-Bass), has a great collection of homographs and homophones and all sorts of other great stuff.

The Hard Stuff: Remembering Especially Tricky Words

Goodness, how much fun can one person stand? In this section we give you a whole bunch of lovely *mnemonics* (memory joggers) that teachers (the cool ones) show their students (especially those with dyslexia) to help them with words that always trip people up. You get sayings that help your child do the following:

✔ Sort out the *cause* part of *because*.

✔ Choose wisely between *stationery* and *stationary*.

✔ Organise every incarnation of *to* (*to*, *too* and *two*).

And that's only half the fun!

Rhymes and other mnemonics that help you order letters inside a word may be particularly useful for your child with dyslexia because poor visual recall (which letter goes where) can be a big part of her dyslexia. Show your child any mnemonic you know and help her come up with some of her own too. Make them as funny as possible and fix them in her mind by singing, saying and using them often. If repeating them ten times straight or writing them down helps, do that as well.

Table 11-6	Mnemonics for Remembering Tricky Spellings
Tricky Spelling	*Helpful Mnemonic*
because	'Big elephants can always understand small elephants.'
stationery/stationary	'There's an envelope in stationery.'
to/too/two	In 'too much' you see too many *o*s.
	'Two twins.'
necessary	'Wear one cap, two socks.'
friend	'Friendship never ends.'
they	'There's no 'hay' in they' (it's not '**thay**').
principal/principle	'The principal is your pal.'
here, there, where	'There' and 'where' both have 'here' in them because they're both about positions.
bought/thought	'**O**nly **u**gly **g**irls **h**ate **t**oothpaste.'
four/fourteen/forty	'If **u** bet, **u** should stay in for four and fourteen dollars but not for forty.'
beautiful	'**B**are **e**legant **a**rms are **u**sually beautiful.'
business	'Catch the bus to your **bus**iness.'
secretary	'The secretary keeps **secret**s.'
rhythm	'**R**hythm **h**elps **y**our **t**wo **h**ips **m**ove.'

The *ight* spelling is an important one for your child to remember because several common words use it (*light, right, bright, tight, sight* and *might*). How on earth can your child with dyslexia remember the order of all those unexpected letters? We haven't come across a really great mnemonic yet, but here are two that are better than nothing!

'Indian girls have toys'

'Isabel goes home today'

We warned you they weren't great! Maybe you and your child can think up something infinitely better and, for that matter, change any of the suggestions we give you into things you think may stick better. If these methods don't work, don't give up! Every child is different; you just need to find the right method that works for her and which enables her to start learning.

Chapter 12

Playing with Phonics

· ·

· ·

*W*hen you take a look at what happens in dyslexia programmes, phonics is key. *Phonics* is the teaching method in which you show your child that single letters and chunks of letters represent the sounds he hears inside words. Phonics is pretty much the backbone of learning to read (and the thing that catches people with dyslexia out the most), so of course leading your child through phonics systematically and thoroughly is important. Luckily, teachers have taught phonics for decades and figured out great strategies, so all you really have to do is recognise them and run through a few at home.

In this chapter, we explain how you can make sure your child gets the structured, sequential instruction in phonics that experts recommend. We show you how to give your child the full story on single letters, make sure he's friendly with word families, help him with blends and digraphs and get on top of tricky vowel and consonant sounds.

You can help your child get a strong handle on letters and spelling with the use of memorisation, visualisation and rhyming tricks. Chapter 11 has the full story. (For more tips on spelling, check out Tracey's book *Teaching Kids to Spell For Dummies*, published by Wiley.) To find out just how much your child already knows, you can run him through the quick tests we provide in Appendix A.

Emphasising Single Letters

When you lead your child with dyslexia through phonics, start by making sure he knows the sound of each letter of the alphabet. If he knows the letter names already, tell him to forget them for the time being and instead talk of 'a' (like in *apple*), 'buh' (like in *big*) and 'cuh' (like in *cup*). After your child can sound out a few consonants and the short sounds of the five vowels, he's ready for sliding them together into three-letter words (see 'Building Three-Letter Words in Word Families', later in this chapter).

If you're not 100 per cent confident you know the correct sounds of the alphabet, have a look at the DIY Parent's Pack from Dyslexia Action. This excellent resource helps parents improve their children's reading at home and includes a DVD of how to pronounce the correct sound that each letter makes. You can find more information about pronunciation at the end of this chapter and obtain a copy of the DIY pack from DI Trading (www.dyslexia action.org.uk) for around £40.

Cosying up with consonants

A great way to help your child come to grips with consonant sounds is to draw features into each letter that turn it into a memorable individual character that behaves in its own distinctive ways. Great idea, huh? We'd like to take all the credit for it, but a few people have come up with this idea before us and produced whole programmes based around it. In Chapter 4, we give you details on Letterland and Jolly Phonics, two programmes you may want to buy bits and pieces of or at least get ideas from. For more immediate ideas, here's a list of consonant-coping activities teachers typically use.

✔ Teach your child only the 'hard' sounds of the consonants *c* and *g* ('cuh' and 'guh') to start with. See 'Sounding out the softies', later in this chapter, to get a few details about the soft 'see' and 'jee' sounds these letters also make.

✔ Focus on one letter a week and talk every day about things that start with that letter, like milk, medicine, mud, melon, mops, moss and mum.

✔ Get library books (from the picture books or early reader sections) that focus on your letter and read them together, paying special attention to your letter sound. If the letter's written on the pages, point it out to your child and, if it's written big enough, have him trace over it with his finger while saying the sound (like 'mmm').

✔ Make posters adorned with pictures or magazine cutouts of items that start with your letter. Say each picture's name.

> ✔ Eat foods whose names start with your letter and make the letter out of breadsticks, pasta, chocolate sauce and anything else you can arrange or squeeze into shape. Say the sound as you go.
>
> ✔ Draw the letter for your child to trace over and glue things onto. Finger-paint your letter and have your child draw over your letter in rainbow colours. Draw the letter in chalk on your pavement. Make the letter's sound.
>
> ✔ Sing songs and listen to alphabet tapes and CDs.

Multisensory learning, which we talk more about in Chapter 14, is a great way for your child with dyslexia to grasp new things. In fact, just about anyone who knows anything about dyslexia says multisensory learning's the very best way for a child with dyslexia to go. When your child sees a letter, says it and traces it, he's engaging in multisensory learning – he's using a few senses at pretty much the same time, so information comes to him from different angles and therefore sticks in his memory better. That's why we always encourage you to have your child say the sound out loud when he sees or draws a letter or an object whose name begins with that letter.

Taking a long look at short vowels

Vowels are especially important because almost every word has a vowel (the exceptions are words like *my* that have *y* in them, making a vowel sound – in this case, long *i*). Because all vowels make at least two sounds, they're especially tricky to learn.

When your child learns the vowel sounds, start by teaching him only the short sounds: *a* like in *apple*, *e* like in *egg*, *i* like in *ink*, *o* like in *octopus*, *u* like in *up*. He learns the long vowel sounds (like in *ape*, *eagle*, *ice*, *open* and *uniform*) later, along with other vowel combinations like *ee* and *ei*. (Check out 'Opening up to long vowels', later in this chapter, for details.)

Show your child the vowel sounds by going through the routines we describe in the preceding section on consonants. For children younger than about Year 2, you can also add the following game to your repertoire of activities. It's fun, so your child wants to play, and the more practice he gets with vowels the better. Here's how to prepare for and play the game:

1. **Cut up a sheet (or two) of paper into 20 pieces, each about 1 × 2 inches in size.**

2. **Write a vowel on each card (a mixed bunch of vowels), leaving four cards blank.**

3. **Draw a smiley face on each of these blanks.**

4. **Have your child hold the cards in a face-down pack and turn them over one at a time, telling you each letter sound as he turns it over.**

5. **If he turns over a smiley face, he claps three times, runs to the door, and knocks on it.**

   You can make the smiley face mean any kind of action, depending on the age of your child and the available space.

Before you start this game with your child, he can pencil drawings into the letters (like an apple in the *a*, an egg inside the *e*, an ink spot for the dot on the *i*, an octopus in the *o* and arrows on top of the vertical lines of the *u* to signify 'up') if it helps him recall the sounds.

Introducing letters by name

What about letter names? Your child with dyslexia has probably watched a few episodes of *Sesame Street* or other TV shows for pre-school and young children, and that's good. These shows are jam-packed with instructions about the alphabet, so chances are your child has discovered the names of one or two letters from them. Songs are another great way of getting letter names into your child's memory. Have your child sing the ABC song as often as you can stand so the rhythm and sheer fun make the letters stick in his mind.

The ABC song is the one you hear all over the place. Your child sings the letter names to the tune of 'Twinkle Twinkle Little Star'. Because they're catchy, songs help your child grasp the letter names more than just about any other activity.

Your child knowing the letter names early on is great, but knowing the letter sounds is much more important. After he establishes a firm grip on letter sounds and can read words like *sat* and *fat*, which are made of single letter sounds joined together, then he can take a look at letter names. You can show him that in words like *ape* and *eve* the long vowel sound's the same as the vowel name. Ta-da, vowel names now become relevant! (And he's probably grasped the other letter names along the way anyway.)

Building Three-Letter Words in Word Families

The first words your child sounds out by himself are usually short-vowel, phonetically regular words like *hat*, *hen*, *hit*, *hot* and *hut* that sound out just the way your child expects them to. But how do you help him move smoothly from single letter sounds ('a', 'buh', 'cuh') to reading complete words? By starting with the word *at* and building up from there.

You can start your child off with *it* or *ot* if you want, but *at* is best because it's easy to pronounce, it's a word in itself and from it your child can build a lot more new words.

Good readers read words in chunks. They get to know common chunks like *at* and read them quickly without labouring over each single letter sound. That's why teaching your child to read chunks like *at*, *an* and *in* very early on is a terrific reading strategy.

In the following sections, we show you how to start your child off with the word *at* and from that build the *at* word family (*at*, *sat*, *fat*, *mat* and *bat*). Then we give you a few more word families for extra practice.

A *word family* is a group of words that follow a spelling and sound pattern. Using word families early on is a great idea because recalling a group of words that share a pattern is easier for your child than recalling each word separately and without the pattern cue. He has plenty of families (like *fight*, *light*, *tight* and *sight*; *round*, *sound*, *pound* and *found*) to choose from.

Putting together 'at'

The best way for your child with dyslexia to read *at* is to discover physically for himself, by sliding letter cards (or tiles) together, how he can join *a* and *t*. Find a quiet time to do the following activity and spend a few minutes on it until your child feels comfortable with *at*.

In the following game, by sliding *a* and saying its name and then sliding *t* and saying its name, your child's doing a multisensory activity. We talk at length about multisensory activities in Chapter 14.

Take an index card and cut it in half. Write *a* on one half of the card and *t* on the other (calling them 'ah' and 'tuh') and give them to your child. Now here's what to do:

1. **Have him tell you the letter sounds.**

2. **Ask him to put down the *a* (pronounced like in *apple*) and slide *tuh* next to it, saying each sound as he moves it.**

3. **Have him do this a few times until he hears the word *at* and gets the very core of reading – that letters represent the sounds that join together to make words.**

When you make the letter cards in this activity, use lower-case letters. In school, your child's taught that capitals are only for names and the beginnings of sentences, so you help him by sticking to those rules at home.

Moving on up with 'bat', 'cat', 'fat' and more

After your child's well acquainted with *at*, he's ready to meet members of the whole *at* word family. The next activity shows you how to have your child build eight words – *bat, cat, fat, hat, mat, pat, rat* and *sat* – by joining letters on to *at*.

Have *at* written on one whole index card. Cut four other index cards in half and write the single letters *b, c, f, h, m, p, r* and *s*, one on each of the eight card halves. Give all the cards to your child and ask him to put *at* down in front of him. Have him slide each single letter in front of *at* and read the words he makes.

Now's a great time to have your child make a set of flashcards. Have him write each of the *at* words (*bat, cat, fat, hat, mat, pat, rat* and *sat*) on a separate index card and read them to defenceless family members and friends.

Running through additional word families

In Table 12-1 you get more word families, so your child can practise the activities we discuss in the previous sections (with *at* words) on a whole new bunch of words. Show your child the chunks *an, ap, ug, in* and *ip* and then let him read you the words. He may start feeling like this reading thing isn't so bad after all!

Table 12-1		**First Word Families**		
an	*ap*	*ug*	*in*	*ip*
an	cap	bug	bin	dip
ban	gap	dug	din	hip
can	lap	hug	fin	lip
fan	map	jug	in	nip
man	nap	mug	pin	rip
pan	rap	rug	tin	sip
ran	sap	tug	win	tip
tan	tap			zip
van				

Mixing It Up with Blended Consonants

After your child reads words like *cat* and *fat*, he's ready to read consonant blends like *st*, *str* and *bl* in phonetically regular words like *stand*, *strap* and *blink*.

The term *blending* describes how your child blends letters (like *a* and *t*) together to read whole words (like *at*), but the consonant blends we talk about in this section are chunks of two or three consonants, like *st* and *str*.

In the following sections, we cover blended consonants at the start and at the end of words.

Blends at the beginning

By the time your child masters the easier words in Table 12-1, he's probably eager to flex his newly developing reading muscles. Table 12-2 gives him words that look impressive but are, in fact, fairly easy to sound out. Initially, your child needs to say and hear the blend in the first column, but that done, he can whizz through the words in the second column. Your child may want to read the table in two or three separate sessions, but if not, he can blast through all the words in one go. Whichever of these options you take, you need to do plenty of re-reads. An easy routine to use for this and other tables is to choose whether to use the whole table or just a few rows and then have your child do the following:

- Read out the table words top to bottom.
- Read out the table words bottom to top.
- Read out random words as you point to them.
- Find words that you call out.
- Write two or three words that you dictate and increase the number of words as he becomes more confident. Use pictures to go with the words if that helps.

Words like *draft*, *crisp* and *trend* can be particularly challenging for your child at first because they have double blends (at the beginning *and* end). You may want to write them out larger for your child so that he can underline each blend before tackling them.

Table 12-2	Easy Words with Blends
Blend	*Examples*
bl	black, blast, blimp, blink, blocks, blot
br	Brad, brag, brick, bring
cl	clamp, clap, clasp, cliff, clip, clock
cr	crab, craft, crest, crisp, crust
dr	draft, drink, drop, drum
fl	flag, flan, flash, flick, flip, flood
fr	Fred, fresh, frog, frost, fry
gl	glad, glen, gloss
gr	grand, grass, grin, grip, grub
pl	plan, plant, plod, plug
pr	prick, print, prod
sk	sketch, skin, skip, skunk
sl	slant, slim, slip
sm	smack, smell
sn	snap, snip
sp	spank, spell, spill, spin
spl	splash, split
spr	spring, sprint
st	stack, stand, stem, stink, stop
str	string, strip
sw	swell, swill, swim, swing
tr	trap, trend, trip
w	twig, twin, twist

Blends at the end

Your child can get to grips with blends at the ends of words in the same way as he can master blends at the beginning, except that a couple of ending blends may need special attention. Walk your child through Table 12-3, taking extra care over words ending in *nk* and *ng*. Sometimes these blends can be harder to distinguish than other blends. If your child needs extra practice, grab paper or a whiteboard and have him write the relevant words, underlining the blends. Reading these words is easier for him when tricky letters are highlighted so he can give them extra thought.

Table 12-3	Easy Words with Blends on the End
Blend	**Examples**
ct	fact, insect, inspect, pact
lk	bulk, milk, silk, sulk
mp	bump, cramp, hump, lump, jump, lamp, limp, stamp, stump
nd	band, bend, end, fend, hand, land, lend, pond, stand, spend, trend
ng	bang, bring, clang, fling, hang, long, lung, ring, sing, song, sting, tang, wing
nk	blink, bunk, chunk, mink, sink, skunk, think, trunk, wink
nt	bent, blunt, sent, spent, tent
sk	ask, mask, risk, task, tusk
st	best, cost, dust, frost, last, list, mast, mist, nest, past, pest, test, trust

Delving into Digraphs

Your child needs to know chunks of speech sounds and how those chunks are written; or in other words, phonics. He needs to move forward systematically so that he first learns simple words like *hat* and then harder words like *last*.

But when your child looks at books, he finds that all sorts of easy and hard words are together. How do you help him deal with that? Pretty much at the same time as you lead him from easy to harder word families, you show him (a few at a time) new sounds, like *ch*, *sh* and *th*. These sounds are called *digraphs*.

A *digraph* is a sound/spelling chunk made by two letters that join to make their own distinctive sound (that's not like their two individual sounds blended together). The consonant digraphs are *ch*, *sh*, *th* and *ph*, and you can think of *wh* as a digraph too.

In Table 12-4 is a whole load of easy *ch*, *sh* and *th* words for you to launch your child straight into. Your child needs to be comfortable with *ph* and *wh*, but this section focuses on the other consonant digraphs (*ch*, *sh* and *th*) because words with those digraphs are much more common.

Move through the table, having your child read and say the words, and write some as you dictate them; then for variety, read out these quiz questions and ask your child to write the answers.

1. A turtle and a crab both have this (shell).

2. A board game with a castle, a queen and a knight in it (chess).

3. Another name for a talk (chat).

4. The bottom front part of your leg (shin).

5. A baby chicken (chick).

6. The part of your face below your mouth (chin).

7. Opposite of fat (thin).

8. A large boat (ship).

9. Opposite of 'this' (that).

10. The short word for 'chimpanzee' (chimp).

Table 12-4	Words with *ch*, *sh* and *th*	
ch	*sh*	*th*
champ	shack	than
chap	shall	thank
chat	shelf	that
check	shell	them
chess	shift	then
chest	shin	theft
chick	ship	thick
chill	shock	thin
chimp	shot	thing
chin		think
chip		this
chomp		thrash
chop		thrill
chum		thrush
chunk		thump

You may want to tell your child that *th* has two sounds: one for words like *thank* and *thin* and one for words like *this* and *then*.

A number of *sight words* (words so common that your child should be able to recognise them automatically) include digraphs and may be a little tricky for your child with dyslexia to sound out. However, memorising sight words is really worthwhile for your child, because the English language uses them so often. For tips on committing sight words to memory, turn to Chapter 11.

Mastering Tricky Vowel Sounds

Vowels represent two sounds, called short and long sounds, and can join together with other letters to make a few more sounds besides. *Short vowel sounds* are the vowel sounds you hear in *apple*, *egg*, *ink*, *octopus* and *up*; *long vowel sounds* are the sounds you hear in *ape*, *eve*, *ice*, *open* and *uniform*. Long vowel sounds are also the sounds you hear when you say the letter names.

In this section we show you the different ways long vowels are written and the simple rules that help your child recognise them. We show you how the letter *y* can take the place of a vowel in words like *my* and *by*. Finally, we show you how vowels can appear next to other letters to make special new sounds that can trip up a child with dyslexia if he's not primed to watch out for them.

Opening up to long vowels

Your child needs to hear the different vowel sounds in words like *met* and *meet* so he can read and spell them for himself. A million words (like *meet*, *pain*, *road* and *cute*) have long vowel sounds in them, but luckily two easy phonics rules apply to most of these.

Chapter 11 gives you the complete ins and outs of the *Bossy e* and when-two-vowels-go-walking rules, but here's a lightning summary:

- To help your child read and spell words such as *bake*, *like* and *cute*, show him the *Bossy e* rule. When *Bossy e* sits on the end of short words, such as *cut*, or word chunks, such as *bak*, it bosses the vowel into making its long sound. *Cut* becomes *cute* and *bak* becomes *bake*.

- To help your child read and spell words like *meet*, *road* and *rain*, show him the rule that says 'when two vowels go walking, the first one does the talking'. When he sees the vowel pairs *ee*, *ea*, *oa* and *ai*, they nearly always work as a partnership in which the first vowel shouts its name while the second stays silent.

Hearing 'y' sound like a vowel

One special letter you want to point out to your child is *y*. In words such as *yellow* and *yam*, *y* makes its simple alphabet sound, but in words such as *merry*, *mystery* and *my*, it makes the sounds usually made by long *e*, and short and long *i*.

The tables in the following sections give you easy words for practising *y* sounds. Have your child read through them, saying, hearing and seeing how *y* can make long and short *e* and *i* sounds.

When 'y' acts like a long 'e'

On the ends of words with more than one syllable, *y* usually sounds like long *e*. Table 12-5 gives example words that your child can easily read so that this long *e* pattern becomes clear. Have your child highlight the *y* in each word, saying the 'ee' sound as he goes, and then have him mark and say other long vowels, in *creepy*, *bravely*, *breezily* and *really*. Lastly, have him read out the words, choosing his own order. He can read columns or rows until he's read all 40 words or he can save some words for another time.

Your child with dyslexia can easily become tired or disheartened, so gauge the amount of work he does and the time he takes, to make sure he stays motivated and on track. Also try to make it fun by thinking up games to play with the words. Your child with dyslexia's usually better off working slowly on tasks and repeating them so he gets a firm understanding than moving forward more quickly but less surely. He needs frequent short breaks, too, so he can concentrate better after he's refreshed (just like everyone else).

Table 12-5		*y* Sounding Like Long *e*		
baby	chilly	funny	lumpy	simply
berry	copy	happy	marry	skinny
body	creepy	helpfully	merry	sorry
bravely	dizzy	holly	milky	spotty
breezily	empty	hurry	nanny	sunny
bumpy	enemy	jolly	plenty	ugly
bunny	entry	lanky	really	very
cherry	family	lucky	silly	windy

When 'y' acts like a short 'i'

The letter *y* turns up in the middle (or near the middle) of quite a few words. Tell your child to watch out for this. It means an *i* sound, short or long but more often short. The best way for your child to work out what sound *y* is making is to try out the short *i* sound first. Table 12-6 gives you some words to get started on. Have your child mark each *y* in the words and then figure out whether the *y* is on the end (in which case it's a long 'ee' sound) or in the middle (in which case the sound's short or long *i*).

When *y* comes after *c* or *g*, it makes those letters make their soft ('ss' and 'juh') sounds.

Table 12-6	*y* Sounding Like Short *i*	
crypt	gypsy	symbol
cryptic	hymn	system
cymbal	mystery	
gymnastics	myth	

When 'y' acts like a long 'i'

In a few short one-syllable words, *y*, when it's the last letter in the word, sounds like long *i*. Table 12-7 gives you this small group of fairly common words so that your child can whizz through them a few times and mentally file them under 'got it'!

Table 12-7	*y* Sounding Like Long *i*	
by	cry	dry
fly	fry	my
pry	shy	sky
sly	try	why

Teaching your child spelling patterns can be an ongoing process. If your child gets quickly on top of the words in Table 12-7, you may want to show him another bunch of words that have the same '*y* acting like long *i*' pattern, only with the *y* in the middle (not the end) of the word. Longer words like *style*, *type* and *python* fit into this group, and so do the words *cycle* and *cyclone*. The rule for 'cy' words is that when *c* is followed by *y*, it makes its soft sound ('s'), while the *y* can make either a long *i* sound (like in *cyclist*) or a short *i* sound (like in *cyst*). How can your child remember words like *style*, *type* and *python*? By taking a good look at them, saying them out loud and jotting them down a few times. No hard and fast rules exist for spelling them, but bunching them together (in the '*y* acting as short or long *i*' word family) helps.

A strategy that can help your child remember a group of words like *style*, *type* and *python* is to keep a personal dictionary. Your child writes groups of words in it, adding new group members (like *dynamite*, *typhoon* and *hype*) as he comes across them.

Surveying schwa vowels

When you say words like *ago* and *around*, you pronounce the first *a* as 'uh'. This 'uh' sound's called a *schwa*, and you need to tell your child about it so that he doesn't spell the words *ugo* and *uround*. You don't have to mention the technical schwa stuff though; just say that sometimes the letter *a* has an indistinct 'uh' sound.

Schwa is technically an unstressed vowel sound. You can hear it most easily in the vowel *a* (like in *ago*, *again*, *above* and *about*), but other vowels can be schwa sounds too (like the *o* in *melon*). Because this is a tricky concept, and an even trickier thing to hear – especially since your dialect affects your pronunciation (and stressing) of vowels – we don't go into the concept too deeply. Your child learns about schwa better in context (and without mention of the technical term *schwa*) than in a theoretical explanation.

The best way for your child to read these fuzzy sounds is to pronounce them phonetically and then correct himself ('a-go', uh-oh, that's really 'uhgo'). One good tip though: the names of many countries end with a schwa, including Argentina, Australia, Austria, Canada, China, Cuba, Uganda and Venezuela. Many British place names also end with a schwa, including Manchester, Windsor and Chester.

Singling out sound-alike chunks featuring vowels

Reading teachers show your child plenty of sound/spelling chunks. In the following sections, we give you spelling chunks that any teacher worth her salt shows to students so that they can push forward with harder, livelier text. Here you get the tricky, but well worth knowing, chunks *oy/oi*, *ow/ou* and *aw/au*. Take your time showing them to your child and coming up with words of your own that follow each spelling pattern.

Practise one spelling (like *oy*) of each sound with your child before telling him about the second spelling (like *oi*). He needs a lot of exposure to one spelling before he can comfortably assimilate the other spelling or he gets overwhelmed.

The best way to turn your child off reading and make him think he may never get this nut cracked is to overload him. Any time you show him a new spelling chunk, like *oy*, take a slow and sure approach. Have him read, say and write plenty of words that fit the spelling pattern, such as *boy*, *toy*, *coy*, *joy* and *soy*. Then when he's really sure of that spelling, slowly introduce a new one, like *oi*.

Oy and oi

In Table 12-8, we give you some *oy* and *oi* words for your child to sink his teeth into. Make a copy and have your child highlight (or circle or underline) the *oy* or *oi* part of each word, saying the sound as he goes. Point out that *oy* shows up on the ends of words (like in *toy*) or at the end of the first syllable of a word (like in *royal*), whereas *oi* features at the beginning or middle of words (like in *oil* and *soil*). After your child has marked the words and is comfortable with the positioning of the two different spellings, have him read the words in the table out loud to you and then dictate them for him to write. Warn him of other special spelling features if you want, like the *s* in *noise* (sounds like *z* but spelled with *s*), the two *n*s in *annoy* and the *al* in *royal* (sounds like it can be *al* or *le*, or even another combination a person with dyslexia may use, like *el*, *ul* or *il*).

Table 12-8	*oy* and *oi* Words
oy	**oi**
annoy	boil
boy	moist
employ	noise
joy	oi
Roy	soil
royal	spoil
toy	toil

Ow and ou

Show the *ou* sound to your child by explaining that whenever he sees either *ow*, like in *cow*, or *ou*, like in *out*, he needs to make the sound he makes if you pinch him. After that, have him highlight the digraphs (*ow* and *ou*) in Table 12-9 while he makes the sound, and then have him read the words to you. Then he can write a few that you dictate to him. Ways to prompt him along include the following:

- Give him several soft and timely pinches when he reads *ow* and *ou*!

- Have him jot down the two versions of a word (like *brown* and *broun*) when he's spelling them, to see if he can spot the right one.

✔ Tell him which digraph to use when he's struggling to spell a word.

✔ Have him draw his own two-column table and randomly dictate words from Table 12-9 for him to fit into it.

Table 12-9	*ow* and *ou* Words
ow	*ou*
bow	around
brown	bound
cow	cloud
crown	found
down	house
drown	loud
frown	mound
growl	mouse
how	noun
now	pound
scowl	proud
sow	round
town	sound

Aw and au

The digraphs *aw* and *au* are pretty tricky, so here's what you can do to show them to your child in a slow and sure way:

✔ Show your child the *aw* spellings first. He's seen the word *saw* plenty of times, so start with that. Have him write and say the word *saw* five times. Now ask him to change the *s* in *saw* to an *l*.

✔ Have him change the *s* in *saw* to *dr*.

✔ Have him write the three words *saw*, *law* and *draw*.

✔ When he's happy with *saw*, *law* and *draw*, show him the words in the *aw* column of Table 12-10.

✔ Have him highlight the *aw* digraph in each word and then read the words to you, top to bottom, bottom to top and then randomly as you point a pencil at a few words.

✔ Have him write the *aw* words as you dictate them.

✔ When your child has a firm understanding of *aw*, you can drop the bombshell about another *aw* sound, spelled *au*, and repeat the same procedure. Generally though, the *au* sound comes at the beginning of words (like August) and *aw* at the end like (haul).

Table 12-10	*aw* and *au* Words
aw	*au*
awning	applaud
caw	auto
claw	author
crawl	fraud
dawn	haul
draw	laundry
fawn	maul
jaw	sauce
law	taut
lawn	
prawn	
saw	
straw	
yawn	

When your child comes across spellings like *auntie* that have a different *au* sound, just explain that words often fall outside a rule. This exception doesn't mean that the rule isn't useful; outsiders or rule breakers do exist and your child gets to know them eventually.

Partnering vowels with 'r'

If you've skimmed through the phonics tips in the preceding sections of this chapter, this section may be a good time to slow down. Your child needs a firm grip on the vowel + *r* spelling that we tell you about here, because it crops up often and its sound's never the straightforward blended sound of its two letters.

Quickly tell your child that a vowel + *r* spelling makes its own new sound and then have him look at Table 12-11. Ask him to cover the first two columns and look only at the last three columns, *er*, *ir* and *ur*. You can also put pictures at the top of the columns or be imaginative – use a toy car, a fir cone and a fork! When he reads a few words (you can help him do this) from each column, what does he notice? Be sure to have your child discover, or point out to him, that *er*, *ir* and *ur* all sound the same. After your child appreciates the sound these three digraphs make, have him highlight the digraphs in each word, sounding them out as he goes, and then read the words to you (top to bottom and so on like you do in the previous sections). Have your child write out the words from your dictation and extend the activity to putting the word in a sentence of his own. If he gets stuck writing a word, have him jot down the possibilities (like *her*, *hir* or *hur*) to see whether he can spot the right-looking spelling. If he can't see the right one, tell him the spelling and have him jot it down a few more times.

Table 12-11		The Five Vowels + *r*		
ar	*er*	*ir*	*or*	*ur*
art	her	bird	corn	burn
barn	herd	dirt	for	curl
car	nerve	firm	fork	curse
dart	perch	first	horse	hurl
far	person	flirt	north	hurt
farm	serve	girl	or	nurse
hard	stern	shirt	storm	purse
large		sir	torn	surf
marsh		stir	worn	turn
star		third		

When you dictate a few words to your child, doing so helps him consolidate what he's already practised. Your child with dyslexia needs to read, say and write words he's already gone over, so give him as much repetition as you can, within the reasonable boundaries of bribery and coercion!

If your child doesn't like being dictated to, try getting him to read the sentence onto a dictaphone and then play it back to him so that he hears his own voice instead of yours! You could also try cutting up a sentence and putting it into an envelope for your child to reassemble. When he works out the correct order he can then read it aloud, try to remember it and write it down from memory. You can gradually increase the words in the sentence as he grows in confidence. This multisensory self-checking exercise helps not only with understanding sentence construction but also helps his short-term working memory.

After your child feels happy with *er*, *ir* and *ur* words, you can show him the *or* and *ar* columns of Table 12-11. Go through the reading, marking and writing routine as with the other columns and then, if you're both feeling creative and energetic, have your child write all the words on small pieces of paper and spread them face down in front of him. Can he turn over and read out loud all of the words? Can he spell each one if he turns each card over, takes a quick peek and then jots it down? Can he spell each one if you dictate the word and he doesn't get to take a helpful peek? When your child's finished with the word cards, have him keep them. After a few days, have him run through a shortened version of these activities to see how well he recalls all the words. Keep any words that slipped through the net. Pin them on a wall and have your child read them to you and write them down a few more times over the next week.

Lopping vowels off the ends of words

Like many children, your child with dyslexia may have trouble reading and spelling words like *riding*. Should he write *rideing* or *riding*, and how can he remember the right way in future?

The easy rule for sorting out *ing* words is drop the *e* (pronounced 'ee') when you add *i-n-g* (pronounced 'eye-en-gee'). Want practice with it? Check out Table 12-12.

Show your child how the *e* gets dropped. Dictate the base words (the ones without the *ing* added on) for him to write down. If you need to revise the 'Bossy e' rule that all these words follow, flip to Chapter 11. Have your child add the *ing* ending to his base words, saying the 'Drop the *e* when you add *i-n-g*' rule as he goes.

Have your child verbalise what he's doing, because sounding out or saying rules out loud is a helpful multisensory strategy. Seeing, saying and writing at the same time is a more effective way to learn than doing any of these three things alone.

Table 12-12	Adding *i-n-g* to Words Ending with *e*
bake – baking	ride – riding
bite – biting	shake – shaking
drive – driving	skate – skating
fake – faking	slide – sliding
glide – gliding	smile – smiling
hide – hiding	take – taking
hike – hiking	time – timing
make – making	wave – waving

Terrific tips for handling any difficult words

As soon as your child starts to read, he comes across words like *they* and *was* that don't sound out regularly. How can you help him with these kinds of words? Where do you start? In addition to the activities we provide in the rest of this chapter, here are some general strategies that can make those words seem easier.

✔ Notice the shape of the word. Draw an outline around the word to show tall and short letters and the length of the whole word.

✔ Circle, or mark with a highlighter pen, the tricky parts of words. In *words*, for example, the *or* is tricky because it sounds like 'er'.

✔ Have your child tape words onto walls where he sees them often. Bathrooms and bedrooms are good.

✔ Run your child through the look, say, cover, write routine: he looks at the word he wants to learn, says it out loud, covers it over and writes it from memory.

✔ Use the word envelope routine we describe in Chapter 11. Your child puts up to 10 words, each one written on a small piece of paper, in an envelope. Every day for a week he takes them out of the envelope and plays games that help him fix the words in his memory.

Bringing Consonants under Control

You need to show your child the quirky but common sounds that consonants can make when they get together with certain other consonants or vowels. Otherwise, stuff like the *z* sound that *s* makes on the end of *friends*, and the soft sounds that *c* and *g* can make, may throw him into confusion. In the following sections, we deal with those spellings and others that can be similarly troublesome.

Unmasking consonants in disguise

This is where we talk about innocent-looking letters that make sneaky little sounds. Here you take a look at *s* sounding like *z* in words like *dogs* and find out how to deal with the three sounds of *ed*. The ones you never even noticed until now!

When 's' sounds like 'z'

A single letter you may want to alert your child to is *s*. In words like *friends*, *hands*, *loves* and *dogs*, your child hears the sound of *z* but sees the letter *s*. A quick advance warning from you may save him from feeling that words are put together pretty randomly.

In words like *foxes*, *horses* and *boxes*, your child sees *es*, but actually hears a sort of 'iz' sound. The *e* is there because it makes the word easier to pronounce – saying a word written *boxs* would be difficult.

When your child with dyslexia comes across a word that doesn't follow a particular rule, have him consider it a rogue, pretty much an all-by-itself word, or see whether he can find a few other words like it and make it into a whole rogue word family. For example, take the word *friend*. It doesn't follow the usual *ie* pronunciation, like in *field*, *piece* and *believe*, and you don't get several common words like it, so the easiest approach is to brand it as a loner renegade word to watch out for. However, a word like *love* is a renegade, but not a loner. Show your child that it breaks the usual 'Bossy e' rule but does so in good company. Its word family includes *dove*, *glove* and *above*. Spell talk can also help by saying 'fri-end' when writing *friend* (remember – you have a *friend* to the *end*) or with words such as parliament or government.

When 'ed' sounds like 't' or 'duh'

If your child *hopped*, *skipped* and *jumped*, he did three things ending with the 't' sound spelled as *ed*. Tell your child that the *ed* ending can sound like 'ed' as in *chatted*, 'duh' as in *smiled* or 'tuh' as in *hopped* (make sure you don't add the schwa though!). And so that he gets to see this for himself, have him read out loud the words in Table 12-13. As usual, writing down the words as you dictate them helps him fix the words in his mind, and reminding him to say the word as he writes it (which adds multisensori-ism!) helps too.

Table 12-13	The Three Sounds of *ed*	
'ed' Sound	*'t' Sound*	*'duh' Sound*
batted	hopped	dreamed
chatted	jumped	planned
shifted	skipped	smiled
shouted	stripped	waved

Sounding out the softies

When your child discovers that *c* and *g* make the soft sounds 'see' and 'jee', he may start switching between hard and soft sounds pretty erratically.

Here's a rule that can help your child. Briefly explain it and then have him read the words in Table 12-14 so that he makes his own hands-on discovery. The rule is 'Soft *c* and *g* are followed by *i*, *y* or *e*', as in *city*, *cyst* and *cent*.

Here are some general help-with-reading tips:

- **Break words into syllables.** Whether your child puts his break in exactly the right spot doesn't matter, as long as he hears the distinctly separate parts of a word. For example, the word *city* is made from the two syllables ci-ty, but your child may choose to break it up into cit-y. The break he puts in for himself is probably the most useful to him, because he remembers his own creation better than someone else's.

- **Highlight tricky parts.** In the word *peace*, for example, your child may highlight *ea* and/or *ce* (because *ea* and *ce* are next to each other, he may mark them in different colours, or circle one and underline the other).

- **Look for spelling rules.** Review 'Bossy e' and 'When two vowels go walking, the first one does the talking', and in this case, of course, 'Soft *c* and *g* are followed by *i*, *y* or *e*'.

Here are some general help-with-writing tips:

- Sound out the word (out loud, not just in your head), from beginning to end, and in syllables if your word has more than one syllable.

- Jot down possible spellings of a sound (like *ase*, *ayse*, *ayce* or *ace*) before you commit to one.

- Encourage your child to jot down the spelling possibilities he thinks of even if you know some of them are impossible. His own discoveries stick in his mind better than your instructions, and the more spelling discoveries he makes, the better he gets at making future spelling guesses.

- Exaggerate pronunciation if that helps. For example, you can pronounce the word *bandage* as 'band-age', not the 'band-ige' of normal people-talk.

- Listen for short and long vowel sounds so you can use spelling rules ('Bossy e' and 'When two vowels go walking the first one does the talking').

Table 12-14	Soft *c* and *g*
Soft c	*Soft g*
ace	age
cell	average
cent	bandage
centre	bulge
chance	cabbage
city	cage
dance	gem

Soft c	Soft g
dice	general
face	gin
fancy	gym
fence	hostage
France	huge
glance	luggage
grace	page
ice	plunge
lace	rage
lice	stage
mice	wage
nice	
pace	
peace	
place	
price	
prince	
race	
rice	
cinoo	
slice	
space	
twice	
wince	

Spotting the silent types

Silent letters are a challenge for just about everyone, but for your child with dyslexia they may be especially tricky. To help your child remember where these letters pop up, have him read through Table 12-15 and try these strategies:

✔ Get the right spelling of these words by pronouncing the silent letters. (For example, for your child to say 'k-nife' every time he spells *knife* is okay, until after plenty of this overpronouncing he remembers the spelling *without* the weird talk!)

✔ Remember words with silent letters like *balm*, *calm* and *palm* in their families (see 'Building Three-Letter Words in Word Families', earlier in this chapter, for details of this concept).

✔ Devise mnemonics (such as '**I** g**e**t **h**ot **t**oes') for remembering letter combinations like *ight*.

✔ Sound out the parts of words that can be sounded out and highlight other silent (or otherwise tricky) parts so that you remember the look of them.

Table 12-15			**Silent Letters**			
k	*b*	*l*	*gh*	*w*	*t*	*g*
knack	bomb	balm	blight	wrap	bristle	align
knead	climb	calm	bought	wreath	bustle	campaign
knee	comb	could	bright	wreck	castle	champagne
kneel	crumb	embalm	brought	wren	gristle	diaphragm
knew	debt	folk	delight	wrench	hustle	design
knick	doubt	palm	fight	wrestle	rustle	sign
knife	lamb	should	flight	wretch	thistle	resign
knight	limb	would	fought	wriggle	whistle	
knit	plumber	yolk	fright	wring		
knob	thumb		high	wrinkle		
knock	tomb		light	wrist		
knoll	womb		might	write		
knot			night	writhe		
know			ought	wrong		
knowl-edge			plight			
knuckle			right			
			sight			
			slight			
			sought			
			thigh			
			thought			
			tight			

Doubling up

When Tracey was a child, she had a lot of trouble spelling *written* and *writing*. Do you use one *t* or two? Then she discovered the following (and got a computer spell checker for all the other words she can't spell!).

So here's the rule that helps Tracey with *written* and *writing* and can help your child with words like *pinned* and *pined*, *hopped* and *hoped*, *bitten* and *biting*. When your child reads or writes a short word with an ending added to it (like *written* and *bitten*), the rule is 'double the letter to keep the vowel short'. The double letter in words like *pinned* and *hopped* prevents you from mistakenly musing about things you *pined* and *hoped* for (like sweethearts or chocolate).

Make a copy of the words in Table 12-16 and have your child read them out loud to you. Let him use his pen to identify the double letters, and after he's marked them all, dictate several for him to write. Have him say each word out loud as he writes it so that he hears that short sound.

The 'double the letter to keep the vowel short' rule works on short words like *hop* and longer words like *drip* that have a blend (in this case *dr*) at the front. But if a blend's at the end of a short word (like in *sing*), forget this rule. It doesn't work on blend-at-the-end words or on blend-on-both-ends words, like *stamp*.

Table 12-16	Adding *ing* and *ed* to Short Words
Base Word	*'ing' or 'ed' Added*
clap	clapping, clapped
dot	dotting, dotted
drip	dripping, dripped
drop	dropping, dropped
flip	flipping, flipped
flop	flopping, flopped
hop	hopping, hopped
hug	hugging, hugged
jot	jotting, jotted
mop	mopping, mopped
nod	nodding, nodded
prod	prodding, prodded

(continued)

Table 12-16 *(continued)*

Base Word	'ing' or 'ed' Added
rob	robbing, robbed
rub	rubbing, rubbed
skip	skipping, skipped
slip	slipping, slipped
slop	slopping, slopped
sob	sobbing, sobbed
spot	spotting, spotted
step	stepping, stepped
stop	stopping, stopped
top	topping, topped
trot	trotting, trotted

Chapter 13

Sprinting Ahead with Reading Basics and Practice

*W*hen you read out loud to your child she's a picture of happiness, but when you ask her to read out loud to you she dissolves into tears. That's how kids who have dyslexia feel. This chapter shows you what your child must grasp in order to be a good reader, how you can help her get those skills under her belt with a reading routine and which reading strategies really work. We also show you how to handle your child's reading errors and difficulties gently but effectively.

Looking at Reading Fundamentals

You can read an awful lot of theory about how kids learn to read if you want to, or you can take it from us (people who've read stacks of theory and spent more than a combined 35 years helping children read): in order to read, your child needs to:

✔ Automatically recognise the most common words, or *sight words*, like *the*, *was* and *they* (because these words crop up so often).

✔ Be able to sound out or have phonics under control. 'But the English language is so irregular,' you may say. Ah yes, some words definitely defy sounding out, but you can sound out more than half, and some people say almost all, as long as you know which letters, and clusters of letters, make which sounds. *Phonic Awareness* means being able to match written letters, and groups of letters, to their corresponding sounds.

✔ Get a lot of reading practice by having someone (that's you!) help her read books that are at the right level of interest for her. (Too hard's overwhelming, and too easy's dull.) This reading practice shows your child that all the work she does on sight words and phonics leads to a great end, gives her on-the-job practice of sight words and phonics (rather than getting the hang of them through isolated practice tasks) and improves her comprehension (the fancy word for understanding). The more reading she does, the more familiar she becomes with typical plot elements, style and grammar; and if she talks text over with you, even better.

An acronym you can use to remember these three reading essentials is SPRint. Help your child regularly and systematically with the following:

✔ Sight words

✔ Phonics

✔ Reading practice

If you do, you see her SPRint forward! And that, in a nutshell, is what you need to know about how basic word reading works. We can talk about grammar, tenses and punctuation if you like, but if you wanted that extra jazz, you'd probably have picked up a book about English usage.

In the rest of this chapter, we discuss the reading (or R) part of SPRint. Before that, though, we give you the basics on sight words, a lightning rundown of sounding out and a quick explanation of what 'comprehension' means.

Being quick to recognise sight words

Your child with dyslexia can't read fluently without having instant or 'sight' recognition of sight words because these words are so common that 220 of them comprise about 70 per cent of all text. Did we just say 'all text'? That's right. Pick up any book, comic or leaflet and you see sight words all through it.

In Chapter 11, we give you a list of 220 sight words and a bunch of nifty ways to help your child get the instant recognition she needs.

Feeling good about phonics

When your child learns phonics, she learns how letters and bunches of letters represent the sounds inside words. She starts off by learning single letter sounds, like 'a' (as in 'apple'), 'buh' and 'cuh'; progresses to sounds like 'st', 'cl' and 'ch'; and much farther down the line, gets to know tricky sounds like 'ough'. Particularly for struggling readers with dyslexia, mastery of phonics is huge.

Most people use the words *phonetic*, *phonological* and *phonemic* interchangeably to mean sounding out. You may encounter the odd person (and you can interpret 'odd' any way you like here) who tells you that we're oversimplifying, but you'd be here a long and fairly boring time if we got into the fine distinctions.

Essentially, *phonics* means sounds of language, and we use *phonic awareness* to match written letters, and groups of letters, to their corresponding sounds. This essential skill for reading's been around a long time, and many teachers know how to teach it well. They know that structured and sequential phonics instruction is best and that learning letter-sound associations is easier when you group them in word families or bunches of words that all have the same chunk of sound in them.

In practical terms you need to teach your child the following things, in roughly this order:

- Each single letter represents a sound and sometimes more than one sound.
- Vowels always represent at least two sounds (usually called short and long sounds).
- Every word has a vowel, but *y* can take the place of a vowel and be a pretend vowel (like in *my* and *by*).
- You need to know all the common sound chunks, like 'ch', 'ea' and 'ow'.
- The best way to remember sound chunks is to put them into word families, like *pain*, *rain*, *drain* and *brain*.

Check out Chapter 12 for more details on dealing with phonics.

Understanding about comprehension

If you worry that your child reads and then has no idea what she's just read, this section, all about comprehension, is for you.

Comprehension means understanding. If your child comprehends something, she gets it. Whatever she reads, she gets the point and understands who did what and why. If she doesn't have good comprehension, she just doesn't get the gist of something, can't remember who did what and hasn't a hope of fathoming out why.

Things that cause or signify lack of comprehension include:

✏ Your child reads so slowly that she loses the point along the way. By the time she gets to the end of a sentence, she's forgotten what the beginning was.

✏ Your child makes so many mistakes that the meaning of a sentence is muddled or lost on her.

✏ Your child doesn't care what the text says. It's boring.

✏ Your child has trouble remembering names and keeping a sequence of events in its right order.

✏ Your child doesn't know some of the vocabulary in the text. She may have missed or struggled so much with reading in class that she never got the chance to learn, read and re-read new vocabulary.

✏ Your child misunderstands the inferences and unstated parts of a text. She grasps only the concrete, openly stated parts, so that things like implied jealousy, love or scheming are lost on her.

You can take the following steps to improve your child's reading comprehension:

✏ Enhance your child's recognition of sight words and phonics skills so that she reads more fluently. (We cover this in Chapters 11 and 12.)

✏ Listen to your child read manageable and fun text often.

✏ Help your child figure out words by starting at the beginning and moving forward, chunk by chunk. Children often misread words because they focus on just one chunk of a word and then guess the rest.

Technically these 'chunks' are syllables, digraphs, phonemes and morphemes.

- A *syllable* is a word chunk that has a vowel in it (or vowel equivalent like the *y* in the single-syllable word *my*).

- A *digraph* is two or more letters that together make a common word chunk, such as *ai*, *oa*, *ch* and *ing*.

- A *phoneme* is the smallest unit of sound in a word, and it can be just one letter, like in *c-a-t*.

- A *morpheme* is the minimum meaningful element in a word, so it includes suffixes like *tion* that make *act* mean something different from *action*.

These classifications can overlap; for example, *unable* is made of both three syllables and two morphemes. Your child gets to know all the chunks inside words, no matter what you call them, through saying, reading and writing them a lot.

✔ Aim to read with or to your child often. Let your child read material she wants to read, including comics and joke books, so that she reads more often and gets the practice she needs. Your child's better off willingly reading three easy books than struggling through one harder book and becoming disheartened and angry. See 'Choosing the right books', later in this chapter, for more about selecting great reading material.

✔ Teach your child to distinguish between the main and secondary points in a text. Children with dyslexia often have poor inferential skills, so try to encourage her to work out any deeper meaning in the text. To help her with this task, have her jot down words as she reads so that she ends up with a list of words that roughly describes what she's reading. Alternatively, you could read it all first, then talk about it afterwards, writing down the key words and discussing any underlying inference in the text.

✔ Encourage your child to draw diagrams of the book's plot and jot down the names of key characters.

✔ Read some of your child's homework to her (otherwise she may not be able to get through it all) and explain new vocabulary. Ask her to use new words in context so that she remembers them, telling her what they mean or getting her to look them up in a dictionary. All children who don't read as much as classmates can fall a long way behind with subject-specific vocabulary. We cover teenage dyslexia issues in more detail in Chapter 16.

✔ Talk about what's happening in stories and fiction and ask your child questions about the plot. What's openly said and what's implied? What feelings, motives and undercurrents can you detect? Could a character face surprises up ahead?

Getting in the Habit: Establishing a Happy Reading Routine

Read regularly with your child. Of course you have other obligations, such as meal preparation, a job and a mammoth pile of laundry. But the thing is, we're compelled to drive you! You must read with your child every day – no putting it off – because right now, this very day, is the best time to help your child.

The sooner and more often you help your child read, the easier reading is on both of you. Older kids and adults have more catching up to do because all through school they've missed years of reading. The sooner you help your child and the more help you give her, the better. We cover specific techniques that you can use in the next section.

Older children and adults who are dyslexic can usually learn to read. Learning to read takes a lot of time and effort, but the feeling of accomplishment's big too! Don't be set back by feeling guilty that you didn't help your child sooner or never learned to read well yourself. Instead, establish a manageable routine of grasping a repertoire of sight words and phonics and doing some daily reading. Reading out loud's a useful strategy for any age because the act of looking at words and saying them out loud helps you get the multisensory learning that works best. Find out more about multisensory methods in Chapter 14.

What kind of things can ease your way on the path to reading regularly with your child? Here are some practical tips to help your child enjoy reading and help you save time and energy. (Your personal energy that is – we're not asking you to turn off the heating or lights.)

- Choose books that your child wants to read, rather than books you think she should read. Comics are fine, and so are joke books or any other kind of book with short blasts of print. Get plenty of easy books rather than one book that's too hard, which is likely to turn your child off. See 'Choosing the right books', later in this chapter, to get started.

- Set a regular time for reading, ideally 20 minutes each day, and stick to it. Bedtime suits many families, but some early birds like to read at the breakfast table. Right after dinner is a good time, too. I've heard of parents initially posing the choice 'Do the dishes or work on your reading'. Somehow reading always wins out!

- If you occasionally miss out on a day of reading, that's okay, but don't let those times sneak up on you until you miss more sessions than you get through.

- Have a record-keeping system. Your child likes to know how she's doing. Just like everyone else, she feels good when she knows that she's making progress and has checked a few things off her list. Help her keep a record of the books she reads, something like the one in Figure 13-1.

  The chart you use to record books read could include columns with:

  - The name of the book

  - Categories for bad, average and good books – just mark the column that applies to a given book

  - The date that your child finished the book

  You don't need to make it complicated or formal if this method doesn't work for your child. Just a checklist your child could use to tick off the books she's read, or somewhere she could draw a picture to remind her of the book.

- Establish a reward system. A good reason for rewarding your child is that she's doing something she wasn't keen on in the first place, and another reason for rewarding her is that she likes rewards!

But maybe rewarding isn't for you. Older kids can be all rewarded out, and besides, you may want to stick with reading's intrinsic rewards. The fact that your child gets through those books can be a reward in itself.

Whether you give extrinsic rewards (like extra TV, extra play or a later bedtime at weekends) or not, always give your child your attention. A simple smile, hug or 'good job' may sometimes work better than all the other rewards.

Book	Bad?	Average?	Good?	Date
Hop on Pop			▓	June 24
Fat Cat		▓		June 27
Happy Family			▓	June 30
Cat Chocolate				
Green Fingers				

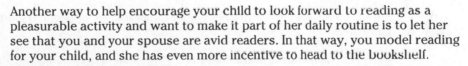

Figure 13-1: A chart can help you reward your child with dyslexia for finishing books.

Another way to help encourage your child to look forward to reading as a pleasurable activity and want to make it part of her daily routine is to let her see that you and your spouse are avid readers. In that way, you model reading for your child, and she has even more incentive to head to the bookshelf.

Using Special Strategies for Reading Success

You want your child to read interesting and fun books early on so that she can see what all the fuss is about and feel motivated to keep going. But even with the best intentions, many parents find great ways to switch their child right off reading! They ask their children to read books that are too hard for them or don't manage to get into a happy reading-out-loud routine. In the following sections, we show you how to select the best books for your child, and we provide you with some proven reading strategies.

You can very easily turn your child off reading with just a few impatient words at the wrong time. So no losing your patience, heavy sighing or saying things like 'You just saw that word!' If you feel your patience being tested, take a break, change books (this one may be too hard) and refocus (remind yourself that everyone learns by making mistakes). Turn to 'Handling Your Child's Difficulties with Kindness', later in this chapter, for more tips.

Your child may tell you that reading's boring, stupid or just not for her. Don't believe her. Not everyone loves reading, of course, but everyone at least wants to be able to read. Struggling readers with dyslexia often pretend that they don't want to read; otherwise, they have to admit that they can't read and that's too crushing. Let her whining wash over you and persevere. With carefully chosen books, sensitivity and commitment, you can help your child (no matter what age) make progress.

Choosing the right books

To make sure that your child can read out loud to you smoothly and compre-hend what she's reading, you need to choose the books she reads carefully. She can choose her own books for browsing later on, but you need to select her first reading-all-by-herself books. To achieve the perfect choice, forget about levels and about titles with 'beginner' in them. (We see plenty of so-called beginner books containing words that are too hard.) Look instead for books that are phonetically controlled and/or pass the 'one-hand rule' (which we explain later in this section).

Phonic books have titles like *Fat Cat* and *Jake and the Snake* and follow two guidelines:

- ✔ They are written with a phonetic rule in mind, like using short *a*, and use mostly words that follow that rule ('a fat cat sat on a mat').

- ✔ Other words that they use are either words your child learned in earlier books in the series or newly introduced words that the author lists in the front or back pages (only a few new words are introduced in each book).

With phonic books, you know what you're getting. You don't find words like 'enough' and 'furious' thrown in with 'cat' and 'fat', so you don't have to wonder what on earth to do about it. When reading these books, you show your child the new words (listed at the front or back), remind her about the phonetic rule (short _a_) and off you go. (Check out Chapter 12 for more about phonics.) Ta-da, your child can read the book pretty much all by herself and everyone's happy.

Our shelves are stocked with series of phonic books, and we don't dream of helping struggling readers without using them. They work. Even if you think to yourself that they're boring, your child doesn't think that way. She wants to read by herself and these kinds of books do the trick.

Books with a particular level and books with controlled vocabulary aren't the same as phonic books.

✔ Allocating levels, or controlling the vocabulary in a book, means that a book's classified (usually as Level 1, 2, 3 or A, B, C) by degree of difficulty based on how many hard words are in it. The hard words are selected and counted by using one of several methods (like Reading Recovery or Paired Reading) that ask things like whether a word's easy to spell and whether its meaning's clear.

✔ Phonic books are classified by difficulty too, but the classification is according to the phonological difficulty of the words in the book.

What this all means in practice is that a book at a particular level or with a controlled vocabulary can have mixed text in it with all kinds of spellings, as long as they're within the level. A phonic book sticks to a phonics rule or two, so its content is repetitive; for example, all the words may be from the _at_ word family, with only two or three other words, like _the_ and _was_.

Flip through the pages of a book before buying. The best books for beginners are phonic books that list new words that are hard to sound out (like _the_, _was_ and _who_) before or after the main text. You can walk your child through the list of new words and avoid nasty surprises in the middle of reading, and all the other words sound out in a predictable way.

Your child's comfort level for reading any book is when only 5 per cent of what she reads (5 words in every 100) poses a challenge.

To find this just-right text, give your child a page of 100 words to read (or a few pages that together make up 100 words) and tell her to close one finger on the same hand every time she reaches a word she doesn't know. If she runs out of fingers on one hand before she finishes the words, the book's too hard. That's the 'one-hand rule'.

To find series of phonic books, head to your library or ask at school. You can also take a look at `www.standards.dfes.gov.uk/phonics/programmes` which offers loads more information about the wide range of phonics books available. If you want to buy, check out these series (roughly in order from easy to more advanced):

- ✔ **Fuzzbuzz:** Many schools use this very popular reading series for reluctant readers. You can buy books and CDs from Oxford University Press. Find information about the Fuzzbuzz series on the Oxford University Press website (www.oup.com/oxed/primary/specialneeds/fuzzbuzz).

- ✔ **Dandelion Readers:** This series of decodable texts is based on the Sounds-Write reading and spelling programme. The books are ideal for either Reception/Year 1 children or for reluctant readers at Key Stage 2. The readers consist of 50 books in the Initial Code Series and are available from Phonic Books (www.phonicbooks.co.uk).

- ✔ **Read with Ladybird:** Ladybird makes several great book series, but Tracey's favourite is the Ladybird Learning to Read series. You get small hardback books with short stories (which children often like better than long stories). These books are perfect after your child has easier books under her belt and needs slightly harder books. Book 1, Set 1 is *Happy Family* by Shirley Jackson. Visit www.penguin.co.uk for more information.

- ✔ **Read Write:** This fun-to-read series of books is based on Ruth Miskin's synthetic phonics programme. Look for titles like *On the Bus* and *My Dog Ned*, along with writing activities. The Book People (www.thebook people.co.uk) is a good source for well-priced copies of these books.

- ✔ **Oxford Reading Tree:** Biff, Chip and Kipper from this structured reading scheme with 60 titles are well known to many children. Book sets with titles such as *Dad's Birthday* and *Poor Old Rabbit!* include handbooks with advice, games and activities, typically for £9.99 from The Book People. Or visit www.oup.com for a handy parents' guide and further information about the series.

Don't make your child stick exclusively to phonic books that confine the text to sentences like 'Dan can fan' – that's so boring. Let her pick plenty of her own books (about things like gymnastics, ocean life and pets) for browsing. That way, she gets to have books she's really interested in (the whole point!), and as long as you have her read phonetically controlled books too, text that's beyond her reading skills doesn't matter.

When your child's flipped through plenty of phonic reading books and is ready to move to harder text (but not too much harder), you may want to stock up on favourite, but fairly simple, book series. Finding books in a series is easier than searching randomly, so here are our suggestions for book series that appeal to nearly all kids:

- ✔ *Captain Underpants* by Dav Pilkey (published by Scholastic). Available at all bookshops.

> ✔ *I Got a D in Salami* is part of the series of Hank Zipzer books by Henry Winkler (better known as the Fonz). Winkler, who has dyslexia himself, tells the story of Hank Zipzer who can't read or spell and is always getting into trouble. The books are available from Waterstone's bookshops.
>
> ✔ For more ideas try Waterstone's Guide for Young Dyslexic Readers, which you can download from www.waterstones.co.uk. The guide's full of ideas for parents to help reluctant readers and includes plenty of recommended books such as *The Twits* by Roald Dahl.

For reading books for adults with dyslexia, check out the Quick Reads series by a wide range of popular authors, available from all bookshops at £1.99 each.

Reading to your child first

To prime your child (at any age) for reading a book, read it through to her first. This gives her the sense of the text so that, when she reads alone, she's better able to use contextual and grammatical cues to figure words out more easily.

> ✔ *Contextual cues* are indirect clues you get from diagrams, headings and a general understanding of the topic. If, for example, you see the word 'horse' in a heading and a diagram of a currycomb, you can guess that the text's about horse care.
>
> ✔ You get *grammatical cues* from understanding how words fit together in sentences. For example, if you read 'they wants to gets swimming', you know you've misread because the words don't flow together and the sentence is grammatically incorrect.

We cover these concepts in more detail in 'Helping your child find contextual cues', later in this chapter.

Pairing up to read

If you leave your child with dyslexia alone with a book and expect her to read it, you're going to be disappointed. Her reading's slow and laboured, so she gets no pleasure from it – only frustration. The solution's to read along with her. You can choose from a few great ways to do 'paired reading', and in the next sections we take you through them step by step.

Having your child read out loud to you regularly is one of the best ways to help her become more fluent. Psych yourself up to do a good job of listening to her. She's a beginner, so she makes mistakes and you have to gently help her through them. The most important thing your beginning reader needs to get from reading out loud to you is the feeling that she's moving forward and making you both happy.

We're not the only ones who make a big deal out of reading out loud. The 'Teaching Children to Read Report', published in 2002 and based on extensive studies carried out in the US, states that reading out loud's one of the most effective strategies you can use to help your child read better.

Paired reading

Paired reading means reading out loud with your child, the same text at the same time. You read together, in unison, and your child gets to hear your voice, guiding and supporting, all the while. When she's not sure of a word she can listen to you. When she's reading smoothly without having to use your cues, she still has you right there joining in the fun. Because it's so easy to do, paired reading's especially good for re-engaging a child who's avoided reading for a long time. As you get in tune with one another, try reading very slightly after your child says the words. You get to hear her better, and she still gets to listen to your voice when she needs to.

A nice modification of paired reading, when you really get into the swing of the method, is the tap-or-nudge routine. Decide on a signal, like a tap or nudge, that your child gives you when she wants you to stop reading. She taps for you to stop reading and then taps again when she wants you to read again. The tap can be on your arm or on the table, and the nudge pretty much speaks for itself. Try it; after you get a rhythm going, it's easy. This modification gives your child more control, which in turn makes her a more confident reader.

Taking turns

Taking turns reading out loud together from the same book is a nice step up from paired reading and is ideal when your child's a little more independent.

Always start small with this technique. If you tell your child to read a page to you she may balk, so ask her to read just a sentence (or even a word) on each page to start with. Gradually ask her to read more and let her choose the sentence or paragraph she reads. If she's reluctant, don't get annoyed, but don't give up either. Make deals. You read an extra three pages if she reads three sentences per page, say.

As always, a terrific book does half the work for you. Your child soon gets hooked into the story and wants to know what happens next, so she keeps reading.

Interrupted reading

Interrupted reading is a great way to take advantage of engrossing stories. If you want your child to try reading all by herself, read to her at bedtime and then stop reading at a crucial point in the story. Excuse yourself by saying you have to let the dog out, clean the kitchen or tuck her sister in. Then graciously allow her a few more minutes of reading time on her own if she wants it (*if* she wants it – are you kidding?). Usually she gets several more pages under her belt.

For interrupted reading to work, you need to be well into the book (so that your child's completely familiar with the characters and plot), and your child should be feeling confident about reading.

Running through multiple readings

Reading a book several times makes your child faster and more fluent at reading it and, as a result, more confident to tackle new books. The DIY Readers' Support Pack from DI Trading is a fantastic resource for parents to use at home. The accompanying CD goes through the pure sounds so that you can confidently correct your child, and the kit contains a stopwatch for timed activities such as reading word chunks. You can purchase the pack from DI Trading (www.dyslexiaaction.org.uk/store) for £39.99.

Try recording stories that are always popular among SENCOs who are in charge of helping students with dyslexia. Children read a story, listen to it on tape or their iPod, practise reading it to themselves and then read it again, timed this time.

You can easily do repeated reading at home without spending a lot of money. All you have to do is get a book that's not too hard for your child and have her read a small section of 100 words from it to you three to five times (whatever suits you both best) against a stopwatch. Draw a chart or graph to plot her progress (see Figure 13-2). Record the number of words she reads correctly (out of the 100) on one page of a book and the time she takes. She usually improves with each reading and gets even better on the next book excerpt. Read about ten successive excerpts like this between the other regular reading you do. Your child gets a quick boost in skill and confidence, and then before the routine gets boring, it's over. After a break of a few weeks, start another ten-excerpt booster programme if you want.

If your child hates being timed, do without the timing part of this activity. You still get good results and your child doesn't get stressed or overwhelmed.

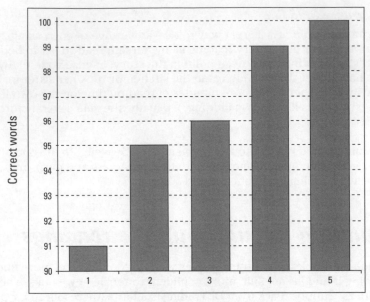

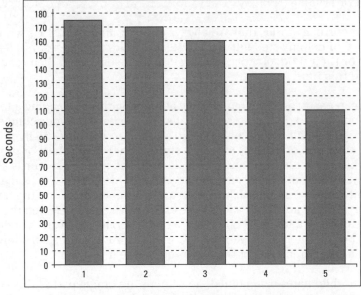

Figure 13-2:
Graphs
can help
you track
your child's
reading
progress.

Handling Your Child's Difficulties with Kindness

When your child reads out loud to you and makes mistakes, which ones should you let pass and which should you correct? Do you simply tell her the word and move on, or should you have her sound out the words? Should you have her jot down the problem words to look at later? In the next sections we give you the answers.

Helping children who have dyslexia is all about modifying their environment and accommodating their needs rather than forcing things on them. If your child's struggling with a book, find another book, empathise and find ways (like taking breaks and reading out loud with her) to make reading easier. If she wants to read the book, use paired reading or other approaches mentioned earlier in this chapter. You can be flexible. Any reading activity is better than none. Some children hate to be told a word and others get frustrated if you don't tell them. Be guided by the child's mood and behaviour, but whatever method you use try to keep the flow going.

Knowing when to give a quick answer

When your child's reading out loud to you and gets stuck on a tricky word such as 'through', give her the answer straight away and continue reading. Hard words aren't worth battling over. Your child gets to know them by reading them often, and meanwhile you can help by having her write them down on paper and read them back to you every day for several days. Stick them up on your walls too.

Don't interrupt the flow of your child's reading to try to get her to figure out all the hard words. If a word sounds out easily, like 'problem', have her sound it out, but don't interrupt her every time she stumbles. She's likely to lose the drift if you do. When you let the reading flow, your child has the chance to understand the text and to feel that she's a reader.

To make headway with reading, your child must feel secure. To appreciate what life's like for someone with dyslexia, imagine getting something wrong time and time again. Imagine someone leaning over you and correcting you every few minutes. You can see why you must limit your interruptions.

Having your child figure out a word

When you're reading with your child, here's when you're fine to take time out and have her figure out words she gets stuck on:

✔ The interruption doesn't make her forget what's going on in the text.

✔ You know that she can sound out the word as long as you prompt her. If she's stuck on 'remain', you can prompt her if she's already learned the 'ai' digraph. (A *digraph* is a two-letter sound/spelling chunk. The two letters – like *ai* – make one sound.)

✔ You haven't stopped to work out words a dozen times already (in which case your child's close to burn-out).

✔ Your child's receptive. If she's had enough, tell her the words! You can always have her re-read the text later.

Knowing when to have your child work out a word for herself is fairly easy, but what's the best way to tell her to do it? You want to avoid tears, furious exits (hers or yours) and damage to her fragile ego with a misplaced word or insensitive demand. Table 13-1 gives you a few dos and don'ts for earning your child's cooperation.

Table 13-1	Asking Your Child to Figure Out Words
Don't Say	*Do Say*
Look at it! You've already seen this word!	I think we just saw this word.
That's not right. Sound it out!	Take this word bit by bit.
That's wrong.	That doesn't sound quite right.
No, it can't say that!	Hmm, does that make sense?
Don't just guess!	Almost. Try that one more time.

Helping your child find contextual cues

Contextual cues are clues that your older child gets about the meaning of text and the words she may expect to find from subheadings, diagrams and key words. Here are some suggestions for how you can be sure you're using all those helpful cues:

✔ **Cover blurb:** You may use the cover blurb, or pictures for a younger child, to help you decide what books you want to read. Make sure that your child knows that this material's a way to find out what's inside and doesn't skip it. (You may think the blurb is obviously there to read first, but that may not be obvious to your child. Many things look different to a child with dyslexia.)

✔ **Table of contents:** If your child's about to read a whole book, she should first check out the table of contents at the front of the book. She can usually get a rough idea of what's coming from the chapter headings.

✔ **Introduction:** If a book or document has an introduction, have your child read it. Children with dyslexia need as much of this kind of preparation as they can get because reading text cold is so hard for them.

✔ **Subtitles:** If your child sees words like 'boy' or 'horse', perhaps underneath pictures, she knows that the text's more likely to be about a boy doing stuff with a horse than a woman getting robbed!

✔ **Pictures and diagrams:** Any illustrations your child can find can be helpful to her. Help her get into the habit of glancing at these any time they appear.

✔ **Key words:** When words repeat themselves in the text, they're probably important. After your child's read factual text for the first time (she probably needs several readings), have her check for nouns that appear often. If she gets words like 'reflection' and 'refraction' in her mind before she reads through a page about light for the second time, she's already won half the comprehension battle.

✔ **Grammar:** Your child can use grammatical cues when she's in the middle of reading. If she reads something like 'They was went to school', she can hear that she needs to read the sentence again. It doesn't sound right at all – it's grammatically incorrect – so she must have misread the sentence.

We don't get caught up in grammatical rules in this book, but if you make sure that your child talks properly (saying, for example, 'we were' and not 'we was'), you're helping with her reading. She knows which words go together and that if she reads things like 'they is' and 'you'd going next', she needs to re-read.

Using contextual cues is a secondary reading skill. If your child relies too much on contextual cues and forgets to sound out, her reading can end up going all over the place. For example, if she sees a word starting with 'trans' that she is unfamiliar with and she's been reading about cars or ships, she might be tempted to say the word is 'transport' and not the correct word, which might be 'transfer'. She then presumes the whole paragraph is about transport.

Chapter 14

Taking Advantage of Multisensory Methods

. . . .

In This Chapter

▶ Clarifying what 'multisensory' means

▶ Letting your child take responsibility for multisensory methods

▶ Turning homework into a multisensory experience

▶ Adding multisensory elements to your child's play

▶ Checking out alternative multisensory methods

. . . .

Multisensory learning's big in the world of dyslexia. Some people have written whole books about it, so we rightly devote a chapter to it now. This chapter tells you, in a nutshell, what you must do to be multisensory, why the approach matters for children with dyslexia and how to fit in a good supply of multisensory tools without having to refurbish your home.

Bringing the Term 'Multisensory' Down to Earth

Fancy terminology can sometimes be really troublesome, but the word multisensory is actually very handy because once you feel comfortable using it, you can cut out a long-winded explanation of what you mean. Without 'multisensory' you have to say something like:

> The things good teachers have always done. Putting hands-on practice into teaching and learning. Adding talk, movement and touch to reading and writing. Being an active, engaging instructor rather than a person who drones on and on and then tells your child to copy things down.

The following sections describe multisensory teaching, explain the differences to traditional teaching methods and detail its importance to children with dyslexia.

Distinguishing multisensory teaching from traditional methods

Multisensory teaching (and learning) is pretty much everything that old-fashioned chalk-and-talk teaching isn't. What happens in chalk-and-talk teaching is simply that the teacher talks about a subject, writes information on the board and asks children to copy it. Every teacher does chalk-and-talk teaching sometimes (they're only human), but too much of it's bad news for children with dyslexia. Chalk-and-talk teaching requires students mostly to use just two senses, hearing (or auditory) and vision. Unfortunately, children with dyslexia happen to be conspicuously poor in both.

Children with dyslexia struggle with auditory memory or processing. They have trouble recalling words and how they're pronounced (saying things like 'pasghetti' instead of 'spaghetti') and they don't hear parts of words well (was it a dairy farm or a dirty farm?). A child with dyslexia may also be weak at *visual tracking* (following words one after the other along lines on a page) and *visual processing* or *visual discrimination* (seeing the difference between different letters and letters facing in different ways). Check out Chapter 3 for more details on the signs of dyslexia.

When you give your child tasks that use just his hearing and vision, without drawing on his other senses, you put him at a disadvantage.

Teaching in a *multisensory* way means helping a child gain knowledge through the use of more than two senses. It especially means adding touch (the tactile sense) and movement (the kinetic sense) to his activities so that his brain has information in a format that it can process better and so that he has more to hang onto. If you teach your child things in a multisensory way, he doesn't merely sit down and copy words – he does things like make 3D words from modelling clay or act out phrases. Adding multisensory teaching feels less like a one-way exchange, from you to your child, and more like a cooperative. It should also be fun.

Researchers know that the multisensory approach works because they've done studies that prove its effectiveness. In rough terms, they know that people learn equally well by seeing or hearing a thing, they do a bit better when they talk the thing through, they do better still by doing the thing and they learn best of all by seeing, hearing, saying *and* doing that thing. So you can take away a couple of messages from the research:

✔ Creative play's really important because when your child plays, he does *all* this fancy learning quite naturally (and seeing him constructing and creating and happily talking to himself all the while too is *so* great!).

✔ To maximise your child with dyslexia's learning potential, ask him to see it, say it, hear it and do it!

Dr Samuel Orton and his colleagues introduced multisensory learning back in the 1920s at a mobile mental health clinic in the US state of Iowa. Orton had children trace, copy and write letters while saying the corresponding sounds and called this method 'kinaesthetic-tactile reinforcement of visual and auditory associations'. Now his multisensory method is called the Orton–Gillingham method (Gillingham was Orton's colleague) and is hugely popular among educators. Teachers can be specially trained in Orton–Gillingham methods, and Orton–Gillingham is mentioned just about everywhere people talk about how to address reading problems

The notion of visual, auditory or kinaesthetic learning styles is a popular one. Most people who know anything about dyslexia warn that even though you hear terms like 'a kinaesthetic learner' all the time, identifying an individual in this way's simplistic, because people learn from all of their senses, especially in combination (also known as multisensory). That said, if you're interested in taking a free online test to see whether you have a dominant visual, auditory or kinaesthetic learning style, go to `www.ldpride.net` or `www.vark-learn.com`. The test's good for adults too, and the idea is that if you know your dominant learning style, you can try to use it most, but also get more practice in your weaker styles so that you improve them too.

Fitting together multisensory and structured and sequential teaching

When you hear the word multisensory, chances are that you also hear a load of things about 'structured and sequential' learning. When a teacher puts explicit instruction of phonics rules into a programme (instead of teaching them as they crop up in stories and other text), she's taking a structured approach. Teaching those phonics rules in a logical order also makes the teaching sequential. (Chapter 12 gives you the full story on phonics.)

On the subject of using a multisensory and structured, sequential approach, Dyslexia Action says that students with dyslexia don't need more of the same instruction in class but a different type of instruction. They need to get to grips with basic language sounds and the letters that make them, starting from the very beginning and moving forward in a gradual step-by-step, thorough way. And to help pull all that together through their own discoveries, they must use their eyes, ears, voice and hands.

Setting the Stage for Multisensory Success

Before you can start helping your child with multisensory learning, you need to assume the role of facilitator or partner. When you demonstrate activities, replenish dwindling supplies of materials and join in the fun but take a facilitating rather than a lead role, your child has ownership and control of a task and feels more inclined to get right into it (eyes, ears, voice, hands and all!).

Following are some ways you can let your child assume ownership of his own learning so that he can get multisensory:

- ✔ Let your child hold his pen, paper and book. He should feel that his work really *is* his work and not something you want him to do. Small acts like holding his book or peering over his shoulder make him feel that you're taking over, so hands off!

- ✔ Have a schedule and remind your child to follow it. Say things like 'It's 5 o'clock now, time for homework' and calmly turn off the TV if you have to. Don't overtalk and get into monologues like 'Turn off that TV. You never turn it off when you're supposed to. It's homework time, you know that. Go and get your homework. Where have you put it? Have you got your pens? Have you been keeping your pencils sharp?'

- ✔ Offer your help in small doses as needed. Say things like 'I'm here if you need me' or 'Call me if you get stuck'. You probably don't need to sit with your child the whole time, but if you do, stop giving your help as soon as you can and give it again only when he needs assistance.

- ✔ Have your child take responsibility for the things he's capable of doing, like putting his books away, sharpening his pencil and bringing his diary to you to sign.

- ✔ Give your child small responsibilities at home so that he can feel valuable and independent.

- ✔ Praise your child for doing what he's supposed to do and getting on with things independently.

- ✔ Teach your child to ask for help in normal, polite tones. If he whines and acts rudely, tell him calmly that you're happy to help and sympathise with his frustration, but remind him that he needs to ask you courteously.

Helping your child plug into multisensory mode at home is important for two reasons:

- ✔ He may get a lot of traditional chalk-and-talk instruction at school and not much hands-on stuff, so you can compensate for this at home.

> ✔ Much of what you do rubs off on your child, so taking stock of what you do makes sense. Are you stepping back and allowing him to try out new things for himself? Do you typically model a skill and then give him plenty of practice? Are you more of a doer than an armchair expert?

Making Homework Multisensory

Good teachers help children apply what they know in concrete ways. They take information that seems abstract (like a foreign language) and show students that it actually does count in the real world ('Here's a French magazine with Orlando Bloom in it. See! Children like you use French!'). You can help your child at home by doing the same thing with his homework. In this section we tell you how to set up the right environment and then surge forward.

Setting up a happier homework environment

The traditional idea of children doing homework at a desk in a quiet and brightly lit spot may not be right for your child with dyslexia. Experiment with different ways of doing things and, as always, if something isn't working, don't force it on your child. Instead, try doing things a different way. You may want to give the following simple, practical strategies a whirl:

> ✔ Let your child stand or alternate between standing and sitting to do his work if he wants. He may feel more comfortable switching positions than sitting for a long time and, in any case, movement helps his wandering thoughts refocus.

> ✔ Let him chew gum or nibble on a snack while he works. Even really small movements like these can help his mind stay on track.

> ✔ Let him sip from a water bottle. Again he gets the benefit of small movement, and of course he's hydrating too.

> ✔ Many children with dyslexia are easily distracted by background noise, so you need to experiment. The same thing applies to light; some children with dyslexia find that an open or closed curtain makes a lot of difference in their ability to concentrate.

> ✔ Give him brightly coloured highlighter pens and help him mark key words. Highlighting can be a nice change from writing or keyboarding, it draws his attention to small bites of important things and it makes his page look cheerful.

✔ Give him a bookmark to keep track of how far he's read. Otherwise he wastes time searching for his place and probably gets irritated in the process.

✔ Give him something, like a set of beads or a squishy ball, to manipulate in his hand. Many children with dyslexia have trouble being still, so things that allow your child some slight movement can be really helpful. You may even want to ask an occupational therapist about the range of devices, like squishy seat cushions and wobbly foot rests, you can buy.

✔ Let him take short breaks. At best, most children have an attention span of about 20 minutes, and the same goes for adults. Frequent quick breaks give your child a learning advantage.

✔ Help him represent information in diagrams and pictures. A few paragraphs of text can look infinitely clearer when your child summarises them in simple bubbles and arrows.

Adults with dyslexia also need to find their preferred learning environment and routine. Take rest breaks and experiment with background noise, lighting and things like gum and squishy hand devices that help you get a little movement.

Helping your child understand new information

Back in her schooldays, Tracey had to study Shakespeare's *Henry V*. Her teacher had the class read the play word for old-fashioned word, though no one understood it. The whole experience was extremely boring and put most of the class off Shakespeare for life. You can't easily learn something by starting from unknown territory. You need familiar ground to get a footing, which in the case of *Henry V* is a modern-day explanation (Who can you compare Henry with in modern times? Who did he argue with? What kind of playground scenario's similar?).

To help your child with schoolwork or new information that seems foreign to him, link it to something he already knows, and do so in a multisensory way. How exactly? Here are some practical pointers:

✔ Put historical information into a current context that he's aware of ('Imagine if I made you walk to the petrol station. That's how far the children had to walk to get water.')

✔ Use new words in a familiar context ('How many *fearsome* people do you know?').

✔ Act out and discuss new words.

✔ Make models, pictures and diagrams when you can (like drawings of fearsome and tranquil scenes).

Having Practical Stuff for Playing at Your Fingertips

Time to home in on the materials teachers use to add the multisensory element to kids' reading, writing and spelling activities. You may not be surprised to see modelling clay featuring first, but did you ever see a teacher use sandpaper as an aid to literacy? In this section we talk about these and other materials that teachers use to give their students educational, feel-good (inside and out!) play.

Modelling clay

A lot of people feel that children with dyslexia learn to read better when they see 3D models of letters and words, so modelling clay is a favourite medium. To make your own soft modelling clay, see the recipe in the nearby sidebar 'Mixing up some modelling clay'.

Gummy mixtures

If you want to have your child with dyslexia remember letter shapes through drawing them in media that give him all sorts of soft or tasty sensations, make him some gluggy, gooey gummy mixtures to run his fingers through. For delicious mixes, try chocolate pudding, coloured sugar or whipped cream, or get dirty with sand, play cement or good old garden mud. Have your child finger-write letters with these concoctions. Hopefully, he licks his fingers only after using the edible mixes!

Sandpaper

When your child uses modelling clay, he gets to squeeze, mould and pull apart the nice soft dough using his whole hands. When he feels sandpaper letters, his tactile sensations are fine-tuned further down to his fingertips, and through them he literally feels the letter shapes. Cut letters out of fine sandpaper so that your child can run his fingers over them to help fix the shapes in his brain. Montessori schools regard this activity so highly that every classroom uses it. (We talk about Montessori schools in Chapter 7.)

To create other textured surfaces, have your child glue things on top of letters you write on paper. Use items like dried beans, rice, wool, buttons, pencil shavings and pasta shells.

Mixing up some modelling clay

If you're like us and have recipes jotted on bits of paper all over the house, with good intentions of one day collating them, you're sure to want to keep this recipe handy as an easy tool for your child with dyslexia.

Easy (and edible) modelling clay

You need the following ingredients:

- 2¹/₂ cups flour
- ¹/₂ cup salt
- 3 tablespoons cooking oil
- ¹/₄ teaspoon food colouring
- 2 cups boiling water

Mix the flour, salt, oil and food colouring in a bowl. Add the boiling water. Mix well and then knead until smooth. (Use the kneading hook on your food mixer if you have one.) This dough keeps for several months in a plastic bag, but don't freeze it.

No food colouring? Try mixing jelly granules or fruit-drink powder into the boiling water instead.

Laminate

A roll of clear adhesive book covering is a great investment. Write letters and words on regular paper and then stick this covering over them. Your child can trace over the letters with his fingers or use whiteboard pens and then re-use the sheets after a quick wipe. He gets plenty of hands-on practice of writing on a nice smooth surface, you can make big and small copies of the same letter and erasing and starting over is a breeze. If you want the deluxe version of the same thing, take your letter sheets to an office supplies store to be laminated.

Teach your child to write in stages with laminate:

1. **Have your child practise tracing over the letters of the alphabet.**

2. **Have him write the letters by joining dots (which you already drew out for him).**

3. **Have him copy the letters, while looking at the originals on a separate sheet of paper.**

4. **Have him write the letters without any props at all.**

Scissors

Scissors are a handy thing for your child to have so that he can cut up lists of words and end up with a pile of single words to move around. By grouping the words (*rain*, *pain* and *main*, for example) and using them like flashcards (see the following section), he gives himself a more interesting way to get to know words than just studying a list. For more games you can play with cut-out words, flip to Chapter 12.

Flashcards

Flashcards should come with a warning saying something like 'WARNING: These cards are pointless and tedious unless basic procedures are followed.'

In the right hands flashcards are a terrific tool for children, especially children with dyslexia, because the cards give small pieces of clear information that you can control. For example, you can use just ten cards for a few weeks before adding more, and you can go as slowly and with as much repetition as your child needs. But never buy a pack of 100 words and flash every one in front of your child in the hope that some of the information will stick.

Following are some specific ways you can make the most of flashcards with your child with dyslexia:

- ✔ Give information in small bites. Select five to ten cards. Most people can retain only between five and ten pieces of new information at any one time.

- ✔ Use only cards that your child's already primed for (like *bug*, *hut* and *luck* and not *bug*, *promise* and *treat*) and progress to the other cards only after you show your child their spelling pattern (like *cheese*, *peel* and *deep*).

- ✔ Allow your child ownership. So your child feels in charge of his learning, invite him to choose the words for himself.

- ✔ Have a hands-off policy. Your child should handle the cards himself and put away the remaining cards himself. When you handle the cards, the paper, the book or whatever's in front of your child, you take over. Offer your help, but don't touch unless your child asks you to. If you handle the material, your child immediately feels that the work's really yours.

- ✔ Have fun. You should launch yourself, with much enthusiasm, into making discovery fun. Games and changing tempo do this.

- ✔ Give praise and encouragement. Provide a flow of praise for each accomplishment.

- ✔ Watch for mastery. Until your child's grasped the information you're giving, don't give more. To test for mastery, you can simply say, 'I can see you're really good at this. I wonder if you can still tell me the words if you first turn them over so you can't see them, and then mix them all up. Do you think you can turn each one over and read it?'

When your child gets to know a new letter pattern (like *ai*), he can easily grasp dozens of new words that use that pattern (like *pain*, *rain* and *main*). Put words into sound families such as the *ou* family – *out*, *shout*, *found*, *around* and *proud*. Have your child make his own 'sounds' posters or give him a notebook and have him make a separate page for each new sound he needs. His pages will have sounds like *ee*, *ea*, *ing*, *ou*, *ai*, *oa* and *ight*. But learning words with no shared pattern's a different matter. So that you don't overload him, use only up to ten new unalike words at a time. See Chapter 12 for more details about sound families.

Board games

If you own games like Boggle, Hangman and Junior Scrabble, don't let them stay buried under other games for months on end. They can help your child with dyslexia practise his phonics skills in a supportive group environment. Bring them out and have games evenings and championships. How many other times does your child get to see everyone in the family modelling the stuff you tell him to do?

Any time you do the same activity your child does, you're *modelling* the activity. Modelling's an effective way to teach your child because you give him a concrete example of what he needs to do. Also, when he sees you or any other person he admires doing something, he wants to do the same. That's why your child needs to see you doing good (not bad) things. Like the saying says, kids do what you do.

Tracey's all-time favourite game is Junior Monopoly. It's so much better than the adult version because only a little money counting's required, you finish within the decade and you can easily see if the banker's corrupt. Your child gets to practise his reading, by the way, when he grabs the Chance cards and figures out street names.

Computer games

We don't go into great detail about technology in this book, but we can safely tell you that computer play can be productive for your child with dyslexia. Good software dishes up straight reading with plenty of sounds and cool effects so that your child gets reading practice *and* a fun time. Computer games can limit your child's social play and get out of hand too of course, but these issues are mostly a matter of using your common sense. Anyway, here are some good computer games you can buy for your child on CD-ROM (Wordshark, Numbershark and Jump Start Phonics are available in formats for both PC and Mac users):

✔ **Wordshark** from WhiteSpace is a very popular resource in schools and at home. The CD-ROM contains more than 55 games that aim to reinforce word recognition and spelling, and the latest version contains 'Letters and Sounds', a detailed phonics course. WhiteSpace also produces the equally popular Numbershark, which contains more than 50 games to reinforce addition, subtraction, division, multiplication, fractions and decimals. Children love both products. Wordshark costs £69; Numbershark costs £59. You can obtain both directly from WhiteSpace on 020 9748 5927 or DI Trading at www.dyslexiaaction.org.uk.

✔ **Nessy Learning Programme** was developed by the Bristol Dyslexia Centre and contains a detailed multisensory teaching approach that children really enjoy, especially games like Whack the Rat. The programme costs £102. You can use the Nessy Games Player in conjunction with the Learning Programme or independently (which costs an additional £17). For further details and a free demo visit www.nessy.co.uk.

✔ **Jump Start Phonics** is a popular title in the Jump Start series. This series has five distinct activities, each with an associated game, and three skill levels that cover everything from letter recognition to spelling and rhyming. Children choose to read and speak their responses, using the programme's 'Read 'n' Respond' technology, or they can simply point and click as appropriate. The programme offers a user-friendly approach to teaching phonics and early reading to young children. Visit www.knowledgeadventure.com for more information.

✔ **Catch Up** was developed in conjunction with Oxford Brookes University and is an intensive programme containing 22 games that aim to help children with reading difficulties. Two CD-ROMs for children ages 6–11 cost £50. Visit www.dyslexic.com for further details.

CD-ROMs aren't cheap, so check out (figuratively and literally) your local library's CD ROM collection. If you don't see what you want, ask the librarian to borrow the product from another library for you. For more recommendations on the newest products, leaf through a few parenting magazines or surf websites such as www.parents.org.uk.

See Chapter 9 for more tips about using technology.

Other great tools to have on hand

Classrooms in which multisensory learning really rocks have shelves full of things for children to manipulate and make discoveries with. This active learning indirectly boosts your child with dyslexia's reading by developing his handwriting muscles (writing makes him think about building words) and encouraging him to be inquisitive. Later, when you show him that reading's a discovery process (what sounds can these letters make?), he's already comfortable with problem solving. The following items all help your child develop the dexterity and thinking skills that stand him in good stead for reading:

✔ Bags of buttons

✔ Blocks and construction sticks

✔ Brushes and paints

✔ Buckets of beads and thread

✔ Clothes pegs and rope to put them on

✔ Dolls and puppets

✔ Jigsaw puzzles

✔ Oversized sewing kits

✔ Paper, scissors, glue and lolly sticks

✔ Plastic building bricks

✔ Playing cards and commercial word games

✔ Rock collections

✔ Shoeboxes full of cut-up sentences in envelopes

✔ Trains, cars and model towns

These kinds of kits are fun, and you may say that multisensory learning's as much about fun as about getting the full complement of seeing, hearing, saying and doing. Gather interesting items that your child can sort through, construct or create with, and you can be a multisensory mogul without even realising!

Older kids don't want to use the same materials as little kids, of course, but they aren't as different as you may think! If you present a doll to older kids and call it the mascot in a quiz game, they love the doll. If you make a competition of building things out of modelling clay, they roll up their sleeves. They can have hours of constructive fun with puppet shows. So don't rule out buttons, blocks and board games; instead, modify them according to who's getting in on the act.

Working Physical Activity into Your Child's Routine

When you do physical exercise, happy hormones (endorphins) race through your veins and make you feel great. Sure, you may take a while to push yourself into going for a walk (or to push yourself into last summer's shorts for that matter), but after you're moving, you feel good.

So you may not be surprised to hear that psychologists and educators recommend exercise for struggling readers and have evidence that children who get fresh air and do physical activities, like running and skating, focus better in class and read more books.

Children who engage in physical activity every day do better in reading and writing than kids who don't. Simple. You don't have a bunch of expensive sports teams to help your child get active, but you should at least throw a ball to him once in a while, take him to the playground often and fit some walking into your weekly schedule.

If you can manage to get active outdoors every day, that's a bonus. The great outdoors is a natural tranquilliser, and a good old-fashioned walk can help you and your child settle and focus on work afterwards. Natural light, fresh air and exercise make a great prelude to a reading session, especially if your child's restless or hyperactive.

Experimenting with Alternative Multisensory Methods

Some ideas that are a far cry from the usual catch on and eventually become popular. Here are a few such alternative ways to treat dyslexia. They all involve the senses, and we think they're pretty interesting.

You often see claims to cure or rapidly improve dyslexia, even though their originators have no valid evidence to support these claims. If the person making these claims cannot cite evidence or actual experience of a method working, be wary. Before you put your child through treatment or spend large sums of money, ask for advice from the British Dyslexia Association or other reputable, professional, non-profit organisations that keep abreast of the research. Go to Appendix B for contact info.

Colouring pages of text

Some children read a page of text better when you place a transparent coloured overlay over it. They say that the words look clearer and sometimes that they stop moving. You have to experiment with colours to see which one, if any, makes a difference.

Eye specialists warn that although children with dyslexia can benefit from using overlays, you're not treating the cause of dyslexia. Coloured overlays help with visual tracking problems, often called *eye wobble*, but not with the auditory processing problem that children with dyslexia have. (Other names you may hear for eye wobble are *visual stress* and *visual dyslexia*. Symptoms range from seeing letters move or fade to feeling nauseous and getting headaches when you look at words.)

To buy coloured overlays and read more about using them, check out these commercial websites:

- ✔ Crossbow Education (`www.crossboweducation.co.uk`)
- ✔ How to Learn (`www.howtolearn.com/filters.html`)
- ✔ Irlen Syndrome (`www.irlencentralengland.co.uk`)

Other ways to treat poor eye control are to wear eye patches or coloured glasses and/or do eye-tracking exercises (your head stays still but your eyes follow, or *track*, an object moving within your field of vision). Be sure to consult an eye specialist before embarking on any of these, though. The best age for eye-tracking exercises to work is up to age 8. Scientists in Britain say that children with dyslexia who wear a different-coloured contact lens in each of their eyes can read up to three times faster.

Reading a new font

A graphic designer with dyslexia has developed a new typeface called Read Regular that's being hailed as a breakthrough for children with dyslexia. What's special about Read Regular? The developer is dyslexic himself and he says that none of the letters can be inverted or mirrored to make another letter. Teachers in UK schools report that students in general prefer it, and students with dyslexia report that Read Regular allows them to read more quickly and that they no longer suffer from blurry vision and headaches. Chrysalis, a book publisher, has adopted Read Regular in some of its books but is still in the early days of production. You can find titles at `www.chrysalisbooks.co.uk` (click on Children's) and then buy the books at `www.amazon.co.uk`.

If you don't have access to the Read Regular typeface then use Arial or Comic Sans (at a minimum point size of 12) or others without *serifs* (the short decorative lines you see added to the tops and bottoms of traditional typefaces).

Listening to different messages in each ear

Children with dyslexia have difficulty hearing word parts, so plenty of manufacturers have designed listening products that they say (not surprisingly) give great results. The products typically include a set of earphones and do things like:

> ✔ Play music in one ear and instructions (like 'colour the ball') in the other.
>
> ✔ Play different music in each ear while your child works on a paper-and-pen task.
>
> ✔ Let your child play games that require him to match a different sound coming through each earphone to symbols on a screen.

The theory behind having your child receive a different message in each of his ears at the same time is that the right ear needs stimulating because it connects to the left hemisphere of the brain, which controls speaking, reading and writing. When the right ear becomes dominant, it gives the left hemisphere a great workout.

To read more about this technique, visit The Sounds of Wellness website at www.mozartcenter.com and Audiblox at www.audiblox2000.com/dyslexia_dyslexic/dyslexia.htm. Be aware, however, that these are commercial websites.

Eating fish

When Tracey was a child, her mother tried to persuade her to eat fish by telling her that it gives you brains. Well, don't you know, like so many old wives' tales this one turns out to be true. Some researchers are saying that many children with dyslexia are deficient in Omega-3 unsaturated fatty acids, which keep the brain cells, especially those involved in reading, healthy. Omega-3s come from fish oils, so to keep up your Omega-3s, eat oily fish (like salmon and sardines) or take fish-oil supplements.

Chapter 15

Handling Everyday Activities and Difficulties

*W*hen the average person hears the term 'dyslexia', he probably thinks of reversed letters, word blindness and sentences jiggling around on the page. Every child with dyslexia does indeed struggle with written print, but for many that's only the half of it.

In this chapter, we show you how dyslexia can be a whole lot more than jumbled words. We cover the importance of fostering a positive, independent attitude in your child, and we give you tips on how to help your child figure out space, time and sequence.

Routine and repetition go a long way to help your child with dyslexia succeed in life. To help her master skills and remember concepts, you need to give her every opportunity to practise. You need to present the same information to her often, in different guises. Doing so certainly takes patience and perseverance, but don't think the effort's all uphill. The biggest part of overcoming dyslexia is facing it head on and moving straight into action. After you realise that your child needs to do more of everything (so that she can hold on to the knowledge she's gained), you can both simply get on with it!

And when you're helping your child practise skills, remember to point out her strengths and interests. Otherwise, all that practice is like you're saying, 'You're weak at this, weak, weak, weak; oh and by the way, did I mention that you're weak?'

Talking Your Child into Feeling Good

You want your child with dyslexia to feel happy, confident and loved, no matter what, and ultimately you want her to have her own positive self-talk to rely on when you're not there. Your child needs to tell herself that she's okay, even though she has dyslexia, and that other people accept her – dyslexia and all. When she can 'wear' her dyslexia, explain it to other people and ask for help without embarrassment, she gets rid of a whole load of anxiety.

To that end, we give you some tips in the following sections on recognising your child's feelings, listening carefully to her, fostering her independence and handling her mistakes calmly.

Understanding your child's feelings

Dyslexia may affect your child's memory, ability to follow instructions and chances of getting where she's supposed to be going. With all this going on, not surprisingly she can sometimes feel scared and unhappy. Ask a child with dyslexia to explain her feelings and you hear things like this:

- ✔ I always knew I was different.
- ✔ I felt isolated and jealous. How come all the other children could easily do the things I struggled so hard with?
- ✔ I just couldn't get it, no matter how hard I tried. I was frustrated all the time.
- ✔ I couldn't find the words I wanted and knew I looked stupid because of it.
- ✔ I'd find myself at the cupboard not knowing what I'd gone there for.
- ✔ The teacher would ask me to do something, but I'd mix it up. I'd bring her a pen instead of a book or find myself wandering around school not knowing which class I should be in.
- ✔ I forgot people's names even when I'd known them for years. I knew I ought to know something that basic and felt so humiliated.
- ✔ I could never gauge what time it was and couldn't understand clocks.
- ✔ I was never sure if what I thought I heard someone say really was what she'd said.

And as if all this weren't bad enough, check out the kinds of things other people tell children with dyslexia about themselves:

- ✔ You're lazy.
- ✔ You don't want to learn.

- You never listen.
- Your writing's very babyish.
- Follow the words!
- Think!
- You need to try harder/listen better/concentrate more.
- You have to look for an easy job.
- You can't go to college.

Children with dyslexia take a lot of knocks. They can easily feel weird or below par, so a big part of parenting a child with dyslexia must be building, protecting and at times repairing her self-esteem. Your child can't move forward unless she feels valued and productive, so you have to step up your nurturing skills to meet her needs. Let her know you have a sympathetic ear. Help her figure out ways to deal with life's knocks. Then, when another child calls her thick, slow or stupid or when an adult calls her lazy or distracted, she's ready to tackle it.

Listening carefully

Most people think of themselves as pretty good listeners, but if you ask their friends and families, few of them really are (not that friends say this to your face, of course!).

You can do several things to be a better listener, and most of them don't come naturally, so you need to grasp them first. If you follow the tips in this section, you can improve your chances of steering your child towards confiding in you. When she does, you become a bigger part of her life and, especially as she gets older, you're better equipped to help her with any trouble she gets into. As a nice spin-off, you get to be a better friend, teacher and all-round parent too.

Just reading these tips and nodding sagely doesn't do you any good. You have to make a conscious decision that your listening skills need an overhaul. Then, the next time your child (or father, friend or workmate) talks to you, try out these tips. And keep trying them!

- **Listen *much* more than you talk.** Your child really doesn't want your opinion unless she asks for it. She wants you to hear her. Resist the temptation to butt in. Pauses are fine. Let her sort through her thoughts and put them out there, in her own way and time.

- **Don't judge.** Resist the urge to say things like 'You did *what?*' or 'That was silly of you' or '*Why* did you do that?' Instead (if you think you need to say anything at all), say things like 'That must've been hard' or 'That must've felt bad'. You're encouraging your child to open up to you. If you judge her, she just stops talking and makes a mental note not to confide in you again.

✔ **Encourage more conversation.** Help your child go into more detail by paraphrasing (saying back to her) what she says. For example, if she says 'The teacher said I was silly and disruptive in front of the whole class and Jade laughed at me', respond with something like 'She said that?' or 'She told the whole class?'

Don't try to clarify what your child says by asking her probing questions like 'How do you know Jade was laughing at you?' or 'Did the teacher use the word *silly*?' Your child then gets annoyed at your interference!

✔ **Let your child do her own problem solving.** Most of the time she can come up with her own problem-busting strategies. She knows better than you how 'kid world' works and feels more capable when she sees that she has control and choices. Most fears come from a feeling of no control, so you don't do your child any favours by always ruling over her.

Big kids are, of course, more able to solve their own problems than little kids, but even your little child can think stuff through if you give her just a little prompting and probing. Say things like 'Can you think of anything you can do to solve the problem?', 'What kinds of things help you out in class?' or 'I expect you have a few ideas of how you can fix this problem'.

✔ **Try to keep your child talking for ten minutes.** When your child feels really down, ten minutes of talking works wonders. After this time her spirits lift a little, her mind clears and she's over the worst.

✔ **Follow up with an action.** When you end your conversation, steer your child into saying what she's planning to do next. 'Do you feel like having a hot chocolate?' or 'What do you want to do now – maybe a soak in the bath?'

If you're thinking that your child just isn't the talking type, you may want to polish your football skills. When you simply hang out with your child, having a kickabout and shooting at goal, or doing whatever else your child likes, you provide just as much therapy as you do when you have a heart-to-heart chat with a more conversational child. As with everything else about having dyslexia, communication preferences are personal, different for each child.

Empowering your child

One of Tracey's kids is a born worrier. She worries about making friends, hanging onto them, going to the dentist, going anywhere new and, of course, whether this pair of trousers goes with that jumper. Because Tracey isn't blessed with vast reserves of patience, this sends her into near paroxysms.

She wants her child to make instant friends with everyone, deal stoically with the dentist and wear – along with a great big radiant smile – whatever clothes she can put on quickest.

As you can imagine, Tracey has had to curb some pretty unattractive impulses and instead train herself to tell her child that she's okay and that she has some control over what happens to her. At some point your child with dyslexia needs you to do the same. Here are tips from experts:

✔ Help your child solve her own problems. Instead of providing her with answers (assuming you have any!), help her come up with her own. She often knows more about school problems than you do, and besides, her own solutions are more meaningful to her than any you give her. Your 'answer' may be exactly what your child doesn't want. For example, you may want to march to school with a complaint about another child, but your child may want to keep a low profile. She may simply want to offload to you, knowing that soon her disagreement may resolve itself.

✔ Work hard at being a receptive listener so that your child comes to you with her problems. Take care not to interrupt her or make judgements. Instead, just listen (take a look at 'Listening carefully', earlier in this chapter, for some tips) and pass the odd comment like 'That must've felt bad'. The simple relief of offloading to you may be all the solution your child needs.

✔ Help your child role-play behaviours like listening, smiling and making positive comments that can help her make and keep friends. If your child has trouble making friends, she doesn't want you pointing the fact out. She knows what's happening and feels embarrassed if you put a spotlight on it. Help her practise positive behaviours *without* giving the message that she's doing everything wrong. Good luck!

✔ Without making her feel responsible for her problems, help her get out of unhelpful habits like not sharing, not speaking up for herself or wearing a permanent scowl. Notice her every time she does good things, like sharing and speaking up, and say things like 'You look great when you smile'.

✔ Help your child explain herself. She needs to ask for help in class, and outside class she needs a standard line for explaining (to friends) any difficulties she has.

✔ Have your child do a lot of activities outside school. Sports and social clubs are great, but doing fun activities with the family builds her confidence too.

✔ Encourage your child to have friends round to play. Make your house a fun place for your child's friends to be.

✔ Help your child deal with bullying. If your child complains of being bullied, simply saying 'Stand up for yourself' is bad advice. Get good advice from your child's form teacher and check out Childline (www.child line.org.uk), one of the clearest and most straightforward sites on bullying. Childline's helpline number is 0800 1111. You may want to let your child see this crisis number too. Even if you're the best parent in the world, older kids often prefer talking to a stranger.

Responding calmly to your child's mistakes

Everyone makes mistakes, but when your child has hardly any sense of space and time and usually can't follow a string of directions – all of which we talk more about in the next section – she makes more. Parents should handle the mistakes that a child with dyslexia makes as calmly as possible because a stirred-up child feels agitated, angry or nervous, none of which helps her fix her mistakes. Try the following tips:

- Most of the time when you talk to your child, you need to phrase your comments in personal terms, such as 'You did a good job' or 'I want you to come here now'. When you're bringing up a potentially sticky issue, however, such as 'You didn't clean your room', you're best not to be personal. Instead, focus on the task. Talk about what you want and not what your child has or hasn't done. That way you don't end up criticising and probably waging war with her.

- Before giving your child important directions, make sure that you have her full attention. She should be looking at you, and ideally, you should talk to her away from distractions like TV and noisy siblings.

- Phrase directions in short, clear sentences. Having your child repeat them back to you can be helpful, just to be sure she understands and has sequential points in the right order.

- Use precise wording. Instead of telling your child to do her homework, tell her to sit at the table after her snack and stay there until she's finished every piece of homework. You may want to specify whether she can get her own drinks or more snacks or whether she must stay put until you call her for breaks.

- Be on hand to help your child with homework and let her know you're there for her if she needs someone to explain what she has to do.

- Create ways for your child to lend you a hand so that she can feel valued and successful. Be very careful, though, to have realistic expectations of what she can achieve; otherwise your best intentions can backfire. You certainly don't want to end up saying things like 'Not *that* way!', 'Why didn't you ask me?' and 'I only asked you to do one simple thing!'

Table 15-1 shows you the kind of positive talk that children with dyslexia say makes all the difference. You already talk sweetly to your child most of the time. However, when you lapse into moaning and criticising because you're tired, hungry or just plain grouchy for no good reason, you may need a reminder!

Table 15-1	Talking Sweetly
Talk That Damages	*Talk That Moves a Child Forward*
You didn't post my letter. What's the matter with you?	Go to the postbox first and then to the shops. The postbox and then the shops. Tell me what you do?
Left, I said left!	Your watch is on your left wrist. If you look at it, you know which way's left.
This isn't the tea we buy!	Look for the box that has a red rose on it.
Why are your socks in the bottom drawer?	Socks go in the drawer with the sock sticker on it.
Look at this mess. I told you to clean up!	Time to clean up now.
Where's your homework? How come you think watching TV's okay?	You must do your homework before you watch TV.

If you want to read a whole book about refining the way you talk to your child, check out *How to Talk So Kids Will Listen and Listen So Kids Will Talk* by Adele Faber and Elaine Mazlish, published by Piccadilly Press. This is particularly great for parents of children with dyslexia because you get clear, explicit phrases (just the kind your child appreciates) to try out.

Helping Your Child with Space, Time and Sequence

Besides struggling with reading and writing, some children with dyslexia may face difficulties that fall into these three categories:

- Space
- Time
- Sequence

Your child with dyslexia may struggle in any or all of these categories, in big or small ways. Dyslexia's different for each child, and that's why it's such an interesting and often contentious disability.

Children with dyslexia are often said to have strengths in spatial and mechanical skills, and that's why we stress that only *some* children with dyslexia struggle in these areas. Tracey has one friend with dyslexia who's 100 per cent reliable at getting things done (she has no trouble with strings of instructions) and has an amazing sense of direction.

In the following sections, we provide tips on helping your child figure out space, time and sequence in fun and easy ways.

In this chapter we discuss space, time and sequence as difficulties apart from reading and writing because we talk a lot about reading and writing in other chapters. However, all the home-based activities here still offer wonderful opportunities for you to build your child's language and early literacy skills – and organisational skills too.

Spacing out

A child with dyslexia can have trouble telling left from right, up from down, and front from back. But that's not where the space thing ends. She may also struggle with hand–eye coordination and be unable to do things like draw a straight line or copy text and pictures accurately. The next sections explain more of the practical problems your child may face and what you can do about them.

Telling the difference between left and right

When Tracey was a child, she wrote an *L* on the back of her left hand and an *R* on her right. She replenished the ink a few times and by then she knew to do without; left and right became second nature.

With a child with dyslexia, things are very different, however. Left and right can stymie her for weeks or forever because she just can't recall which word (left or right) is the one to use. She needs things on which to hook the concept of left and right.

One item that parents use to help their children get to grips with left and right is a watch. The watch kills two birds with one stone because your child can look at it to be reminded which ways the numbers face and know that it normally sits on her left arm. Want to go left? That's your watch arm. (Check out 'Timing is everything', later in this chapter, for details on helping your child figure out time.)

Older children can remember left from right by recalling which hand they write with. If you put your left hand out, the thumb and first finger make the *L* shape if your stretch out your thumb. The advantage of this method is that they always have their hands with them (and there's no frantic searching for watches left in lockers!).

To help your child get into the watch habit, play left-and-right games. Have your child move toy trucks along carpet roads and find treats you hide on the left or right side of rooms.

Distinguishing between under and over and other spatial terms

Your child with dyslexia struggles to recall the names of familiar things, and when choosing the right word from a bunch of conceptually similar words, like under and over or before and behind, she may struggle even more.

A good way to help your child with the concepts of in and out, under and over and top and bottom is to team up for some routine activities around the house. First, head to the kitchen, where your child can put the eggs *in* the bowl, flip the pancake *over* and pour *on* the syrup. To work off the calories, head outside with a ball. Throw it *into* a hoop, roll it *under* a swing and lob it *over* a trampoline. When you're back indoors, build cardboard-box forts and plastic-brick towns and move figures *in* and *out* of rooms.

Navigating new places

Because left and right and other directional concepts may get into a muddle in the mind of your child with dyslexia, getting to new places may be a life-long hurdle for her. Even adults with dyslexia often report that they're afraid of going to unknown locations. They worry that they may never get back out.

When your child starts a new school, you need to help her navigate her way around it. Explain your situation to the form teacher or head, and plan a few visits to help familiarise your child with the school layout. For older kids pocket maps are helpful, but before your child tucks a map into her pocket, you need to show her how to visualise herself on the map and use landmarks, like the office, the library, the cafeteria or the big art mural in the hall, for gathering directional facts. For example, she can remember that her locker's opposite the library. The more your child uses this technique of taking mental snapshots, the more she can use it in places beyond school.

If your child with dyslexia's very visual, she may want to take photos of these landmarks (her locker or classroom) from a distance so that she can refer to them in the same way a hiker refers to mental images of landmarks he passes in order to find his way back.

Putting everything in its place

Remembering what goes where can be a big problem for your child with dyslexia. She may wear mittens on the wrong hands, shoes on the wrong feet and jumpers backwards. Her book may turn up in the tool shed, her lunchbox may disappear altogether and her pens may make an appearance just about everywhere.

One thing that children and adults with dyslexia all agree on is that lists of what you need and colour-coded boxes for storing things in make life easier. Try these tips for getting as close as possible to having a place for everything and everything in its place:

✔ Assign each child a different colour for identifying her belongings (your towel, flask and lunchbox are blue, and your sister's are red).

✔ Use colours to label things like subject-specific files and books. Use pictures (rather than words) to label boxes of toys.

✔ To keep your child wearing clothes facing the way they should, have her look for labels on the back of garments or pictures on the front.

✔ Mark the inside soles of each of your child's shoes with a dot at the inside edge (the edge that touches the other shoe). Dots go together. (See the nearby sidebar, 'Putting the shoe on the right foot'.)

✔ Establish a set-in-stone morning routine! For example, wash and get dressed before eating breakfast.

✔ Make wall charts with pictures that show the sequence of a routine. This way, on Monday she can look at it and see the picture of PE on Tuesday's space and know she has to pack her PE bag, for example.

✔ Have your child do a check before she leaves in the morning. Is she clean? Does she have her lunchbox, books and shoes? She can touch each item to be sure she has it. (Alternatively, she can give you the 'duh' treatment and bolt out with last night's pizza stuck to her face and her sports kit sitting on the hall table.)

Classifying stuff helps your child sort out all the information her eyes and ears bring her. Have her categorise and classify objects at home as much as you can: by type, colour, texture, number, size and so on. You can do this with groceries, items in the cupboard or wardrobe or pebbles at the beach (if you're lucky enough to get to hit the waves). At school, she can put her classification know-how to good use on disorganised desks and fully loaded lockers.

Boosting hand–eye coordination during play

When your child starts school, she uses a lot of fine motor skills that require good hand–eye coordination. Every day she manipulates blocks, beads and other small things, and steers her pen and scissors along lines and curves. Strong hand–eye coordination doesn't come easily to children with dyslexia, so prepare her by having crafts and toys in your house and making sure that she uses them. Get into the action with her. Keep pens, tape, scissors, building blocks and Barbie out so that you can construct, play and watch TV at the same time. If you can, have one parent cook dinner while the other one updates Barbie's spring outfit.

Ever heard the saying 'You can't make an omelette without breaking eggs'? Try to apply it to your child's play. If she builds a Barbie village and tapes half your Tupperware together to do it, look past the mess. The cutting, taping and general fiddling she does builds strength and coordination in her fingers. And we haven't even started on the tremendous brain value of creative play! (We go into full detail in Chapter 14.)

Putting the shoe on the right foot

In most households, mornings are chaotic enough without having to worry about your child putting her shoes on the right feet with the laces properly tied. To ease the morning madness, here are a few shoe-taming tips:

✔ Have little kids wear Velcro shoe straps!

✔ Teach your child to make two loops and then knot them (rather than going through the alternative right-over-left-and-under routine).

✔ Draw things on the inner sole of each shoe, up against the edge that touches the partner shoe. Put lips to kiss each other or, for older kids, tiny dots, so that your child knows to join them together.

✔ Put different-coloured laces in your child's shoes. Have the left lace match the colour of her watch (worn on the left wrist).

Copying print and pictures

Copying's very hard for a child with dyslexia because when her eyes leave the page, her brain doesn't seem to hold onto the mental image of what she just saw. Your child with dyslexia may always have trouble copying things from a blackboard (or from any other place, for that matter), so you need to help her in two ways:

✔ First, stick with a routine of helping her read so that she can identify the words on the board, which we talk about more in Chapter 13.

✔ Second, ask her teacher to take her difficulties into consideration and make simple accommodations for her, such as having her copy only key words. We talk more about classroom accommodations in Chapter 10.

The following suggestions can help your child keep her writing level and centred when she's copying:

✔ Tape her page to the desk (positioned at a comfortable angle).

✔ Put a strip of tape at the bottom of the page to remind her to end there.

✔ Put a pencil grip on her pencil.

✔ Put an elastic band above the bare wood part of her pencil to remind her to grip above it.

✔ Remind her to leave a finger's width of space between words.

✔ Have her use lined paper so that she knows to write on the lines.

At about Year 2, handwriting becomes a big issue at school. Your child is asked to practise and practise her handwriting – and then practise some more. The only trouble is that she may never develop a neat hand or win a penmanship award. See your child's teacher and ask for her consideration. Explain that you want to ensure that your child doesn't start to dislike school totally simply for the sake of a skill that she can never really master and that isn't, in the big picture, worth hammering at – especially if her writing is legible.

Not taking points off for penmanship is an accommodation you can request for your child and add to her Individual Education Plan (IEP). We explain IEPs in Chapter 8.

Timing is everything

Your child with dyslexia may have trouble figuring out months of the year, days of the week and what time of day it is because she can't match the word (even if she can recall it) to the right concept. Even if you tell her, for example, that yesterday was Monday, she may not be able immediately to work out that today's Tuesday. She may also struggle to put personal stories into a time frame. For example, she may not know whether Fred lived in his house years ago, a little while ago or still lives there today. In the next sections, we talk about big time – years, months and weeks – and smaller time – days and hours – and how to give your child a lot of practice with each.

Reading routinely to your child offers the opportunity to address space, time and sequence difficulties (like when Fred lived in his house). See Chapter 13 for more info on reading with your child.

Understanding a calendar

To give weeks and months meaning for your child, you need to pin her personal information to them. Have your child make a calendar. Most computers have calendar software, so help her plot birthdays and school breaks on the months, print them out and staple them together. Block out school times in one colour and evenings and weekends in another. Have your child cross off the days as they pass. And why stop there? Your child may love finding out about the solar system and how days and years are measured by it. You can add as much detail as you like, with pictures to make it more fun.

Whatever you do to fix calendar information in your child's mind, the key is to personalise and attach physical action to it.

Reading a clock

Whenever you can, have your child do hands-on activities to get to grips with things. Telling the time lends itself nicely to hands-on discovery because you can use all kinds of timers to get your point across.

Digital clocks make life easy, but your child still needs to understand analogue clocks. Make or buy a clock for her to play with and explain how each hand on the clock works by itself. The little hand's pretty much the boss because it tells you the hour, but it has to keep a check on what the big hand's doing (so it can gauge its own slower movement). A handy rhyme for remembering which hand tells minutes and which tells the hour is 'The little hand has all the power, it's the one that tells the hour'.

Try out these progressive activities to help your child tell the time:

- **Counting by 'One Mississippi':** When you say 'Mississippi' after saying each number up to 60 (like 'one Mississippi, two Mississippi, three Mississippi . . .'), you count an accurate minute. Explain to your child that a minute contains 60 seconds and that 'one Mississippi' is a second while 60 of them get you to a minute. Then have her practise. Ask her if she can hold her breath for a minute, guess how long a minute is (by doing the Mississippi counting to herself) or do press-ups for a whole minute. After that, you're ready to help her grasp the idea of intervals of five minutes.

- **Using an egg timer:** You can *still* find old-fashioned egg timers – the kind with real sand. (A lot of children's games include old-fashioned timers.) A sand-filled timer's great to play with, and if you're really smart you can make your own version (rice in two taped-together plastic bottles). Cook up some eggs (three minutes for soft-boiled, five for hard-boiled!), let your child get used to waiting for five minutes, and then show her what five minutes looks like on an analogue clock.

- **Counting in the kitchen:** After your child knows how long 5 minutes is, she needs to experience 15 , 30 and 60 minute intervals. A nice way for her to do this is to roll up her sleeves and head to the kitchen. Help her rustle up some muffins or pizza and, in the process, use your oven timer. For fun, you can both try guessing the time without using a timer – so long as you don't burn the cakes!

Telling time is a complicated skill that requires your child to know other things too. For example, she needs to know how to multiply by 5 and how to tell minutes past and minutes before the hour. Provide your child with plenty of opportunity to practise and ask her to repeat explanations back to you. She can find her own way to gather and organise her thoughts if you give her the chance.

Teach your child one concept at a time. Begin with the role of the little hand on an analogue clock. Have your child move the little hand and tell you the hour time as she does it. Do a lot of this before adding a new concept. When your child's comfortable with 'o'clock time' (one o'clock, two o'clock, three o'clock), coach her on how to multiply by 5, and explain how that ties in with how the big hand moves. Later, when she's secure with that concept, you can follow the hour with half an hour and quarter of an hour.

Following a sequence

Children with dyslexia often have trouble expressing *linear thoughts* (this, then that then the next thing), following someone else's line of conversation and remembering things such as telephone numbers and lists of instructions. Remembering strings of numbers and instructions is a skill, called a *short-term memory skill*, that's often used in assessments of dyslexia.

If you know that your child has trouble remembering several things in sequence, help her by breaking the sequence into small steps. Tell her just one or two steps at a time and add more only when you're sure she completely understands them.

The fancy name that psychologists use to describe the way you can break tasks into small sequential steps is *task analysis.* Good teachers do task analysis naturally. They start at the beginning, work steadily forward and have classrooms full of kids who know exactly what's going on!

Task analysis and sequence may sound easy, but in practice not all teachers achieve that state of grace. To be effective in explaining any given task sequence to a child with dyslexia, try the following:

- ✔ Make an analogy or comparison that relates what you're introducing to your child to something she already knows. For example, when you show your child a compass for the first time, you can start by saying: 'Does this look a bit like something you already know?'

- ✔ Point out large features of a new concept before homing in on the specifics. For example, ask your child: 'A compass fits in your hand and has a pointer like a watch does. Can you ever tell the time with it?'

- ✔ Ask your child to make guesses about a new concept and tell you anything she already knows. For example, 'If this compass doesn't tell you the time, what do you think it *does* tell you?'

- ✔ Explain the specifics you're leading up to, in small bites. For example, 'The compass has four main points. Can you see them?'

Asking your child broad questions, having her compare new information to what she already knows and making her take guesses engages her with the task. She becomes an active learner. When she tries doing the task for herself, keep this active learning in motion by stepping back and allowing her to learn by trial and error. She gets more confident and independent if you step in to correct her only when she can't move forward without your interruption. Reminding yourself to stop talking and step back is an excellent teaching strategy!

Doing something's better than just talking about it. You need to show and tell rather than merely tell. The story in the nearby sidebar, 'Getting comfortable with a compass', shows (hopefully) the importance of both task analysis and modelling a skill for your child.

Getting comfortable with a compass

Tracey once went on an outdoor education course for scout leaders. Along with all the other parents who came, she got to do a lot of hands-on things and was fed good barbecued food too. The trainers really knew their stuff.

One of the skills everyone gained that day was teaching children to use a compass. The trainers got right into the role, teaching the leaders as if they were the children they would soon be showing this skill to. They walked the leaders through the ins and outs of compasses and, taking one step at a time, everyone got the hang of it.

When it was time to practise what they'd learned, the trainers put the new leaders into pairs. One person in each pair was to act the part of a child and the other was to be the parent. Tracey offered to play the child's role and, without preliminaries, her partner said, 'You look at 120 degrees and you face that way.'

Tracey and her partner had heard and experienced the right way to introduce a compass, but even so, Tracey's partner launched straight into what should have been the last part of the

learning sequence. Her partner just wasn't used to teaching. Unless you have experience, you tend to launch into the end stage of a whole sequence of instructions. You don't break up your task. You don't start at the beginning.

Instead, Tracey's partner should have started with something like this:

'This is a compass. You use a compass for finding your way around. It looks a bit like other things you see, like a stopwatch, but it doesn't tell any sort of time; it's only for finding your way around. The way it helps you to find your way around is by showing you the four direction points. Do you see N on your compass? What does it mean? Can everyone see it? (Help the person next to you if she can't see it.) Very good. Now, what's the right way to hold the compass?'

This is how task analysis works. You teach one concept at a time, building from simple to harder and letting your child practise at each stage. Help your child takes things step by step like this, with plenty of practice, and she doesn't become lost or disheartened.

Maintaining Harmony in Your Home

Dyslexia exerts its influence beyond the classroom. While your child's core problem's with reading and writing, her dyslexia affects her whole self-concept and this, together with her academic struggles, affects your whole household. You may worry about her sadness and frustration and tread warily, trying not to upset her. You may over-protect her or expect too much of her. Brothers and sisters may resent the extra time you spend with your child with dyslexia, and she in turn may resent the greater freedom they have or the fact that younger siblings outperform her academically. With a child with dyslexia in your household, you can easily find yourself managing a big, hot, volatile boiling pot. In the following sections we give you tips for keeping the temperature down and avoiding spills.

Sharing the load

Shared chores and responsibilities help households run more smoothly. You need to include your child with dyslexia in your household's duty roster. However, to avoid misunderstandings or mistakes, select her responsibilities wisely from the outset. She probably isn't the best candidate for remembering to put out the rubbish, but walking the dog (who makes his presence known) may be a much better choice. Of course, your children all get plenty of homework and probably fit sports into their evening too, so you want to make sure that chores are helpful and not more trouble than they're really worth. Small responsibilities, like loading the dishwasher, tidying up the pile of shoes by the back door and setting and clearing the table, are enough to give children with dyslexia and non-dyslexic children alike a sense of responsibility.

Toeing the line

Disciplining a child with dyslexia can be a bit different from disciplining other children because your child with dyslexia may do things that appear intentional when in fact they're not. To help you distinguish between genuine infractions and forgetfulness or distractedness, and choose a measured rather than impulsive response, here are some behaviour-management guidelines:

- ✔ Your child with dyslexia easily forgets instructions, misunderstands instructions or understands them but gets them in the wrong order. You need to be quite sure that she hears what you say and understands your meaning before relying on her to carry through.

- ✔ Punishing your child with dyslexia can make her feel resentful or humiliated. Repeated punishments can desensitise her and make her wonder why she should bother being good anyway because she can't see beyond the here and now of the punishment. The best response to misdemeanours is to find ways for your child to make up for them. If she breaks or loses something, she can do an extra chore to pay for it. If she needs to make up homework that she failed to do earlier, she can forgo her TV time to do it. If she fails an assignment because she lost her book, she can spend an hour organising her room so she's less likely to repeat the same mistake any time soon.

- ✔ Your child with dyslexia already has a fragile ego because her dyslexia keeps her from being an academic high flyer. Your understanding can help her pass through bad times. If she yells and cries for seemingly small reasons, there are underlying bigger ones. Stay calm, encourage your child to talk about her anger and then refocus and get active on other things.

- ✔ An immediate response to your child with dyslexia's behaviour is the best approach. If your child does something out of line, ask her right away what's going on. Is she aware of how her behaviour seems to you?

What's her line of thought? If you save your response for later, your child may not remember the incident in question. If you say something like 'You can't go to the cinema on Friday', by the time Friday comes you may both see the incident in a less harsh light, and besides, your child may stew on it in the interim period. She may get more and more resentful, so now you have another situation on your hands.

✔ Your responses to misdemeanours should be firm and consistent but manageable. Clearly and calmly tell your child with dyslexia why her behaviour's unhelpful. Tell her what your response is. Make your consequences small and helpful ('Instead of watching TV tonight you must tidy your room'), not big and reactionary ('No TV for a month!').

✔ Give your child consequences only when you feel calm and with the intention of solving the problem, not blaming the child.

Strengthening bonds between siblings

Other people in your child's life may come and go but siblings are forever. So they'd better get used to the idea and start being nice to each other!

Here are some strategies that psychologists recommend for helping your children talk respectfully to one another, willingly share their stuff and refrain from the theft of socks, friends and best ideas. Dyslexia-specific tips are peppered throughout.

✔ Make sure that everyone in your family understands what dyslexia is and that your child with dyslexia needs enabling rather than protecting.

✔ Explain to your other children why your child with dyslexia needs extra help with academic matters and that all your children get the help they need rather than an exactly equal share of all things, including your time. Be sure to explain that the amount of time you give to your children is not a measure of how much you love each one but a response to need. So that your non-dyslexic child doesn't feel resentful, make sure that you give her plenty of attention when you can. Giving all your children a few minutes of your undivided time for talk and hugs at bedtime can be a great way to help each one feel noticed and valued.

✔ In sports and family events in which the difficulties of your child with dyslexia make little or no difference, treat your children the same.

✔ Listen to your children. You can dissolve a child's jealousy and resentment by hearing her out. Let her say how she feels, even if that includes hate, so that she can vent and move on. Resist the urge to say things like 'You really don't feel that way' or 'You shouldn't say things like that', because then your child bottles up those (natural) feelings and they may grow. The adage 'Better out than in' is really what this kind of non-judgemental listening is all about.

Part V
Moving Beyond the Childhood Years

'When I took you on as an apprentice,
you didn't tell me you are dyslexic.'

In this part . . .

Teenagers, students and adults with dyslexia have such a need for information on the special challenges they face that people write whole books for them.

In this part, you get all that information condensed into practical essentials. You get friendly guidance for tiptoeing through your child's teenage years, solid advice for helping him walk confidently through college applications and an inside tour of college itself. Also, we provide sensible information and timesaving tips for adults with dyslexia in the real world.

Chapter 16

Assisting Teenagers with Dyslexia

In This Chapter

▶ Building your teenager's life skills

▶ Helping your teenager handle schoolwork on his own

▶ Strengthening your teenager's work skills

Katrina's son is about to become a teenager, and she's edgy. At any time, she may make a remark that her almost-teenager interprets as teasing or an outright insult. There may be tears, breakages and language that's not very nice at all – and her son can get pretty upset too. But you didn't buy this book to read about teenager-raising traumas, so in this chapter we let you off that particular hook and instead get right down to teenage problems that have dyslexia at their heart.

Teenagers with dyslexia have more self-esteem issues than other teenagers do; they have to know how to speak out about difficulties they prefer to hide (so that they receive help); and on top of that, they have to work even harder at school than regular overloaded secondary school students do. In this chapter, you find out about these and other issues facing teenagers with dyslexia.

Instilling New Life Skills

Your teenager's surging bumpily forward into adulthood. He's learning a mountain of new things fast (like how to speak in monosyllables and grunts and buy trainers that look like the rest but cost three times as much). And he can make you feel like you're the only one who doesn't understand. Much as we sympathise, we leave all that in your capable hands and confine the next few sections to the big, dyslexia-related questions that relate to new life skills. How can you help your self-conscious teenager with dyslexia feel good when his dyslexia makes him look 'stupid'? How can you persuade him to become more independent? And when he feels good, dyslexia and all, where can you hide your car keys?

Aiming for high self-esteem

Poor self-confidence blocks your child's learning. Yes, you've heard that to death, so we don't dwell long on this topic. The following list is a lightning review of things you need to bear in mind when you can't see the nice child behind the surly teenager and you feel like throttling or at least avoiding him. He could tell you these dozen things if only his teenage bravado and paralysing self-consciousness loosened their grip:

- ✔ I can figure out problems in my own way if I have enough time.

- ✔ I have my own system for keeping track of school stuff. (Please don't move my things.)

- ✔ I don't deliberately do things wrong or miss doing them altogether. I just forget and get muddled.

- ✔ I get frustrated. I wish I could do things perfectly, and when I can't, I don't want to do them at all.

- ✔ I try to listen when you talk, but things (like small noises and background TV) distract me. (If you have something important to tell me, please choose a quiet time and write me lists.)

- ✔ When my work looks all over the place, remember that I put in twice as much time and effort as everyone else (even when you don't see it).

- ✔ If I mess up, I need you to give me a gentle hint. (Please don't call me lazy or lose your temper with me.)

- ✔ When you see me acting tough, it's a fair bet that I still feel stupid inside.

- ✔ Making friends is hard enough for me, so please try not to dismiss out of hand the ones I have.

- ✔ Telling me how other people do things doesn't help me. It makes me feel that you don't like me for who I really am and that you secretly wish I were them.

- ✔ I have a sense of humour, and it helps me when we joke good-naturedly about my mistakes and clangers.

- ✔ I really, really want to please you.

So how can you build up the self-esteem in your teenager with dyslexia? The following strategies can work wonders:

- ✔ Keep a positive and respectful tone with him that tells him that he determines his own progress and development (but that you can help out too).

- ✔ Have him tutored and help him learn labour-saving strategies like efficient note taking so that he keeps up in class. See 'Taking notes', later in this chapter, for more information.

✔ Help him keep abreast of technology that may assist him. He's probably just as informed as you about gadgets (and maybe more!), but you can at least check out dyslexia websites to see what's new in the way of devices like handheld spell checkers and speech-to-text software. Chapter 9 has additional information on technology.

✔ Help him feel more independent by making him responsible for certain chores (within reasonable limits, given that he gets a lot of homework) and encourage him to belong to clubs. See the next section 'Fostering more independence at home' for details.

✔ Work in time for sports, music and other non-academic pleasures (see 'Making time for rest and play', later in this chapter).

✔ Maintain your own social life and outside interests so that he has a good role model.

Fostering more independence at home

A few years ago, Tracey's morning routine included following her kids around the house screaming things like 'Have you brushed your teeth?' and 'Is your bag packed?' (Sound familiar?) Then she read a magazine article that advised pulling yourself together. 'Just tell your children, calmly, what time it is,' the article said. So she did. Now she yells out only digits and chiefly from the kitchen.

Most self-respecting teenagers have enough sluggishness and obstinacy in them to wear down the perkiest of parents. They can make enslaving yourself to them seem like a good idea at the time, and that's bad. Your teenager must be responsible for getting to places on time and for pouring the milk on his own cereal.

The more responsibility you give your teenager, the more chance he has to rise to the occasion. Ask him to help you out with household tasks, like lawn mowing and taking out the rubbish. Allocate him his own chores and tell him what a weight he takes off your shoulders. Let him know that you need and value him so that he wants to please you by being reliable and thorough. When he feels proud of himself, he takes pride in the things he does and develops traits that stand him in good stead in the workplace (see 'Encouraging the Development of Work Skills', later in this chapter, for more details).

Every now and then, parents of capable teenagers lapse. They pick up their teenager's dirty laundry, remind him to brush his teeth and race to school with the lunch he forgot. That's okay; parenting tends to be like that. You can't help overindulging your kids occasionally, but you may want to make a conscious note to get serious next time. Allowing a teenager to be overly dependent on you doesn't help him in the long run because he stops trying to do stuff for himself.

Making time for rest and play

Teenagers do a lot of growing and that, along with all the preening and worrying they do (chiefly about who's looking or not looking at them), can sap their energy. Add to this the burden of having to reread everything, listen harder to everything and refer to a spell checker pretty constantly, and you can easily see why you need to make sure that your teenager with dyslexia doesn't burn too much midnight oil. He actually needs about nine-and-a-half hours of sleep a night! And if you can see that he fits school sports or other types of exercise into his life too, so much the better. Physical activity helps him look and feel good, beat boredom before it takes hold and concentrate better back at his desk. (Chapter 14 has more info about the benefits of exercise for children with dyslexia.)

All work and no play can make Jack not only a dull boy but a sick one too. Studies show that school pressure and boredom (and interestingly, too much spending money!) are risk factors for stress, and stressed teenagers do more drinking, smoking and drug taking than those who are more relaxed.

Getting behind the driver's wheel

Taking a driving test can be nerve-wracking for anyone. If your teenager with dyslexia has trouble with left and right and isn't so great with hand–eye coordination either, he may be terrified. Here are some ways for you to help him:

✔ Help solve the left/right problem by using the terms 'driver's side' and 'passenger's side' instead. You can also try having him write the words on his hands or put stickers on the car windows. Use whatever trick works for your teenager!

✔ Make sure that your teenager takes plenty of practice written tests.

✔ Take your teenager out for plenty of practice driving.

✔ Enrol your teenager in driving lessons with an approved instructor.

The British Dyslexia Association website (www.bdadyslexia.org.uk) has excellent advice for the learner driver with dyslexia, including details of how to go about obtaining special arrangements such as extra time for the theory test.

Facing School Challenges Head-On

Your teenager has many school-related things to worry about now. Does he manage to hand his homework in on time? Has he chosen the right subjects? Does his hair spike up at just the right angle? You want him to worry enough that he's responsible, but not enough that you end up with a nervous wreck on your hands. In the next sections, we tell you how to help your teenager rise to new school challenges with a healthy balance of optimism and realism.

Moving towards self-reliance with schoolwork

When your child's in primary school, you pretty much organise everything for him. You anticipate his needs. You ask his teachers to make allowances for him. You make sure that he gets assessed and that his Individual Education Plan (IEP), if he has one, runs smoothly. (We talk more about IEPs in Chapter 8.)

When you have a teenager to care for, your role changes somewhat. You have to hand over some of the academic reins because your teenager must prepare for taking tests and doing assignments completely on his own eventually. And he needs to know his own needs, speak up for himself and speak up again if need be. Because he's self-conscious enough even before you take his dyslexia into account, he has quite a lot on his plate! What can you do to make the hand-over go well? Give your child frequent (and kind) reminders to do the following:

- ✔ Jot down to-do lists so that he stays organised.

- ✔ Pinpoint his practical needs ('It may take me an extra two days to do this assignment, and I should get the book on tape').

- ✔ Use all the available gizmos to help him read and write (for example spell checkers, laptops and speech-to-text software – see Chapter 9 for the scoop on using technology).

- ✔ Ask friends to help him in specific ways, like talking about assignments and deadlines.

- ✔ Practise describing his dyslexia so that he can easily and without embarrassment tell people that he's dyslexic.

- ✔ Remember that he isn't sponging off other people, causing a nuisance or being stupid. He's explaining himself and asking for reasonable consideration.

- ✔ Remember that if one person doesn't help him, someone else may. (Some people always understand him and other people just haven't had that much to do with people with dyslexia.) Remind him he may not always need to rely on other people. He is probably good at solving problems so speak to him about his concerns and find a solution that works for him together.

Ownership is key. If you do most of your child's school projects for him, he feels like a bad mark really isn't his responsibility. On the other hand, if you type exactly what he dictates to you and no more, you genuinely help and he feels in charge. The work is his alone: a reflection of himself.

Enforcing order on those files

When your child becomes a teenager, he must work out his own system for organising his schoolwork and change it if it doesn't work. For example, he can colour code his homework file and find all his rulers and pens for himself. He must do such tasks himself because any system he thinks up for himself is always more meaningful than a system that someone else gives him. You can lend a hand by doing things like buying storage baskets and other stationery, but make sure that he directs you or at least does most of the brainwork. For more info on managing homework, see Chapter 9.

And in case you think you don't have much to do, remember that you need a plan to ensure that your teenager stays organised, like linking funds to pay for his mobile phone top-ups to him keeping his desk tidy, in case things fall into disarray.

Staying on top of all the reading and writing

Dyslexia hits your child hardest when he's reading and writing. By the time your child reaches his teenage years, he's developed a lot of (hopefully good) coping mechanisms. Here are some strategies to help with reading and written projects:

✔ Have a quiet, properly equipped study area for your child to work in. It can include items such as a big working surface, pens, reference books, a computer and a printer.

✔ Plan out long-term assignments by setting interim deadlines on a calendar or in an assignment notebook.

✔ Ask for extra time from his class teachers to complete assignments.

✔ Read and reread all text. Talk about it with friends so that he's sure he's read it correctly and got the gist.

✔ Find his preferred way of taking notes (in class and as he reads homework assignments). We talk about this in the next section.

✔ Get curriculum books on tape from Listening Books (www.listening books.org.uk).

✔ Mark books and worksheets with highlighting markers or sticky notes to make key points prominent (but guard against marking just about the entire page!).

✔ He should type his assignments whenever possible to cut down the amount of handwriting he has to do. Check whether this is okay with all his teachers at the start of the year so that he doesn't have to ask about each assignment further down the track.

✔ Ask a friend to proofread his writing (handwritten and word processed).

✔ Use a spell checker on word-processed assignments.

✔ Use speech-to-text software for him to speak (not write) text into his computer, a graphic organiser to plan out assignments and any other technology that makes life easier for him.

A graphic organiser helps your child build flow charts and maps to represent information diagrammatically. You can download, for free, all sorts of pie charts, bar graphs and other diagrams at www.edhelper.com/ teachers/graphic_organizers.htm, or you can get software that enables your child to design his own creations. Check out the graphic organisers, Kidspiration and Inspiration (for Years 6–12 and older) at www.kidspiration.com or contact TAG Learning on 01474 537 887.

If you're lucky, your teenager's developed some good reading and writing strategies by now. So what strategies *aren't* productive?

✔ If your child denies having dyslexia or maybe isn't aware that his problems are dyslexia (see Chapter 3 for symptoms), that's not helpful. The sooner he can tag the word 'dyslexia' onto his problems, the sooner he can let out a sigh of relief and get on with asking for help. If you have a teenager who persistently denies the possibility that he has dyslexia, you can take action in a few ways:

  • You can ask him to check out information for teenagers about dyslexia on the web; one site to try is www.nhsdirect.nhs. uk and search on **dyslexia**. Another good site to look at is www. beingdyslexic.co.uk/information/home_education/ teenage_dyslexics.php, which offers information and guidance for teenagers with dyslexia.

  • For some teenagers a GP may help with a referral to organisations such as the CAMS Team (Child and Adolescent Mental Health Service) in your area.

  • You can decide to go along with your teenager because the stress of a prolonged argument may outweigh the potential benefits (especially if your child has only mild symptoms).

✔ If your child acts up in class or sinks into the background to avoid detection, that's not helpful. He needs reassurance that he's perfectly fine but has a problem *processing* (reading, writing, hearing and recalling) words. The problem's manageable, but he needs to know how to ask for help.

✔ If your child avoids reading and writing, he can't improve. You can help him read by doing paired reading with him (see Chapter 13). A computer and good keyboard skills go a long way towards making him a happy writer. For learn-to-type software, check out Easy Type Senior from DI Trading at www.dyslexiaaction.org.uk/store. (Chapter 9 has additional info on the use of technology.)

✔ If your child copies answers from other kids and so covers up his problems (children with dyslexia are masters of cover-up), he can't improve. He needs extra help, and you may want to get advice from his teacher about the best ways to provide it. (Chapter 10 has details on working productively with your child's teacher.)

✔ If your child isn't getting help with phonemic awareness and phonics, he can't improve. (*Phonemic awareness* is the awareness that words are made of sounds. *Phonics* is making sound–letter associations. Children with dyslexia learn to read best by being guided systematically through the alphabetic system – how single letters and clusters of letters represent sounds.) Arrange for a tutor and/or help your child yourself. In Chapter 12, we give you practical advice for helping your child with phonics at home.

Taking notes

Your secondary school pupil needs to know how to take great notes. He needs to find out what kind of note taking suits him and what he should and shouldn't be jotting down. In the following sections, we explore the whys, whats and hows of getting the main stuff down on paper and leaving out the frills.

Clarifying the importance of note taking

Your teenager needs to be especially good at taking notes for the following reasons:

✔ It encourages him to listen carefully and reinforces his understanding of the material.

✔ It forces him to identify key and secondary points.

✔ Personal notes are easier to remember than text.

✔ Writing important points down helps him remember them even before he studies them.

✔ Note-taking skills are important to master before heading to college or university.

Narrowing down essential points

Secondary school pupils often get obvious clues about what they should be jotting down. For example, teachers may give the following signs that something's important:

- Words they write on the board
- Words and concepts they repeat
- Concepts they emphasise by their tone or by the amount of time they spend on them
- Concepts they organise with 'clue' words such as 'first', 'second' and 'in conclusion'
- Overviews they give at the beginning of a lesson and summaries they give at the end

Try talking to the teachers at school. They may be prepared to offer handouts so that your teenager can make his notes on the relevant sections.

Saving time and trouble

If your child's notes are concise and follow a consistent pattern, he doesn't have to rewrite or struggle to figure out what they mean later on. These tips can help him to get the note taking just about right the first time:

- Keep it short. Use a phrase instead of a sentence, or a word instead of a phrase.
- Pick out the meat of the subject and forget the trimmings.
- Think for a minute about what to write instead of taking notes just to be taking notes.
- Keep related notes in one book, not on scattered pieces of paper.
- Use abbreviations and symbols, but use them consistently. Perhaps keep some sort of master list of symbols to avoid later confusion.
- Put most notes, except for facts and formulas, into your own words.
- Indent and number your points.
- If you miss something, just write down a key word, leave a space for the details and fill in the blanks later.
- Leave space around your writing in case you want to add some notes later.
- Date your notes and number your pages.
- Look over your notes soon after you take them. Add extra information that you recall as important and rewrite unclear notes.
- Review your notes regularly. You need to hear/see/do several repetitions of a point before you really remember it.

> ✔ Try to get access to notes or handouts in advance of lessons. This will avoid the need to listen and write at the same time and you can instead focus on what is being said.

If your child has severe difficulties with note taking, he may want to use accommodations, such as recording lessons (see Chapter 9), having a buddy or a note taker or even having a teacher provide a written outline that he can add to as he listens.

Using a specific method

Want to check out a few methods for note taking? Go to some of the excellent university study skill websites such as `http://people.brunel.ac.uk/~mastmmg/ssguide/sshome.htm` or `www.humanities.manchester.ac.uk/studyskills` and get a rundown of the following techniques:

- ✔ **Charting method:** The charting method is for subjects like science that lend themselves to column headings (like 'animal', 'habitat', 'food' and 'population'). You jot down headings in advance and then fit brief phrases into the correct columns.

- ✔ **Cornell method:** Divide your paper into a 2-inch column on the left and a 6-inch column on the right. During class, take notes in the 6-inch column. When the teacher moves to a new point, skip a few lines. After class, add more to your notes, and for every significant bit of information, write a couple of key words in the left margin. To review, cover your notes with a card, leaving the key words visible. Say the key words out loud and then say as much as you can of the material beneath the card. Move the card and see if you were right on most points. The more you can say, the more you know.

- ✔ **Mapping method:** If you like to draw headings with arrows and balloons branching from them, you're using the mapping method. This method helps make text look more attractive and bite-sized, but you need plenty of practice so that your nice balloons don't get into a nasty tangle when you add more information.

- ✔ **Outline method:** This method's good for subjects like science in which you're given facts that you can classify into headings of different levels of importance. You create an outline of the material by writing it in headings that get more indented to signify subdivisions.

- ✔ **Sentence method:** If you receive a lot of information about a subject and don't have time to figure out the main and secondary points, the sentence method's good. Write down sentences, each one on a separate line. You end up with a lot of sentences, but they're more concise than whole paragraphs, and the gaps help you clearly see and edit your notes later.

Studying the right foreign language

Most secondary schools require students to do a few years of foreign language study. It is a core GCSE subject. But learning a foreign language is hard for someone with dyslexia, so when your child takes French, Spanish or any other language at school, he needs extra help and time with assignments. These general tips may make the work easier:

- The easiest foreign languages for children or adults with dyslexia to learn are phonetically regular languages, like Spanish and German, and possibly non-alphabetic languages, like Chinese and Japanese (although no research is available on this latter info, just anecdotes).

  German's phonetically regular because it's a what-you-see-is-what-you-get language. German words typically have only one pronunciation, so you don't have to grasp rules like 'this letter sounds this way except if it's next to this or that letter or has an accent mark above it'. French and Spanish are more variable, although Spanish is easier to learn than French. Talk to a language teacher or two to receive expert advice.

- The best way to help your child read and write in English is to teach him a structured phonics programme through multisensory techniques, and the same methods work for learning a foreign language. (When your child uses a few senses, like seeing, hearing and doing, at the same time, he learns in a 'multisensory' way.) A good foreign language teacher for your child is one who has kids doing things like naming objects while they touch them, writing words in the air as they say them and role-playing while they read and say their lines. See Chapter 14 for more about multisensory activities.

  One way to find out what the teachers at your teenager's school do is to chat with other parents. Talk to the teachers too and explain (nicely) that multisensory teaching is important to your child and why.

- A learner with dyslexia needs plenty of reinforcement and consolidation of information. He needs to practise the same foreign words and phrases often, in different guises, like in quizzes and role-play, and the teacher speaking slowly and clearly in class helps.

- Learners with dyslexia may have trouble with small, tightly spaced print in any class, but in a foreign language class (where everything's *really* foreign to them!), the situation can be worse. A sensitive teacher uses a large, plain, well-spaced font and plenty of diagrams.

- Computer software's a great tool for foreign language classes. For software that tutors your child in a foreign language, check out the Rosetta Stone programmes at www.rosettastone.com. The Level 1 CD-ROM costs £139. Also, your child can learn a language like Italian or Spanish free on the BBC website, at www.bbc.co.uk/languages.

For a teenager who's still struggling with reading and writing in English and is already years below in reading, learning a foreign language can be a huge struggle. Ask the school about the possibility of exemption from taking a foreign language – this may be an option.

Giving great speeches

Some important speech giver once said that no clever speech, one-liner or witty quip is unrehearsed. Whoever that guy was, we're willing to believe him. Every year, Tracey gives a few talks to parents and teachers and knows much better than to start cold with no preparation. She practises what to say and how to link key points together. She jots down key words, transitioning phrases that get from one topic to the next, and always, always, the name of the person to thank for inviting her. However, giving speeches can sometimes be a strength for those with dyslexia and an opportunity to shine.

Encourage your teenager to practise giving talks. Help him jot down (on one sheet of paper or a few cue cards) key words. Have him make marks that remind him where to pause, change his intonation and slow down. When he's nervous, every little cue or prompt helps.

Giving speeches is an important task for teenagers because they get asked to give so many of them in class. Your teenager with dyslexia may find presentations even more daunting than other children do because he has to write and read cue cards and may have trouble remembering the words he wants to use, especially when he's on the spot and has only a few minutes to speak.

Planning for college and jobs

Your child may set his sights lower than he's really capable of and may not have a mindful careers adviser to put him on the right track, so you need to be vigilant just in case. Even if he doesn't plan to go to university or college, he can keep his options open by choosing school subjects that don't limit him. And you can help him start thinking about work skills and how to appeal to employers too. (We show you how to help your teenager with dyslexia develop strong work skills in the next section.)

Many teenagers don't visit the careers adviser at their school until the last couple of years at secondary school, if at all, which is a shame. The adviser can help your teenager start thinking about his future, whether he needs advice on choosing a career, deciding on a college/university, looking for a part-time job or volunteer opportunities or exploring trades and vocational education programmes. The adviser also has information on college/career Open Days in your area and when recruiters may be visiting your school. For additional info on preparing for (and succeeding in) college or university, check out Chapter 17. As well as the careers adviser, Connexions offers advice on education and many other topics for 13–19-year-olds by phone or by email. Your teenager can contact Connexions advisers in confidence by telephone on 080 800 13219 or via their website at www.connexions-direct.com.

And if your teenager has an IEP, planning for the future's part of it. Because this planning's such an important detail, you want to make sure that it's really happening. See Chapter 8 for more IEP info.

Encouraging the Development of Work Skills

Your teenager has huge demands on him at this point in his life. He has to work hard to achieve good marks at school and also spend time and effort developing all-important work skills in areas outside school. At secondary school, your teenager makes subject choices and may be expected to start doing voluntary work as well. You can also encourage him to participate in extra-curricular activities or help him get a part-time job or other work experience.

Obtaining work skills during the teenage years is essential because employers and university interview panels want to hear that your child has an impressive work history. We cover options for gaining work skills in the following sections.

Keeping up with extra-curricular activities

Have your teenager with dyslexia keep up with extra-curricular activities because sports and leisure interests keep him happy and healthy and look great on his CV (see the sidebar 'Writing a knockout CV', later in this chapter). Additional benefits of participating in these activities include:

- Finding activities he likes can boost his self-esteem.
- Extra-curricular activities can lead him towards a future college or university course or job.
- Success in an activity can inspire him to put more effort into schoolwork.
- Extra-curricular activities teach skills like teamwork, punctuality and self-discipline that are important in the workplace.

Help your child divide his time sensibly between schoolwork and extra-curricular activities. Otherwise, he may be running from one extra-curricular activity to another and may not devote enough time or energy to his homework.

Doing some good with voluntary work

Voluntary work holds sway with universities and future employers, and some schools ask students to complete unpaid voluntary work in order to achieve the Duke of Edinburgh's Award. How does voluntary work help your child with dyslexia?

✔ He builds confidence (especially if he's doing hands-on work and no reading or writing).

✔ He's treated well. Everyone loves a volunteer!

✔ He gains job skills under less stressful conditions than if he were getting paid.

✔ He may be able to use the contacts he makes as references for job applications.

✔ He may decide he wants to find paid work in the same field and can ask questions more freely than if he were a paid employee (who wants to keep his job!).

Finding a part-time job

The most straightforward way for a teenager to develop work skills and explore potential careers is to find a part-time job. Children with dyslexia usually enjoy having weekend and evening jobs, especially if they work with friendly, supportive people. Help your teenager make wise choices, fill out application forms and do plenty of mock interviews.

To help both of you make a wise choice, here are a few considerations you want to keep in mind. If they sound like words of caution, they are, but don't forget that even though you must protect your child as much as you can without suffocating him, he receives great experience by doing paid work and gets huge kudos among his friends. And for a teenager, how cool is that?

✔ Your teenager with dyslexia may want to steer completely clear of reading and writing tasks. If this is the case, you need to make sure that his part-time job doesn't require him to fill out forms, write reports or do any other regular pen-and-paper work.

✔ Your child's first paid job is exciting but nerve-wracking. His entry into the workforce may be easier if someone he knows is on site. Ask friends and neighbours if they can offer your teenager a job at their workplaces.

✔ Money's a sensitive issue. Discuss rates of pay with your child upfront. What's the minimum wage? If an employer doesn't pay your child for his work, what should he do? If your teenager's self-employed and does jobs like lawn mowing or babysitting, what does he charge for his services, and does he make any exceptions?

If your child's self-employed, you may want to role-play his first conversation with clients. He must know how to tell people his rates and conditions without embarrassment or delay, and that can be hard for anyone!

✔ A paid job means that your teenager has to be there when he says he will, and on time. He needs to carefully plan his entire life! How many hours does he set aside for homework, paid work, sports and the like? And has he factored in commuting time?

✔ Your child may be so excited to get a job and so eager to please his employer that he's an easy target for people who aren't so honourable. Explain to him that even though he's young and expected to show respect, a good work attitude and a small measure of servitude (he's probably last in the pecking order), his employer must treat him fairly. And if that doesn't happen, he must tell you and not be ashamed.

Keep an eye on your teenager and listen carefully if he tells you about things happening at work that make you worried.

Writing a knockout CV

A CV (or resumé, pronounced 'rez oo may') is one or two sides of A4 paper that briefly outline your teenager's accomplishments. If your teenager writes one at secondary school to find a part-time job, he gets great practice for later CVs and creates a tool that helps him keep track of all the things he does. Your teenager needs to keep the following things in mind when he writes his CV:

✔ It must be typed in see-at-a-glance style (a bit like this list).

✔ It must answer the key question 'Can this applicant add value to my company?'

✔ It must emphasise your teenager's strengths, especially the strengths that relate directly to the job he's applying for.

✔ It should include positive personal characteristics, technical and computer skills, educational accomplishments and skills and experience gained from work experience and other work, including unpaid work.

✔ Your teenager can show his human side by mentioning his hobbies. If they relate to the job he's applying for, all the better.

✔ CV design is just as important as content. Your teenager's CV has about 20 seconds to make the right impression.

To get ideas for CV layout and content, your teenager can go to the library and look at books specifically written for students. He can use a computer template, but if he does, his CV looks just like everyone else's! You can also check out *Resumés For Dummies* by Joyce Lain Kennedy (Wiley).

Chapter 17

Heading Off to College or University

....

In This Chapter

▶ Finding facts about universities and colleges

▶ Narrowing your focus to a few universities

▶ Understanding the application process

▶ Putting together your UCAS Personal Statement

▶ Selecting the right college or university

▶ Looking for financing and tips for success

....

*Y*our child with dyslexia knows what working harder than other people is like. She's used to spending long hours on homework and can never cruise through school tests even though she's bright and diligent. As a result, maybe her teachers have told her to set her sights low. But you and your daughter both want her to go to university, so how can you reach that goal?

In this chapter you hear how to help her aim high and do all the things that good universities want their prospective students to do. We give you the lowdown on writing a good Personal Statement, researching colleges and universities, contacting specific institutions for information and going through the application process. We also help you out with tips on selecting the best college or university, finding financing and successfully sending your school leaver into further or higher education.

Researching Universities and Colleges

Your child chooses a course according to her interests, but she also must take a look at the duration of the course, the costs and the location. In the following sections, we give you a closer look at all these issues.

Deciding on potential fields of interest

What subjects should your child choose to study? To answer that question, your child must weigh her strengths against the career she's interested in to see whether they're a good fit. If they're not well suited, she should re-assess her choice.

Universities place course requirements online so look at those and see how much reading and writing is involved. Check how the course is assessed – is it mainly coursework or exam-based? If your child does choose a subject that involves dealing with a lot of text and has exams, then find out how much support is available at that particular university. If she is really motivated to do that particular course, then don't put her off immediately without looking into course requirements in more depth.

Some people maintain that people with dyslexia are suited to architecture and engineering because they often have great spatial skills and the ability to visualise things in three dimensions. Another field generally thought to suit those with dyslexia is the arts, but that may be because actors and singers are in the public eye, and people therefore hear about those celebrities' dyslexia. Just as many people in other fields have dyslexia too!

Your child can probably surf the Internet better than you and she gets career information from the school careers officer or from a Connexions advisor (see `www.connexions-direct.com`), but you have real-life work experience. Tell her about different jobs and their pros and cons. If you have friends who do jobs that your child's interested in, try to arrange some work experience. For details about finding a part-time job, see Chapter 16.

Go with her to Open Days at different universities. Dates for Open Days appear on university websites. They fill up quickly at popular universities, so be quick to register.

Examining different types of universities and colleges

Your child can choose to apply to a college of higher or further education:

- **Colleges of further education** (which include colleges of horticulture and agriculture as well as colleges of art, dance and drama), where you can study for AS and A2 Levels. You can generally apply to these colleges directly online.

✔ **Colleges of higher education** (which include universities), where you can choose to study for a traditional degree or a Foundation Degree that combines academic study with workplace learning. You can also study at a college of higher education for a work-related qualification such as a Higher National Certificate or Higher National Diploma. Applications to university have to go through UCAS.

To get accepted into a university, your child needs better A level grades than those she needs for a college of further education, and the more desirable the course or university, the higher the grades she needs. For more information on the UCAS points system and the number of points needed to get into certain universities or courses, look at www.ucas.com. This is a good starting point. However, if a university likes your child they may well offer her a place dependent on getting slightly lower grades than predicted. We cover your teenager's options in the following sections.

Your child should start researching university and college options as early as possible. She should ask the school careers officer for help finding good universities and college for the courses she's interested in, knowing the recommended qualifications and finding out about the disability services they offer (see 'Asking about disability programmes', later in this chapter, for details). She should read university and college websites too and start gathering brochures.

Colleges of further education

At a college of further education, your child can study for AS and A2 levels or one of the new vocational Diploma courses. She can also study just about any subject (such as flower arranging, writing or word processing), including preparatory courses for occupations like hotel management, computer programming or dental nursing. Most have remedial or developmental courses to help your child upgrade her basic academic skills. Your child can take these courses either before enrolling in higher-level classes or concurrently because some colleges offer both further and higher-level education. Further education colleges don't tend to have the same residential facilities as universities, where students tend to live away from home, so the students at these colleges tend to live locally. For more information, contact the student services office of your nearest college of further education.

If your child wants to work in a trade, such as hairstyling or mechanics, after taking a course at a college of further education, she needs first to verify with someone working in that job (a manager rather than a shopfloor worker) or with the trade association for that job that the course she plans to take actually counts. If, however, your child thinks that she may want to go to university after a course at a college of further education, where courses tend to be more vocational, she needs to check that the qualifications she gets at a college of further education are transferable, or are an appropriate preparation for university. She can do this by simply calling her nearest university and asking.

Colleges of higher education

At colleges of higher education your child can earn a Bachelor of Science (BSc), a Bachelor of Arts (BA) or another specific degree, such as a Bachelor of Education (BEd) if your child wants to go into teaching. For example, law students receive an LLB degree (Bachelor of Law), while medicine, veterinary science and dentistry have similarly specific degrees. These degrees enable her to get a professional job, such as doctor, dentist or lawyer (though she must go to university for longer than three years to qualify in these professions). Colleges of higher education also offer Foundation degrees or two-year full-time Higher National Diplomas (HND) and Certificates (HNC) which are also available to take part time while working.

You sometimes hear university programmes called 'undergraduate'. An *undergraduate* is a person who is working towards a batchelor's degree. After you have a BSc or BA, you can return to university as a *postgraduate* student to get a higher degree called a master's or, highest of all, a PhD. With these pick-of-the crop degrees, you're looking at jobs like a professor or a scientist.

Before your child opts to attend university, she should go through the pros and cons with her school careers officer. He can outline the general issues that all students face and the special issues that your child may face because of her dyslexia (like extra-long study hours). University student services offices can also discuss issues with your child, and she can get a feel for how helpful each university is.

Focusing on the Right College or University

So your teenager with dyslexia has a few ideas about what she wants to study and the specific colleges or universities she wants to consider. What do you do next? In the following sections, we tell you about visiting the campuses of your teenager's choice and requesting specific information about disability programmes.

Touring campuses

The only way to make a good match for your child is to narrow down your search to two or three colleges or universities and visit them. You want to see the academic facilities and the people who may be helping your child, and your child should have a few specific questions ready to ask. How big are the classes? Is a disability tutor available to help me with the course?

You and your teenager need to go to official college or university Open Days and spend time walking around campus. Check out the halls of residence, cafeterias, bulletin boards and local shops. When your child narrows down her search to two or three favourite options, visit each campus several times just to hang out and get the feel and lay of the land. Strike up conversations with students if you can so that you get the unrehearsed version of what's really happening there.

Asking about disability programmes

Your child can find out more about how a college or university of her choice can meet her needs as a student with dyslexia by emailing, calling or visiting student/disability services. Every campus has an office of disability services or something similarly named (like student support services or student access office) that provides disability help. Your child needs to know the strength of a college or university's disability support services.

University in particular is all about independence, and if your child wants services, she must find out where the office is, walk over there with her documentation and ask for them. To save herself legwork, she should first call and ask, 'What services does your disability programme provide?' Here are the types of services usually offered:

✔ Your university should have a disability service that can offer your child a lot of help and which probably includes a learning centre and several disability staff members. The service can provide screening and assessment for dyslexia and other specific learning difficulties, and can help with getting a Needs Assessment. A student who has been through the Disabled Students' Allowance process is usually entitled to around an hour per week of study skills support from specialist study skills tutors employed by the university. She can also get additional software and sometimes money for extra photocopying and books she may need.

✔ Colleges offer a different kind of support through learning support or disability services, which is funded differently. You need to check out what the college offers before you apply.

So that your child's clear about how she can get help and what that help may entail, she should ask the disability services office additional questions like:

✔ Can I make arrangements for accommodations with each of my lecturers?

✔ Can disability services help me talk to lecturers if necessary?

✔ Do I need to have the DSA (Disabled Students' Allowance) in order to receive services?

Applying to University through UCAS

If your teenager's about to apply for one of the many courses available at university, she has to use UCAS, the University Admission Service (www.ucas.com). You can only apply to UCAS online. Application deadlines for certain subjects and universities are earlier than others. For example, applications for Oxford and Cambridge as well as those for medicine, dentistry, veterinary science or veterinary medicine need to be in by mid-October of the year preceding entry. For other courses the closing date's the following January. Universities make all their decisions by the end of March. Applicants applying in January for entry in September of the same year are able to apply for an additional course in late February or early March, if they have used all five of their choices and have either not received any offers or have rejected all the offers they've received. For those who either receive no offers or substantially better or worse grades, the opportunity exists to go through the clearing process for places in August.

There are seven sections on the UCAS application:

- ✔ Personal details
- ✔ Additional information
- ✔ Choices
- ✔ Education
- ✔ Employment
- ✔ Personal Statement
- ✔ References

Universities want to see the following information about your child on the online application form:

- ✔ Whether she has any disability such as dyslexia
- ✔ Academic results, such as GCSE and AS levels already taken
- ✔ A Personal Statement that gives details of her involvement in the community and extra-curricular activities

The following sections cover all three types of documentation in more detail.

So that your child has all the information UCAS needs, help her start writing a Personal Statement early on. Keep a portfolio or a file full of important documentation. Make sure that your child puts her (still crisp and clean) GCSE results into the portfolio as soon as possible after she obtains them and makes copies just in case.

Find more information on how to apply through UCAS at www.directgov.co.uk.

Providing proof of dyslexia

The transition of your child with dyslexia from secondary school to university is different from that of most children because the Disability Department at the university will be able to make accommodations for her, such as:

✔ Extra time on exams

✔ Extra time on essays

✔ Questions read out loud to her

✔ Test questions written in large print

✔ Use of a laptop in lectures and examinations

To get accommodations, your child must qualify for disability services by applying for the DSA (Disabled Students' Allowance) and submitting her dyslexia assessment results to your Local Authority. Your child also needs to talk to the Disability Department as soon as she has made her choice of university. The DSA isn't means tested and the funding comes from your Local Authority. See 'Disabled Students' Allowance', later in this chapter for information on how to apply.

Even if your child's been assessed for dyslexia in school, your documentation has to be up to date. All universities want a recent assessment, so a test like the Wechsler Intelligence Scale for Children (taken when a child is 5 to 16 years old) is no good. She needs to take a new test, like the WAIS-R (Wechsler Adult Intelligence Scale-Revised). A psychologist can administer these tests but a recognised and qualified assessor can also use a battery of prescribed tests, such as the Wide Range Intelligence Test, that meet universities' requirements.

If your child hasn't yet been assessed for dyslexia in school, you can still get an assessment now. We talk about assessment in detail in Chapter 6.

If you want your child assessed for dyslexia before she enrols at a university, you typically have to pay a private psychologist or a recognised assessor who is a specialist teacher. Universities can give you (when you ask) lists of psychologists who test for dyslexia and organisations such as Dyslexia Action (www.dyslexiaaction.org.uk) have specialists who carry out diagnostic assessments. (Currently, the cost of a diagnostic assessment from Dyslexia Action is £355.) The university doesn't help with payment, but you may be able to claim the cost back from the local education authority (LA).

Good news! Even if your child didn't receive a Statement of Special Educational Needs or even additional help in secondary school, she still may be able to get support at university! For more about the support that students with dyslexia can receive from universities, see 'Asking about disability programmes', earlier in this chapter.

Gathering academic results

Just like any other student applying to university, your child must provide the following on the online UCAS form:

- ✔ GCSE grades
- ✔ Personal Statement
- ✔ School reference

Naturally, your child's already working towards her AS and A2 Levels or even one of the new Diplomas. The good news is that she can get accommodations when she takes the exams, and you can help her with her Personal Statement. In the following sections, we explain exactly how.

Studying for AS and A levels

Getting AS and A2 Levels can be hard for a child with dyslexia. Unlike GCSEs, A Levels place far less emphasis on coursework and more on exams. Make sure that your child gets all the accommodations she's entitled to, such as extra time and use of a laptop. SENCOs usually make exam access arrangements for your child, and to be able to use a laptop there must be a clear history of usage – your child can't suddenly decide mid-way through Year 11 that she wants to use a laptop!

Succeeding in entrance exams

If your child's applying to certain universities or wants to study certain subjects, she may have to take an *entrance exam*.

One university entrance exam is the National Admissions Test for Law, or LNAT, which a consortium of UK universities runs so that they can select the most suitable applicants for their undergraduate law courses. The LNAT is a two-hour on-screen test with multiple-choice and essay questions. Eleven universities currently require applicants to sit the LNAT, including Oxford, Cambridge, Bristol and Exeter. Find more information and practice tests on www.lnat.ac.uk.

Other entrance exams include the Biomedical Admissions Test (BMAT) and the History Aptitude Test (HAT). Find more information on these tests and the universities that require them on www.hero.ac.uk.

Your child with dyslexia can receive accommodations on entrance exams, including:

↙ Extra time

↙ Extra and/or longer breaks

↙ Questions read to her

↙ Large-print text

Without up-to-date evidence of your child's dyslexia, your child can be denied accommodations when she takes AS or A2 Level examinations and entrance exams, even if she's received services at school for years. See 'Providing proof of dyslexia', earlier in this chapter, for more information.

If you get into any disputes when asking for accommodations, contact an organisation like the British Dyslexia Association (BDA) or Skill (the National Bureau for Students with Disabilities). The BDA has members who have been through similar processes, people who can advocate for you and connections with disability lawyers. You can check out the Skill website at www.skill.org.uk and find more information about the BDA in Appendix B.

If your child left school without taking any exams and wants to take a degree course now, going to university as a mature student is still a possibility. Evidence of ability (for example, through an access course) to keep up with the academic content of a degree may well be necessary. You can find more information about access courses and this route to studying at university on the UCAS website (www.ucas.com).

Reference

The final documentation your child needs in the academic area is a reference. The school provides the reference, which includes details such as predicted grades for any exams to be taken and information about your child's suitability for the course she has chosen.

Giving evidence of school and community involvement

As soon as your child starts secondary school, she can start thinking about filling her Personal Statement with evidence of her superhuman involvement in the community. She needs to look to experiences that show her involvement in activities that benefit people, like participating in charity runs, helping at scout or guide meetings, serving food at soup kitchens and achieving awards such as the Duke of Edinburgh's Award. Other useful information may include involvement in World Challenge Expeditions, Young Enterprise and work as a student representative, mentor or Head Girl.

Remind your child that she's probably far more involved in the community than she thinks because every club membership she has or good deed she does around the neighbourhood can count. Have your child grab a pen and paper and jot down things like the following:

✔ Participating in organisations, such as scouts and guides or school clubs

✔ Being involved in religious organisations

✔ Being involved in music groups, such as bands and choirs

✔ Helping at fairs and festivals

✔ Dog walking

✔ Lawn mowing

✔ Babysitting

✔ Delivering newspapers

Make sure that she puts her activities into categories like 'Work experience', 'Social interests', 'Sports achievements' and 'Community service'. Later your child can condense this information into her Personal Statement. When she writes this summary, help her use action words and phrases such as 'achieved', 'implemented', 'organised', 'was responsible for', 'participated in' and 'developed'. She needs to showcase her achievements, and sentences such as 'I helped with netball coaching' sound less impressive than 'I taught 20 primary schoolchildren key netball skills'.

Handling the Application and Interview Process

All students want to fill out application forms competently, write brilliant application essays and breeze through interviews with flair and verve. For your child with dyslexia, these tasks can take extra preparation and commitment. In the following sections, we give you practical advice for helping your teenager present herself in the best light. We look at UCAS application in particular, which is the usual way to apply for admission to university, but the same ideas can apply to college application forms as well.

Completing applications with ease

Your child's university application tells everything about her in succinct but glowing terms. To be an early decision applicant, she starts on the UCAS application at the beginning of Year 13.

Filling out forms effectively

Help your child read and re-read through the UCAS application form online before she fills them out. Proofread her answers when she's finished. Fields that your child usually sees on a form include:

- ✔ **Fee:** Applying through UCAS costs £17, or £7 if you only apply for one course.

- ✔ **Predicted grades:** The school fills out this section. Your child should talk to her form teacher or head of year about her predicted grades.

- ✔ **GCSE and AS Level results:** Your child writes in her GCSE and AS Level grades.

- ✔ **Personal Statement:** Your child includes this as part of her application. (We cover Personal Statements in the next section.)

- ✔ **Reference:** Your child's school supplies this information.

Writing a wonderful Personal Statement

Personal Statements give a university a better feel for what kind of person your child is. Applicants have up to 4,000 characters (including spaces) or 47 lines of text available. Your child should make an early start on her Personal Statement so that she leaves herself time for several rounds of edits and for recruiting the help of a teacher or knowledgeable person for proofreading.

A Personal Statement isn't meant to be a complete life history! It's specifically about the reason your child is applying for higher education, and about one third needs to be about her reasons for applying for a particular course. In this section of the application form, she needs to demonstrate that she's capable (academically) and interested in the course she intends to study.

Encourage your child to use as many of the following strategies as appropriate to create a memorable Personal Statement:

- ✔ Divide the Statement into paragraphs rather than solid text, which is harder to read. Consider incorporating some headings, such as 'Reason for course choice', 'Work experience' and 'Reasons for returning to study' (if this applies to your child).

- ✔ Include reasons why she's interested in the subject and what she's doing to support her interest. For example, mention memberships of societies, relevant visits and any work experience she has (or is applying for, for example during an intended gap year).

- ✔ Supply evidence of research into the course and where it may lead her as a future career.

- ✔ Note examples of outside/social activities, but don't include so many that an admissions tutor may think that she hasn't any time left for serious study!

- ✔ Take care to craft an opening sentence that grabs the attention of the admissions tutor and conveys her enthusiasm for her intended field of study.

- ✔ Incorporate new and original details in the Statement; don't merely rehash stuff she's already said elsewhere in the application form.

- ✔ Keep the writing clear and clean. Less is more! Encourage your teenager to ask herself whether her Personal Statement really does sound interesting and upbeat.

- ✔ Proofread the Statement and check the spelling!

- ✔ Be original. A Personal Statement *must* be the teenager's own work.

The Personal Statement needs to give a sense of what kind of person your child is. Instead of cramming the Statement with details of her accomplishments, she should describe herself in warm, witty ways. Your child needs to show a real passion for what she intends to study. Check out www.thestudentroom.co.uk for inspiration.

Writing a Personal Statement's primarily a marketing exercise. What's your child marketing? Herself! So she shouldn't be afraid of showing off her achievements! Applying to university is very competitive, and your child needs to prove that she's better than the next applicant. Some universities have more than 40 applicants for each place, and all they have to base their decisions on are students' UCAS forms.

After UCAS processes the application, your child receives a personal ID that she can use along with a username and password to track the progress of her application online.

Impressing interviewers

When a university is considering accepting your child onto one of its degree courses, it may notify her about an upcoming interview. Generally the university makes offers on the basis of the UCAS form alone, however for some subjects and at some universities they still like to interview candidates. Your child must prepare. Here are the kinds of things that university interviewers ask:

- ✔ Why have you chosen this subject?

- ✔ What can you offer this university?

- ✔ Why do you think you can be a good historian/doctor/teacher?

- Do you have good study skills?

- Can you tell me more about your work experience/interests/community service?

- Do you think you're prepared for university life?

- Why have you chosen this course?

- Do you have any questions?

Children with dyslexia may have an extra-tough time in an interview situation if they're prone to forget their words. The best way for your child with dyslexia to feel confident about the interview is to jot down answers she may give and role-play giving them. Here are some things that your child can practise (with your help) to improve her chances of doing well during the interview:

- Remember key phrases (she can jot them on index cards).

- Talk at a regular speed (nervousness generally makes people speed up).

- Place her hands loosely on her lap (rather than wringing them together or flinging them wide apart).

- Say 'I will' rather than 'I'll try to' (it's more persuasive and go-getter).

- Iron out nervous ticks (like a tapping foot or swinging a crossed-over leg).

- Lose words like 'um' and 'like' (so she avoids sentences such as 'I like went to guides and, um, like, had fun and like stayed for, um, like, three years').

The more practice your teenager gets, the more comfortable she feels, so be generous about going through the role-playing routine with her often. You may want to talk about interview clothes too and courtesies such as waiting to be offered a seat when she first walks into the interview room, and shaking hands with the interviewers (or main interviewer) when it's all over. You also may want to help her prepare the answers to any questions she might be asked by looking at the online course information, so it doesn't look as if she hasn't bothered to do any research about the course before the interview.

Unless someone with a special interest in disabilities or a disability staff member's on the interview panel, your child's probably best to keep her questions pretty general. She should direct all disability-related questions to the people in the disability services office. See 'Asking about disability programmes', earlier in this chapter, for details.

Picking the Winning University

Your child may find that one university out of her options feels just right. More likely, she's torn between a few universities. In the end her choice may boil down to the 'feels right' factor that she gets from walking round campus and reading the prospectus, but in the meantime her decision should include consideration of the following:

- ✔ **Course content:** Subjects should interest her and test requirements should seem reasonable. Multiple-choice tests, for example, may hold more appeal than essays.

- ✔ **Structure of classes:** Small tutorial classes may interest your child more than lectures to large audiences.

- ✔ **Disability support services:** Your child should find out whether the services she gets are low key or comprehensive enough for her needs. See 'Asking about disability programmes', earlier in this chapter, for details.

- ✔ **Campus and social life:** Does your child want to live away from home? Does she want to get a job to help pay for university? Does she play sports? She wants to answer these questions and may also want to spend time simply hanging out on campus before committing herself.

Bouncing back from rejection

If a university rejects your child's application, she has to learn from the experience. She must move down through her list of options and re-check that she's presenting herself well. For a child who doesn't have dyslexia, all this re-grouping can be distressing enough, but a child with dyslexia has added concerns. Is she better to hide her learning disability instead of telling universities about it upfront? Can she cope without support? May she make more friends if she goes undercover?

For your child to have these doubts is only natural, but the problem with forfeiting help is that unexpected things can happen. Your child may keep abreast of university work for months and then find that she has three essays due and two exams in the same week. The best solution's for your child to register for services even if she thinks she may not need them. Otherwise, she may find herself in a crisis later. You just never know, so why take chances?

If telling people about her dyslexia's a problem for her, practise it with her. Let her run through different ways of saying it. When she can openly and matter-of-factly explain herself and ask for help, she avoids subterfuge and the greater embarrassment of having others find out about her condition by surprise or accident!

Your child, like all children, may not take full notice of a lot of the stuff she hears about her possible university choices. For example, does she really know how far away potential universities are from home? Does she realise how many hours away the university is by bus, car or train? Can she tell you the cost of a bus or train ticket? Is she really aware that universities that are hundreds of miles away can be lonely places? You need to discuss these things with your teenager before she finally decides on a university.

Finding Help with Financing

After your teenager makes her university or college application, you can apply for financial help as soon as student applications open, without waiting for an offer. Funding is different for students with dyslexia at university and college, as is the way support is accessed. We cover your financing options in the following sections, but funding practices for university are constantly changing so keep yourself up-to-date with information from relevant websites, such as www.slc.co.uk.

Loans

If your child is an eligible student doing a full-time course, she can take out a student loan for tuition fees and apply for a student loan for maintenance to help with accommodation and living costs. The interest rate for student loans is linked to the rate of inflation and is 3% at the time of writing. All loans are taken out through the Student Loan Company. Repayment of a student loan begins in the April after the student leaves her course, but only starts if the student is earning more than £15,000. The interest rate is set at the rate of inflation and your child will repay 9 per cent per annum of anything she earns above £15,000.

Student loan for tuition fees

This loan covers any amount up to the full amount charged for tuition fees (up to £3,134 for 2008/9). Student Finance Direct pays the loan directly to the university or college.

Student loan for maintenance

This loan helps towards accommodation and other living costs while studying. The maximum loan for 2008/9 is £6,475. Student Finance Direct usually pays the money into your child's bank account in three instalments. The maximum amount of the loan depends on several factors, including your household income, where your child lives while studying and whether she's in the final year of her course. The higher the amount of parental income, the less you are able to borrow.

Maintenance Grant

The Maintenance Grant is worth up to £2,835 a year and is non-repayable. The grant is paid in three instalments – one at the start of each term, just like the student loan. The amount you're entitled to receive depends upon your household income. If you have a household income of more than £60,000 your child won't be eligible.

Disabled Students' Allowance

The Disabled Students' Allowance, or DSA, is a government grant available to disabled British students to help meet the additional costs of studying that your teenager with dyslexia may face. The local authorities administer this discretionary allowance which relies on diagnostic assessment, the funding body accepting that evidence and assessment by a Technical Needs Assessor. This person assesses the disability of the individual student against the requirements of the course. The recommendations fall into three categories:

- ✔ **Non-medical helper allowance** pays for specialist study skills support that your student with dyslexia may require.

- ✔ **Equipment allowance** pays for equipment such as a laptop, which remains the student's property.

- ✔ **General allowance** covers additional small costs, such as additional photocopying or books that your student with dyslexia may need.

You and your teenager with dyslexia must go through several stages to apply for the DSA:

1. **Complete and submit the DSA1 form to your LA.**

   You need to include appropriate evidence, including an up-to-date psychological assessment of dyslexia. See 'Providing proof of dyslexia', earlier in this chapter, for more.

2. **If the LA determines that you're eligible for DSA, undertake an Assessment of Need.**

   You can arrange for an assessment at your chosen university or college or from a member of the National Network of Assessment Centres (www.nnac.org). A specialist teacher with a current Practising Certificate can also carry out this assessment. Contact Dyslexia Action on 01784 222 300 for more information. The cost of an assessment through Dyslexia Action is approximately £355.

Based on reviewing the recommendations in your completed Assessment of Need, your LA decides whether to fund the requested support.

3. **Based on your LA's recommendations, arrange for support with your university or other education services.**

Find information on DSA on www.studentsupportdirect.co.uk and www.dfes.gov.uk/studentsupports. Further research may sound daunting, but that's how you find current and relevant updates – and save money and stress in the long run.

Other sources

Many universities offer bursaries, which you don't need to repay, for students with special academic, athletic or artistic talent. For example, Portsmouth University offers a bursary worth £300 if you've attended one of the selected local colleges listed on its website. You need to go through the prospectus for each university with a fine-tooth comb!

If your teenager's thinking of a career in the army, navy or air force, all offer generous bursaries to university students.

Many large companies also offer assistance. For example, Shell offers 12 technical scholarships (each worth £2,500 a year) for students starting four-year courses culminating in master's degrees in science or engineering at Leeds or Manchester University. Go to www.moneyextra.com/guides/managing-student-debt-033823.php for more information about these sources of financial help.

For a smorgasbord of information about financial aid that may apply to your child with dyslexia, including a bursary map, visit www.direct.gov.uk.

Campus life versus living at home

Your child may be better off financially living at home rather than in a hall of residence or getting a room or flat close to university. If you encourage her to stay at home, though, consider whether you're doing so because that's best for her or because you're afraid of having an empty nest. Most parents dread their children leaving home and worry about whether they can cope on their own. But you're reading this book, so you obviously support your child and teach her well. More than likely, she thrives. If not, she can always come back to you to re-group before launching off anew!

Successfully Keeping Up with the Work

After your child with dyslexia suddenly finds herself beyond your radar, you may worry that she may not study and keep up her marks like she should. She has to exercise restraint in the midst of all sorts of distractions, so a few pointers from you before she flies the coop can't hurt! Here are some things you may casually mention:

✔ Early on, find a good place to study.

✔ Sit towards the front of class.

✔ Study with a friend from class. Discussing ideas reinforces them and helps you remember.

✔ Use goal charts to break tasks into smaller steps that you set deadlines for (see an example in Figure 17-1).

✔ Use a diary or personal organiser to keep track of all classes, assignments, test dates and so on.

✔ Ask professors for advance lecture notes and notice of due dates on assignments. Go to disability services early to arrange this and make sure that they know about you.

✔ Well in advance, read course requirements and syllabi to get a sense of the workload and to help guide your course selections.

✔ Colour code your subject notes.

✔ Read and re-read, several times if need be, books and important notes.

✔ Jot down questions you need to ask as soon as you think of them.

✔ Plan on two or three hours of study (daily rather than in one frantic block at the end of the course!) per hour of class.

✔ Take study breaks.

✔ Ask a class friend to be your sounding board. Tell her what you think the text means.

✔ Summarise text in point form.

✔ Use gadgets that can be funded through the DSA (such as a digital recorder, speech-to-text software, computer thesaurus and mind-mapping software).

✔ Give yourself enough time for each assignment (allowing for distractions and minor catastrophes).

✔ Head to disability services as soon as you enroll. The people there can help you revise your goals, may tutor you and may ask your lecturers for extra considerations, such as extra time for assignments, if needed. Specialist study skills tutors are often very over-subscribed so don't expect to be seen the next day. Plan ahead!

✔ Make sure that the lecturers understand how dyslexia affects you.

Goal	How	When
Write my final essay for English class and mention the following points:	Take 3 essay skills sessions	16/4, 23/4, 30/4
1. The author's use of symbolism	Have the first draft proofread by T. Olsen	5/5
2. How the author's life experiences are reflected in the book	Have the final draft proofread by T. Olsen	20/5
3. How the author's prose is distinctive	Turn in the final essay on time to Professor Smith	24/5

Figure 17-1: A goal chart can help your child stay on top of assignments.

After your child works hard in and out of secondary school, she deserves a smooth transition into college or university. Of course, she may embark on a career that she comes to dislike, have trouble handing in assignments on time or find that she needs to be pushier than usual to get help. All sorts of things can happen to stress and demoralise your child, so anticipate problems and work with your child to nip them in the bud.

Chapter 18

Succeeding with Dyslexia in Adulthood

For adults who struggle with written words, the term 'dyslexia' can be a lifeline. It gives them answers at last, and may tell the world that their struggles have nothing to do with stupidity or laziness. If you're reading this book because you're wondering whether you have the confidence to call yourself dyslexic, this chapter should encourage you. If you already describe yourself as dyslexic, this chapter should interest you. If your child has dyslexia and you're wondering about his prospects, you can get inspiration here. More and more people are identifying themselves as dyslexic, and that alone has to be great news!

In this chapter, we explain why getting a diagnosis and treatment for dyslexia has advantages even for adults. We tell you why and when adults should let family and friends know about (and help with) their dyslexia, and describe the rights you have as an adult with dyslexia in the workplace.

Benefiting from a Late Diagnosis

Many people leave school without ever knowing they're dyslexic. They struggle with reading and spelling, and maybe maths and following directions, but they manage to scrape through. They get jobs and hide their problems (see Chapter 3 for a list of dyslexia symptoms in adults). Some even hide the truth from spouses by saying things like 'I'm not interested in books' and 'I hate writing'. All the same, when they hear about dyslexia, they're intrigued. Is that me? Did I have dyslexia all along? Should I call myself dyslexic now?

A late diagnosis puts the 'Am I or aren't I?' question to bed. It tells you what's been going on with you all these years. And if you *don't* have dyslexia, it may identify any other condition that you *do* have. It clears the fog and lets you move forward, perhaps with as small a step as calling yourself dyslexic or as large a step as going to adult literacy classes, taking more qualifications or getting help for a totally different condition, like attention deficit hyperactivity disorder (ADHD). Whether a diagnosis takes you one step or many steps forward, you go forward!

Dyslexia is sometimes confused with ADHD or other disorders, such as dyspraxia, and a person can have dyslexia and another specific learning difficulty. We talk about similar and related disorders in Chapter 2.

Where can you get a diagnosis – and do you have to pay? Here are some options:

- ✔ A private educational (or other) psychologist can assess you for a fee. You usually pay between £400 and £1,000. To find a psychologist, log onto the British Psychological Society website (www.bps.org.uk), ask your doctor, look through the Yellow Pages or ask your local branch of the British Dyslexia Association or Dyslexia Action (see Appendix B for contact information).

- ✔ You can refer to an adult checklist on the BDA website (www.bda.dyslexia.org.uk) or take an online dyslexia screening test such as AmIDyslexic on the www.dyslexiaaction.org.uk website. This simple test, which costs £30, gives you a printable report with recommendations about further psychological assessment.

An online test does not give you a formal or officially recognised diagnosis of dyslexia, but does tell you if you're at risk of dyslexia. If you just want this information for yourself, go ahead. If you need assessment results for your workplace or college, verify that it accepts online assessments before you go ahead with one. Most institutions ask you to be assessed by a qualified, listed psychologist.

- ✔ If you're looking for a job, contact your local Jobcentre and ask to speak to the Disability Education Adviser (DEA). The DEA may help organise a full psychological assessment and get finance for lessons afterwards.

Trainees on the postgraduate Dyslexia Action courses need to assess and teach adults as part of the course. Contact the Training Office on 01784 222 347 to see if any trainee needs a pupil to work with.

✔ Organisations such as the Shaw Trust, which is a national charity, have projects like Pathways to Work, run in conjunction with Jobcentre Plus and Dyslexia Action. As part of the project, adults who feel that they may be dyslexic and believe that the condition's a barrier to finding work can have a Skills Profile carried out by a specialist teacher from Dyslexia Action. The profile looks at underlying ability and skill attainment using several diagnostic and literacy tests. The profile doesn't give a diagnosis of dyslexia but can make a recommendation such as tuition, which a specialist can then offer. Contact the Shaw Trust on 0800 085 1001 or `www.shawtrust.org.uk`.

To prepare for testing and screening, have a clear idea in your mind of the difficulties you experience now and those you faced going through school. If you have any copies of previous diagnostic reports or school reports that support the points you intend to make to the tester, bring them along. Be prepared to talk and look at print. Whatever tests the psychologist gives you, she certainly asks you to describe your difficulties and read words (like *snail*), parts of words (like *sn*) and probably nonsense words too (like *urm*).

If you have dyslexia (or if your child has it), you probably relate to many of the symptoms we list in Chapter 3. And even without a diagnosis, you just know that something's wrong. Do you need a diagnosis? Not really. You don't have to be diagnosed, but if you do, perhaps to get the Disabled Students' Allowance, you probably feel better! At least you know for sure and can call yourself 'dyslexic' with absolute certainty. And if you need it, you have the verification to show at work. But if you aren't racked with curiosity and you don't need the diagnosis at work, save your money and don't get an assessment.

Deciding to identify yourself as dyslexic

When you identify yourself as dyslexic, good things can happen. You now have a 'disability' (though you certainly don't have to use that word) rather than a set of vague problems. You got to educate other people so that they understand what's going on for you, and your life isn't a round of excuses and cover-ups.

Being openly dyslexic is sometimes good, but you have to tell people not only that you're dyslexic but (briefly) what that means, which is stuff like this:

✔ You can't always read fast or accurately, but given enough time, you get through all the reading.

✔ You write terrible notes by hand, but you're good with email or a word processor.

These are the kinds of practical issues you must talk about in order to save confusion and embarrassment later. If you don't speak up for yourself, people who don't know any better, and plenty who should know better, may assume that you're less capable than you are.

Looking at Helpful Programmes for Adults

Adults may never have had a better time to catch up with reading, writing and perhaps strategies for better time management. Plenty of literacy programmes for adults are available, and if you don't like the sound of that, you have at-home options too.

Heading to the classroom

If you want to work on improving your literacy and like the idea of getting away from home and learning alongside other people who are in the same boat as you, you may like these options:

- **Your local school or college** almost certainly runs evening adult literacy programmes. Check out its course guides by picking one up from the college itself or from your library (you have no escape!). Often you get a brochure through your door at the start of each session.

- **Learndirect** is a government initiative aimed at getting all adults up to a certain level of literacy and numeracy. You can take online courses in basic English and maths, the Certificate in Adult Literacy and Numeracy as well as courses in IT, business and management and others right up to Master's level. Courses start from £19 and may be funded, depending on your circumstances. You can also take free courses at local centres – most towns have a Learndirect centre. Go to www.learndirect.co.uk or call 0800 101 901 for more information.

- **Skills for Life** is a programme for improving adult literacy and numeracy in England. Established in 2002, the project sought to describe and illustrate theories of dyslexia and resulted in the publication of *Framework for Understanding Dyslexia*. For more information, look at www.dfes.gov.uk/readwriteplus/understandingdyslexia.

  A tutor carries out a diagnostic assessment to determine your level of skills, potentially highlighting difficulties that may indicate dyslexia. Download the diagnostic tests from www.dcsf.gov.uk/readwrite plus/DiagnosticMaterialsDyslexia.

  Through Skills for Life, you can obtain free national qualifications in adult literacy and numeracy, starting at entry level (for example, writing a basic CV and completing forms) and going up to Level 2. Practise the tests online and when you're ready, take the test in one of many local learning centres.

✔ **Move On** is an adult-focused government initiative to improve adult literacy for higher-level learners. The programme is linked to Skills for Life. Find more information on www.move-on.org.uk and information about national qualifications on www.qca.org.uk.

The government programmes, Learndirect and Move On, are basic skills courses taught by basic skills tutors rather than dyslexia specialists. More dyslexia-focused support is available through organisations like the British Dyslexia Association (www.bdadyslexia.org.uk) or Dyslexia Action (www.dyslexiaaction.org.uk) who offer specialist-taught courses, some of which are funded by grants such as the Big Lottery or have government funding such as Train to Gain, and are therefore free.

Improving your reading skills at home

A friend wants to help you learn to read, but where do you both start? The resources that we list next are books or kits designed for adult home use. (That may sound X-rated, but we promise these materials are all on the up and up!):

✔ **Adult Literacy Programme (Version 1.4):** The ALP is a structured, multisensory CD-ROM programme that helps adults with dyslexia build their skills. Learners progress through sections, working from the CD and workbooks. To use the ALP, you must complete the accredited specific learning difficulties/dyslexia training course (AMBDA or ATS including FE/HE) or have completed the course Supporting Adults in Dyslexia at Level 3. Find more details on these courses and requirements on www.dyslexiaaction.org.uk.

✔ **Units of Sound (Version 4.4):** Adults can effectively use this multisensory reading and spelling programme. It includes a test to help place you on the appropriate stage for reading and spelling and encourages you to work independently on the computer. In three separate stages, the programme builds reading accuracy, vocabulary, spelling, sentence-writing skills, automaticity, listening skills, visual skills and comprehension. The three stages cost £90 each or £250 for the complete set from DI Trading at www.dyslexiaaction.org.uk/store.

✔ **Units of Sound: Literacy that Fits:** Although adult learners can use Units of Sound (see the preceding bullet) at home without supervision, the programme's even more effective under the guidance of a teacher. The Literacy that Fits resource is a great home supplement to in-class lessons – or you can use it as a stand-alone programme. A simple placement test and an easy-to-follow guide lead the way. Although children can use the programme, the graphics are very adult-friendly. Like the full Units of Sound programme, the CD-ROM contains reading, spelling, memory and dictation programmes. The cost is around £58 from DI Trading at www.dyslexiaaction.org.uk/store.

✔ **Barrington Stoke:** Publisher Barrington Stoke produces a range of books for reluctant readers, including adults. Its Most Wanted selection of books is for individuals aged 18 and over with a reading age of 8. Popular titles include *Sawbones* and *Dead Brigade* and are £5.99 each. Find out more by visiting www.barringtonstoke.co.uk.

You get the most out of all the preceding programmes if you do them with a 'teacher' – in other words, any capable friend you feel comfortable enough to work with. However this does depend on the individual. If you prefer to have lessons with a specialist tutor, you can telephone Dyslexia Action on 01784 222 300 and ask for details of your nearest centre. The BDA also offers lessons for adults in some Local Associations and you can get further details on its helpline (0845 251 9002). In addition, the Adult Dyslexia Organisation may also be able to help. Its helpline telephone number is 0207 924 9559.

Knowing Your Workplace Rights as an Adult with Dyslexia

Some people choose not to disclose their dyslexia in the workplace. Some let employers know about it in informal, chatty ways because their dyslexia makes hardly any difference to their performance, because they're embarrassed or they think it might affect their career. Others explain their dyslexia upfront before they even start the job.

However you decide to handle your dyslexia at work, you may be more reassured if you know your legal rights. You can call some organisations for in-depth advice, but the basic things you should know are:

✔ The Disability Discrimination Act (1995) is the main disabilities-related act that protects you when you have an assessment or diagnosis of dyslexia. This act bans discrimination in employment against people with disabilities.

✔ Your workplace must provide reasonable accommodations to allow you to do your job.

✔ If you can perform essential work functions, you can't (legally) be disqualified or discriminated against in any way because of your dyslexia.

✔ Your organisation must keep your dyslexia confidential and must not disclose the information to fellow workers or anyone else without your explicit (written) consent.

In the following sections, we go into more detail about accommodations you can receive in the workplace and steps to take if you believe that your employer's discriminating against you because of your dyslexia.

Making small accommodations for big results

The DDA (Disability Discrimination Act) requires that 'reasonable accommodations' be provided to individuals with disabilities. Your employer isn't expected to drain her financial or personnel resources to help you, but has to be 'reasonable'. Small changes (or 'reasonable accommodations') in your work environment, such as the following, can make your life much easier:

- Having special equipment (such as voice-recognition software). To check out software that can help you in the workplace, visit www. dyslexic.com.

- Getting extra services (such as a secretary who, as one of her tasks, proofreads your letters).

    Giving you access to a quiet room if working in an open-plan office becomes too distracting.

- Being allowed to do tasks in ways that are easiest for you (such as typing rather than handwriting).

- Taking modified tests (such as oral rather than written tests).

- Receiving more or alternative training (such as being allowed to keep a work manual for longer than usual so that you have time to read it). Extended mentoring can also help as can a 'buddy' who can spend time telling you what the Health and Safety Notices mean.

- Ensuring that handouts in any meetings are given on the coloured paper that is the best colour for you.

Use technology whenever you can! If you don't know how to spell well, a computer can help correct that problem. If you can't read all that fast, voice to text software can help with that. If doing mathematics with a pencil and paper doesn't become your forte and multiplication tables always slow you down, a calculator can fix that. (See Chapter 9 for more info on using technology.) And for a really low-tech (but still incredibly handy) gadget, buy an erasable-ink pen.

You may have chosen a job in which your dyslexia's hardly an issue. All you need is the occasional helping hand. Or perhaps you need quite a bit of help. In either case, getting workmates on board may be a quick and easy solution to your difficulties, after you take the plunge and ask. Build friendships in which you help each other out. We're sure that this is stuff you already know and do, but maybe you have more bartering power than you think. Most people need lift-share friends, babysitters and emergency contacts, so they're probably more than happy to read over your application or check your time sheet in exchange.

Receiving reliable advice

For reliable advice about your rights and what to do if you think you're being discriminated against, check out the following resources:

- ✔ For the full rundown of the DDA, visit `www.direct.gov.uk/en/ DisabledPeople/RightsAndObligations/DisabilityRights/ DG_4001068`.

- ✔ For free legal advice, find your local Citizens Advice Bureau by visiting `www.citizensadvice.org.uk`.

- ✔ For general help on issues to do with dyslexia, visit the British Dyslexia Association at `www.bdadyslexia.org.uk` or call the helpline on 0845 251 9002.

- ✔ Log on to `www.dyslexiaaction.org.uk` and click on the section for adults. You get clear information about the DDA and case studies of adults with dyslexia. You also find resources and handy gadgets that you can buy to help you at work (such as a pen that reads a word out loud when you run it over text you can't read).

- ✔ *Dyslexia in the Workplace* by Diana Bartlett and Sylvia Moody (Whurr) is another useful source of information.

Organisations like Dyslexia Action (`www.dyslexiaaction.org.uk`) and Working with Dyslexia (`www.workingwithdyslexia.com`) offer *workplace consultations* in which a specialist visits you at your place of work, meets your employer and manager and makes recommendations that can help you work more effectively. The recommendations may be small alterations, such as changing the light fittings, or larger recommendations, such as having access to a quiet place to work with a laptop, when necessary. The consultant supplies verbal feedback straight after the consultation and follows up with a written report, which may recommend tuition. This could be for specific literacy skills or even for help with report writing or time management skills. Your private health insurance may cover the cost of a workplace consultation. The Working with Dyslexia website also includes some useful articles about adults in the workplace.

Similarly, the Access to Work (AtW) scheme, run by the Employment Service (your Jobcentre), provides advice, information and funding for employers and people who have long-term health problems or a disability (including dyslexia) that hinders them in their work. AtW grants can help out with:

- ✔ Specialist equipment to suit your needs at work

- ✔ Adapting premises or existing equipment

- ✔ Providing a communicator at a job interview if you're deaf or have a hearing impairment

- ✔ Providing a support worker, such as a reader, if you're blind or have a visual impairment

- ✔ Travelling to or within work

You can apply for AtW funds through the Disability Service Team at your local Jobcentre.

One of the adults I teach, Paul, is a good example of how AtW can help. Paul worked quite happily in the print room of a large organisation for many years. Suddenly he was moved to work in the post room. Important post started to go astray and Paul became very stressed and nervous that he'd lose his job. He was sent for an assessment with Dyslexia Action who diagnosed dyslexia. Paul then received tuition and his company engaged a support worker through AtW who goes on his rounds with him and ensures that he has strategies to help him through his working day.

Keeping Family and Friends in the Frame

Children with dyslexia sometimes get called lazy. Their teachers think they can read if they only put in more effort and, of course, if parents believe the teachers, they may follow suit. As a result, the child with dyslexia feels awful, so he grows up looking forward to leaving school early and never having to try to read again.

But then, years later, he has children. His wife writes his child's home-to-school notes and signs the birthday cards, and he thinks he's doing fine. But his daughter wonders why he never signs her cards and thinks he doesn't care. 'He can't be bothered,' she thinks. 'He can't even make the effort to sign his name. He's lazy and doesn't really love me all that much.'

This is just one kind of scenario that happens when a parent keeps his dyslexia a secret. Another's that one of his children also has dyslexia, but because no one's looking out for it, it goes undetected. Another scenario is that he misses all his children's important school events because he can't bear to set foot in another school ever again.

Letting your friends and family know what's going on is better than hiding it. You risk weakening your relationship with family members if you deceive them, and besides, if they know about your dyslexia, you may eventually be able to laugh at your subterfuges and mistakes with them. People with dyslexia are resilient and inventive because they have to be. They can be hugely successful, just like anyone else. They can come to terms with their dyslexia and manage to chuckle about it. As one man with dyslexia said at the end of a conversation Tracey had with him:

> Did you hear about the man with dyslexia who called 999? He told the operator, 'My wife broke her leg. Can you send an ambulance?' 'Where do you live?' asked the operator. 'On Rhododendron Drive,' said the man. 'How do you spell that?' asked the operator. 'Never mind,' he said, 'I'm going to drag her over to Elm Street.'

Part VI
The Part of Tens

'We couldn't afford a Pocket Spell Checker, so I've brought my little brother along instead.'

In this part . . .

1f you could limit your children to ten pairs of socks each or serve them ten meals they'd happily eat, think of the Zen-like calm you'd exude. You could buy all your children the same colour socks and fix meals on a rotating schedule.

Alas, that's a mere dream. But in this part of the book, we at least give you a bit of the ten (if not the Zen) thing. For your absolute joy and convenience, here are ten useful tools to make a person with dyslexia's life easier and ten dyslexia programmes and treatments you want to know about.

Chapter 19

Ten Tools for Making Life Easier for Someone with Dyslexia

In This Chapter
▶ Erasing ink and getting a good pen grip
▶ Using colours to get (and stay) organised
▶ Saving time with a wristwatch
▶ Teaming up with technology

*I*n this chapter you get to see what a number of people with dyslexia rank as their most useful gadgets and gizmos for reading, writing and everyday activities. Some of the things we list are high-tech, but others are just nifty ideas that creative people have come up with that don't involve ever laying a finger on a keyboard or plug. Chapter 15 has additional information on making everyday activities easier for a child with dyslexia.

A Pencil Grip

Plenty of children with dyslexia hold their pencils in a fist grip or way down near to the lead, which usually leads to messy handwriting, so make use of pencil grips. Buy a grip from a stationer or a specialist supplier like LDA (www.ldalearning.com) or improvise by wrapping an elastic band around your child's pencil an inch from the lead. When she pushes her fingertips against the band, it keeps them where they should be (by stopping them from sliding down to the point).

Pens with Erasable Ink

A child with dyslexia's handwriting is usually difficult to read and full of spelling errors. Buy your child pens with erasable ink, and she can present her teacher with work that's decipherable.

Discuss this item with the teacher first, because many classes operate on a keep-mistakes-visible policy. The teacher may want to see your child's errors, but if her errors comprise nearly all her work, he may relent.

Colour-Coded Files and Other Handy Items

Children with dyslexia can have an awfully hard time staying organised. To keep your child with dyslexia's life on track and on schedule, she needs to know exactly where she should be, when, and what files to take. Coloured files, towels, pencil cases, water bottles and anything else available in assorted colours make life easier for your child. When she can reach for a colour rather than a written label, knowing that blue stuff is always hers, she does things more quickly and with minimum fuss.

At the start of each school term, help your child colour code anything that can, within human reason, be allotted a colour. Drawers and files are obvious things to stick coloured labels on, but your child may like to colour code other things, like musical notes (on the page and on the instrument), nouns and verbs (using highlighter pens) in a written foreign language and topographical features on maps.

Children with dyslexia also tend to have difficulties with the concept of time. To help, a wall chart in her bedroom can be effective to let her know when coursework is due in.

A Wristwatch

If your child remembers that she wears her watch on her left wrist, she saves herself a lot of embarrassment, potential turmoil and, oh yes, time! When she can't figure out her left from her right, she just has to feel her watch. Simple, huh? Oh, and should she wear digital or analogue? Digital's usually easier for her to figure out, but analogue's helpful if she tends to reverse numbers. When she's not sure which way to face 3 and 5, she can discreetly peek at her watch.

A Pocket Spell Checker

When a word processor puts a squiggly red line under your child's spelling, she knows she's made a spelling error. She's comfortable using her computer spell checker and may even use the thesaurus function in the software too. But has she seen a pocket spell checker? If not, you may want to get her one, since they're inexpensive and, according to many students with dyslexia, really useful. Because they're small and easy to carry, your child can check her handwritten spelling in class or anywhere else.

To find out more about spell checkers, visit these two websites: Franklin Electronic Publishers at www.franklin-uk.co.uk and www.dyslexic.com, which has a range of spell checkers.

A Mobile Phone and a Personal Organiser

Are you wondering whether your child should have her own mobile phone and, if so, at what age? We haven't yet sorted out that dilemma for our own children, but we can tell you this: teenagers and adults who have dyslexia rely heavily on their phones. They avoid writing lengthy emails by talking on the phone instead and use hand-held gizmos like electronic personal organisers to make sure that they're in the right place at the right time with the right company. Fancy phones and organisers can keep the most muddled person on track, so for someone with dyslexia they're especially awesome!

Books on Tape or CD

Books on tape (from your local library, www.listeningbooks.org.uk or www.booksontape.com) enable your children to listen to more advanced or lengthy text than they read by themselves. She could also use an iPod for far more than just downloading music by her current favourite band! (www.i-pod-info.com gives information on how to make iPods play MP4 files, for example). Make digitally taped stories a regular feature in your house. If you drive long distances, use the time to listen to epic stories. If your child's in secondary school, get a list of the books she needs to read for English class and borrow the taped versions. She can whizz through texts that may otherwise take her days or weeks (and plenty of midnight oil) to get through, and especially if she listens *and* reads the text at the same time, she's taking the multisensory route (Chapter 14 has details).

A Photocopier

Even if you're something of a technoflop, you can use a simple photocopier to help your child with her schoolwork. Head with your child to a copier every now and then to copy the teacher's notes, summaries of subject curricula (so you can see what to expect over the whole year) and pages from books that your child may want to paraphrase for assignments. You can enlarge the print from good textbooks and then help your child highlight key parts and rewrite them in her own words.

A Word Processor and the Internet

Do you have to ask your 10-year-old to explain how email and camcorders work? If so, you're in good company. Plenty of kids are more competent with technology than their parents are, but they may not be so smooth about typing. Your child with dyslexia needs to type smoothly so that she's got one less thing to worry about. As long as she can roughly type her ideas into a word processor, she can use the spell-checking feature to fix most spelling errors, proofread and hand in work that's legible and much more accurately spelt than her handwritten version.

Introduce her early on to a fun keyboarding programme like English Type Junior. English Type Junior consists of progressive, step-by-step keyboard lessons for touch typing. The software's for Windows, and available in junior or senior versions from www.englishtype.com or www.dyslexiaaction.org.uk.

The Internet can also give your child an incentive to read and write. Even if she uses only email and writes mostly in text message abbreviations (RU there? CU l8r), she still practises regular writing between abbreviations, and knowing these short forms may be as useful to her as knowing regular spellings.

To check out software and book reviews, visit www.which.co.uk. To buy a used or reconditioned computer, check out:

- ✔ **Apple:** www.apple.com
- ✔ **Dell:** www.dell.co.uk
- ✔ **PC World:** www.pcworld.co.uk

Speech-to-Text Software

Your child with dyslexia, especially if she's in primary or secondary school and gets plenty of homework to write, may find that speech-to-text software saves her time and stress. Speech-to-text software enables your child to speak to her computer and have her words appear in a text document. She can scan other people's text, like notes from a classmate, into her computer and get her own copy to edit or save. She may even improve her spelling in the process because when she says words, sees them appear on her screen, and then edits them, she's using a few senses (so her learning's multisensory – see Chapter 14 for details) and she's poring over the same words a few times (so she gets the repetition that helps her learn).

Speech-to-text software can be like having your own personal secretary in your work or home office. With it installed on your computer, you can dictate letters and notes (to your computer) and have them appear in written form all ready to print up and go.

Chapter 20

Ten (Or So) Well-Known Dyslexia Programmes

In This Chapter

▶ Perusing phonics-based programmes

▶ Checking out programmes using sounds, vision and exercise

▶ Examining programmes focused on the mouth and brain

▶ Considering diet

*W*hen you start looking into programmes for people with dyslexia, you may find yourself feeling overwhelmed. Loads of programmes are available and, as if that weren't bad enough, they can have unusual names like 'Orton–Gillingham' and 'Lindamood–Bell'. These are mainly used in the United States, though, so in this chapter we make things easy for you by summarising ten well-known programmes in the UK that range from the long-standing and trusted ones to a couple that are unusual and, in some people's minds, risky. Chapter 9 also features general information.

You can never be sure whether your child may thrive on a programme (otherwise no competition exists!), so you may have to shop around. And before you put your child into someone else's care and pay money to do it, contact a reputable organisation like the British Dyslexia Association or Dyslexia Action (we give you all the contact info you need in Appendix B). The people in these organisations hear the good and bad of the programmes from parents who use them. Your local branch in particular can give you handy advice.

Phonics-Based Reading Programmes

Your child's school probably runs a remedial reading programme that emphasises small groups of children and phonics (the teaching method in which your child discovers how letters represent speech sounds – see Chapter 12 for details). The school chooses a particular programme because it's well known and trusted and/or the school's teachers have been trained in it.

Some of the more popular programmes that schools choose are Reading Recovery or the DILP (the Dyslexia Institute Literacy Programme). If your child's taught either of these programmes, you can be sure that he's being given instruction that's well thought of and usually gets good results. (Chapter 7 has more info about school programmes in general.) Ask your child's SENCO how you can help at home as well though. Programmes like DILP have reading cards to go through on a regular basis.

Private tutoring (in learning centres and from individuals) in the best-known methods costs between £25 and £50 an hour depending on your location. Here's how to find information on tutors (who may also call themselves therapists or consultants) in those methods:

- ✔ Search the online register of PATOSS, the Professional Association for Teachers of Special Needs, at www.patoss-dyslexia.org. The association can connect you with appropriate and qualified tutors in your area with whom you can discuss method and tuition questions.

- ✔ Contact the British Dyslexia Association's Helpline on 0845 251 9002 or go to its website at www.bdadyslexia.org.uk.

The information you receive from these organisations serves as a good yardstick, but bear in mind that individual tutors vary in their qualifications and services.

Programmes that Tune into Sounds

Your child with dyslexia has trouble identifying and manipulating speech sounds. The programmes in the following sections treat this by having him listen to sounds at varying speeds and frequencies.

Fast ForWord Language

Fast ForWord Language is an intense four- to eight-week programme (five days a week, 100 minutes a day) in which your child plays computer games. Whether your child spends the full eight weeks on the programme depends on how soon he reaches the goals that are set for him by the assessor at the initial student assessment session.

Your child starts off by listening and responding to stretched-out sounds like 'c-a-t' and progresses to other listening-and-responding activities like identifying the missing parts of spoken sentences. The programme runs at a centre near you, or you can have a trainer come to your home. If you're far from a centre, a trainer can sell you the home products and guide you in using them.

Fast ForWord offers programmes in language, language to reading, reading and middle/high school. To check everything out, visit the UK site at www. neuron-learning.co.uk.

Earobics

The Earobics programme is like Fast ForWord (see the previous section) but is simpler and less expensive. The three CD-ROMs (for age 4–7, 7–10 and adults) are for home use (you're not required to go to a centre) and cost £43 each. Push the CD-ROM in (it's formatted for both Windows and Macs), and your child can get started pretty much right away with little need for your help. The programme aims to help phonological awareness and processing skills in a fun and interesting way.

Check out the programme at www.earobics.com or www.donjohnston. co.uk.

Units of Sound

Units of Sound (Version 4.4) is a multisensory reading and spelling programme for learners from age 8 to adult. The programme begins with a test to place the learner on the appropriate stage for reading and spelling, and various resources effectively allow him to work independently on the computer. Divided into three separate stages, the programme builds reading accuracy, vocabulary, spelling, sentence-writing skills, listening skills, visual skills and comprehension. Each of the three stages costs £90, or you can get the complete set for £250 from DI Trading or Dyslexia Action (www.dyslexia action.org.uk).

Programmes that Focus on Vision

The British Dyslexia Association defines dyslexia as a problem primarily to do with *phonemic awareness* (your child's ability to identify and manipulate speech sounds), but people with dyslexia can have trouble seeing letters too, due to problems with visual perception. However, if your child with dyslexia complains that he sees wobbly, fuzzy or moving letters, it could be due to visual stress (sometimes called *Irlen Syndrome*).

The methods we talk about in the following sections pay special attention to your child's visual difficulties.

Davis Dyslexia Correction

At the helm of the ship known as Davis Dyslexia Correction is Ron Davis, severely dyslexic himself and author of the book *The Gift of Dyslexia* (Penguin Group). Davis has centres and individual facilitators around the country in which your child takes a 30-hour intensive programme (one week, Monday to Friday, from 9 a.m. to 4 p.m.). Davis methods work on the idea that dyslexia is due to distorted perceptions of letters and words. Training a child to maintain a point of focus when reading or writing may help your child overcome these distortions by creating mental pictures for words and mastering a list of words that typically cause dyslexic problems in children.

The Davis programme focuses on visual skills, not phonics skills, so it's especially good for older learners who haven't done well with phonics-based instruction. Parents are instructed in the methods so that their child can continue using them when the programme ends. This often means having your child do physical activities, like making things with modelling clay and throwing balls and doing other balance/perceptual training exercises.

The programme costs around £1,400 depending on location. Included in the cost (and in addition to the 30 hours of training) is an initial two-hour assessment, six hours of follow-up tutoring and unlimited phone consultations. Remember to check costs with individual providers before embarking on the course, as costs can vary.

If you want to practise Davis methods without going to a centre, you can do it by reading *The Gift of Dyslexia* (£12.99) and using either a regular kit (£75) or a kit of CD-ROMs (£99 for Windows).

For more information on Davis methods, visit www.davislearning foundation.org.uk or www.thelearningpeople.co.uk. Or call 01227 732 288.

The Irlen Method

The Irlen Method treats a condition that psychologist Helen Irlen calls scotopic sensitivity syndrome. According to Irlen, your child has *scotopic sensitivity syndrome* or Meares Irlen Syndrome if he can read print better through a coloured tint.

An Irlen practitioner called a screener can screen your child for scotopic sensitivity syndrome. The screening, which takes two hours and costs around £60, determines what colour overlay your child should use over print.

An Irlen diagnostician can do a screening and a diagnosis, which determines what tint (mixed from up to 12 colours) your child's glasses should be. Before your child gets a diagnosis, he must first get an independent eye exam. After the diagnosis, which takes four hours and costs £224, the diagnostician sends your child's glasses to a lab for tinting. The lab fee is £95.

To find out more about the Irlen Method and how to find a screener or diagnostician, visit `www.irlen.org.uk`.

The Dyslexia Research Trust

The Dyslexia Research Trust, or DRT, is a charity set up by Professor John Stein (brother of Rick Stein, famous for cooking with fish!) and Dr Sue Fowler, who carries out research into many areas of dyslexia. The trust is currently carrying out visual research. It tries to offer assessments and treatment free of charge for children, but you should expect to join a waiting list for a free appointment. Private, paid appointments are often available within a month for £195, which includes the whole investigation, treatment, full report and follow-up.

Make an appointment at Dyslexia Research Centre, 179A Oxford Road, Reading RG1 7UZ; telephone 0118 958 5950; or at the Department of Physiology, Parks Road, Oxford, OX1 3PT; telephone 01865 272 116.

Find more information on the DRT and its work at `www.dyslexic.org.uk`.

Mind mapping

We can't call Tony Buzan's concept of mind mapping a programme as such, but we include it in this section because it certainly helps most people with dyslexia. Buzan's technique taps into the good visual abilities that people with dyslexia generally have and teaches them to use words, images, logic, rhythm, colour and spatial awareness to help with tasks such as note making and note taking. The only resources you need are blank paper, coloured pens and your imagination! Your child may not want to do a full-blown mind map, but the principles of how to organise thoughts, improve memory and speed up reading are worth introducing to your child at any age.

Buzan's website `www.buzanworld.com` sets out exactly how to mind map and gives many colourful examples. You can also purchase courses to teach memory strategies, mind mapping and speed reading (£295 per course) via the website, as well as books, DVDs and software.

Programmes that Get Physical

If your child seems poorly coordinated (sometimes a symptom of dyslexia), treatment programmes are available. Most give your child a load of exercises to practise at home. (See Chapter 14 for more about the benefits of exercise for children with dyslexia.)

Brain Gym

Brain Gym includes 26 targeted activities (like crawling, balancing and stretching in moves similar to simple yoga positions) for improving your child's balance and concentration and hence his memory, reading, writing and more. A typical session lasts two hours. Your instructor can tell you how many sessions are best for your child, but many parents report that they see improvement after five sessions.

Your pre-teen or teenager can also take a 24-hour Brain Gym for Teens and Pre-teens course stretched over three consecutive days. After taking either private sessions or the course, your child can do the exercises at home by himself and, if he wants, take refresher courses later. The website lists practitioners, course dates, times and centres. You also can buy books, tapes, videos, CD-ROMs and DVDs.

For more information go to www.braingym.org.uk or phone 0208 202 3141. If you're interested in training to be a Brain Gym instructor, courses start at £495.

The DORE Programme

DORE went into administration in 2008, however we include it because we hear some whisperings of the organisation returning. Controversial when it was running, due to the lack of concrete evidence to support its theories and the element of hard sell, the DORE programme took roughly 12 months and cost about £4,000. Some parents, particularly if their child had dyspraxic rather than dyslexic tendencies, did report an improvement. However many found that it was hugely expensive and didn't make any significant difference to their child's literacy skills.

A child would start the DORE programme by completing a screening questionnaire over the phone, followed by a medical questionnaire. After an initial 3½-hour assessment, a provider would run parents through the results and recommended exercises for your child to do. The exercises included things like balancing on one leg and throwing a beanbag from hand to hand, for ten minutes, twice a day.

Participants visited a centre every six weeks to track progress and received updated exercises.

Find out more about the DORE programme at the website, which is still active at www.dore.co.uk. You can make up your own mind by reading a response to the closure of the DORE organisation on the Dyslexia Action website (www.dyslexiaaction.org.uk). Click 'News and events' and then 'Our opinions'.

Lindamood–Bell Learning Processes

Lindamood–Bell centres are mainly in the US, but London now has a centre. The centres provide programmes in reading, spelling, comprehension, critical thinking and maths. The best-known programme is the LiPS, or Lindamood Phonemic Sequencing. Just like it sounds, LiPS has to do with your child's mouth. The programme teaches your child to feel the shape that his lips make when he says speech sounds so that he gets better at identifying and later reading and writing those sounds.

Lindamood–Bell programmes are popular. Dyslexia educators in the US regard them highly and research verifies that these programmes can be effective. Contact the London Learning Centre at Eardley House, 182–4 Campden Hill Road, London, W8 7AS; telephone 0207 727 0660. The website www.lindamoodbell.com gives further information about the programmes.

Audiblox

Designed mostly for home use, Audiblox is a programme of 'multisensory cognitive enhancement' or, in other words, a system of activities for improving basic thinking skills such as concentration, short-term memory and classifying. Children as young as 3 can use Audiblox, and the designer, Dr Jan Strydom, says that you can expect to see progress within three months.

An Audiblox kit includes a book, a manual, a CD-ROM, a DVD, a reading book, word cards and more. Get the ins and outs of Audiblox at www.audiblox2000.com, which features a UK link, or by calling 07899 964 281.

Fish Oils

Research into the use of Omega-3 fish oils by children with dyslexia has been very positive. Have a look at the BBC website for more information on a recent experiment carried out by Madeleine Portwood in Durham: `www.bbc.co.uk/science/humanbody/mind/articles/intelligenceandmemory/omega_three.shtml`.

The Dyslexia Research Trust website at `www.dyslexic.org.uk` has more facts and figures about children's improvements after taking fish oil supplements. According to the DRT, many people with dyslexia – as well as dyspraxia and ADHD – have deficiencies in Omega-3 unsaturated fatty acids, a substance that come from fish oils. (The typical Western diet is low in fish consumption.) These 'good fats' support aspects of brain and visual function, including learning ability, concentration and coordination. A deficiency may contribute to inhibited brain functioning involved in reading and dyslexia.

Supplements such as Efalex are excellent sources of Omega-3 and Omega-6 nutrients, particularly DHA, EPA and AA, all of which play important roles in helping to maintain brain and eye function. The cost of these oils is around £8.99 for 60 capsules. Check around for local pharmacies that sell fish oils over the counter.

Part VII
Appendixes

In this part . . .

This part of the book contains the appendixes. Superfluous, dreary add-ons? Not at all! In fact, these two appendixes are downright exciting.

First, you get a test that's typical of what SENCOs use in school to pinpoint your child's phonics skills. Then you find a whole Aladdin's cave of useful resource information and contacts, plus suggestions about learning materials you can order right away. Now is that handy stuff or what?

Appendix A

An Informal Assessment of Phonemic Awareness and Phonics Skills

• •

Dyslexia is a reading and writing disability (or, if you prefer, difference) that results primarily from weak phonemic awareness and phonics skills. That's quite a mouthful, so here's how it translates into practice: your child can't identify speech sounds (like *ch* and *ick*) and can't match them to the letters that represent them.

Consultants and therapists find out what phonemic awareness and phonics skills your child needs to practise by having her take tests. Very often they design their own. In this appendix we give you a series of tests that we wrote and use with the children we help. They're quick and easy for you to administer, and they pinpoint your child's weaknesses. Use them to check out your child's skills before you have her professionally assessed for dyslexia (see Chapter 6 for details about assessment) or as a supplement to the other activities in this book (especially those in Chapter 12).

The tests in this appendix gauge your child's phonemic awareness and phonics skills at the pre-reading, early reading and independent reading stages in her reading development. Before you start, here are the guidelines:

- ✔ Move fairly quickly from one question to the next.

- ✔ Give your child the answers if she can't quickly get them for herself.

- ✔ Stop testing when your child gets three to five answers (depending on how long the test is) in any test wrong. She needs more practice at that skill before she tries again.

- ✔ Do all the tests in order. Move on to the next test only when your child has fewer than three to five mistakes. This isn't a rigid, error-counting formula; these tests are a diagnosis only of the *areas* in which your child struggles rather than the precise extent of her difficulties. A psychologist can give you an in-depth assessment.

✔ Be supportive and matter-of-fact. Tell your child not to worry about giving incorrect answers, because you're just finding which words she needs to grasp so she doesn't waste time going over old ground.

For additional info about phonics and activities that you can do with your child, be sure to check out Chapters 4 and 12.

Picking Out Pre-Reading Skills

Before your child can read words and sentences, she must be able to distinguish one letter from another and hear the sounds that letters make. The following sections are all about these important pre-reading skills. In an average classroom, most children develop strong visual and auditory discrimination skills and phonemic awareness by about age 6.

Visual discrimination

Your child may pass an eye test and still have weak *visual discrimination* skills – the ability to discriminate the shapes and orientation of letters. This weak visual discrimination can be a pronounced symptom of dyslexia.

Test 1: Make a copy of Table A-1. Have your child look at the letters in the Find column and circle the corresponding answer in the Answer column.

Table A-1	A Test of Visual Discrimination
Find	*Answer*
d	b b b d b
p	q p q q q
u	v v v u v
n	w m w n m
du	bu bu du bu bu
nm	mn mv nv nm nmv
on	an am on om un
dpb	pdb bdp dqb dpb bpd
loas	laes loas loes leas lose
anoe	awon amwa anoe amwa aneo

How to help: Have your child do lots of looking activities; dot-to-dot, spot the difference and *Where's Wally?* activity books are good (*Where's Wally?* is one of those books that has figures and objects hiding in elaborate scenes for your child to find). Activity books with a bit of everything in them, including letter recognition, are even better.

Auditory discrimination

Your child may pass hearing tests but still have weak *auditory discrimination* skills – the ability to identify speech sounds. Weak auditory discrimination is a key feature of dyslexia. In the following sections, we show you how to test the discrimination of various sounds in words, both separately and together.

Surveying sounds in the beginning, middle and end of words

Test 2: Tell your child that she's going to listen for sounds in words. Explain that *dog* begins with the sound 'duh'. Tell her that *map* begins with 'muh' and then ask her what *fill* begins with and then *gum*. When she has the idea, read column one in Table A-2 to her, stopping after each word to let her tell you the beginning sound. Move to column two but before starting it, practise with *map*, *fill* and *gum* again, this time listening for the end sounds. Finish the second column and then move on to the third column. Practise listening for the middle sounds in *map*, *fill* and *gum* and then do the exercise.

Table A-2	**Identifying Beginning, Ending and Middle Sounds**	
Beginning Consonant Sound	**Ending Consonant Sound**	**Middle Short Vowel Sound**
cup	rub	bill
fish	hat	sock
jug	deep	bun
pond	goat	hit
yellow	clock	peg
dinner	hug	log
mask	fan	dot
bend	hood	wig
rabbit	loaf	rug
nurse	room	bag

If your child has trouble with *map*, *fill* and *gum*, you need to leave this test for later. Meanwhile, practise one sound, like 'ss', at a time with her. Talk about 'ss' words (*sock*, *step*, *Sue*, *snail*, *smelly*, *sun*) until she hears the sound and then choose a new sound. After plenty of practice with at least six sounds (a mix of consonants and short vowels), try the test again. If she's still uncertain, keep practising one sound over a few days and then another sound over a few days until she gets the hang of the task.

How to help: Try the following fun activities:

- ✔ Play 'I spy with my little eye', saying things like 'I spy with my little eye something beginning with "mmm"'.

- ✔ Play 'I went to the shop and bought/saw/found . . .'. Every answer must start with the same sound.

- ✔ Play 'I went to Aunt Maud's'. The first player thinks of a sound, like 'ay', and all players must say they're taking something with them (to Aunt Maud's) that has that sound in it ('I took paint, Raymond, an acorn, an apron, mail, raisins').

Pushing sounds together to form words

Test 3: Tell your child that you want her to listen to the sounds you're going to say and tell you what word they make (when you push them together). Practise with *m-a-p* (pronounced *mm-aa-pp*), *f-i-ll* and *g-u-m* and then read the following list of words, pausing after each word so that your child can tell you the answer.

- ✔ m-a-n
- ✔ d-o-g
- ✔ d-u-ck
- ✔ p-a-t
- ✔ w-i-n
- ✔ w-e-ll
- ✔ l-a-m-p
- ✔ sh-u-t
- ✔ s-n-a-p
- ✔ c-r-o-ss
- ✔ s-a-n-d
- ✔ t-w-i-n

How to help: Run through simple words with your child every time (make sure you do this in a fun way to prevent it getting tedious) you're in the car or waiting for the bus or cleaning up after dinner (*b-e-l-t, d-i-sh, s-p-oo-n*). Also, if your child sounds out a word like *bit* as 'buh-i-t' and has trouble losing the extra 'uh' sound, show her how to blend the beginning consonant with the vowel, then add the last letter: 'bi-t'.

Phonemic awareness

Your child may pass vision and hearing tests but still have weak *phonemic awareness* – the ability to identify sounds and move them around (sometimes making new words). Weak phonemic awareness is an extension of the auditory discrimination we talk about earlier in this appendix; auditory discrimination is distinguishing sounds, and phonemic awareness is distinguishing *and* being able to move sounds around. Weak phonemic awareness is a key aspect of dyslexia. In the following sections, we show you how to test phonemic awareness by rhyming and switching letters in words.

Recognising rhymes

Test 4: Read the pairs of words in the following bulleted list to your child. Ask her, 'Do they sound the same or different?' Practise by explaining how *lay* and *may*, *men* and *hen* and *pig* and *wig* all rhyme, but *bed* and *hut* and *leg* and *thin* don't.

- *pet* and *vet*
- *man* and *can*
- *hat* and *pot*
- *tree* and *egg*
- *log* and *frog*
- *mat* and *cat*
- *hill* and *bell*
- *stamp* and *ramp*
- *clock* and *slip*
- *belt* and *dip*

How to help: Play the name-rhyming game, using sentences like this: 'I like Lizzy even though she's dizzy.' 'I like Ben and his big fat hen.' 'I saw Brook reading a book.' When you get to names of more than one syllable, you really have to think! ('I saw Nicky being very picky.' 'I saw Kelly; she was on her belly.')

Switching letters in words

Test 5: Say the first key word in Table A-3 to your child and then read out the instruction that goes with it, pronouncing the letters as sounds (like 'puh', not 'pee', for *p*). Wait each time for her answer.

Table A-3	Changing Letters
Key Word	*Make These Changes*
pat	Take off *p*; put *c* there instead (cat)
bun	Take off *b*; put *f* there instead (fun)
hot	Take off *h*; put *p* there instead (pot)
hut	Take off *h*; put *c* there instead (cut)
tin	Take off *t*; put *p* there instead (pin)
pan	Take off *n*; put *ck* there instead (pack)
pin	Take off *n*; put *t* there instead (pit)
bill	Take off *i*; put *e* there instead (bell)
fun	Take off *u*; put *a* there instead (fan)
bug	Take off *u*; put *i* there instead (big)

How to help: Play the alphabet rhyme. Write the alphabet for your child to see. Say a small word beginning with *a*, like *an*. Your child must give a rhyming word (like *fan*). Do the same for every letter of the alphabet (*an/fan, be/he, cut/gut, dog/log, end/send*) and see how far you can get. Have your child cross off the letters as you go.

Examining Early Reading Skills

Early reading skills are the skills your child has when she can read simple words made of two or more letters. By 'simple' we mean the following:

- Words like *bat*, *pin* and *nut* that have short vowels in them

- Words like *spin* and *plant* that have a short vowel and one or two consonant blends (like *sp* and *pl*) in them

- Words like *chip* and *shop* that have a consonant digraph (*ch*, *sh*, *th*, *ph*, or *wh*) in them

Maybe these sounds seem hard for 'early' skills, but in practice they're not. In the following sections, we give you tests of each word group and you get to see that they really are a straightforward bunch. In an average classroom, most children develop solid early reading skills between ages 5 and 7 and then quickly jump to independent reading of simple texts (see 'Testing for Independent Reading Skills', later in this appendix, for details).

Knowing single letters

Your child should be able to name and sound out every letter of the alphabet, uppercase and lowercase.

Test 6: Make a large copy of Table A-4 and have your child read the letters to you.

Table A-4	Single Letters
Uppercase Letters	*Lowercase Letters*
B C E G K H J N O R S P T U V M W A X Y F Z D Q L I	d c f b g i j k h l n p r t o s u q w x y a v z e m

How to help: With magnetic letters that you stick on your refrigerator, letter tiles and alphabet puzzles, play sorting and naming with your child. Use just three or four letters at a time. Can your child name them if you jumble them up? Can she find and name them if you hide them? Can she straighten them out if you turn them the wrong way? Take turns doing these activities and then make letter posters of the letters you used. A letter poster is chock-full of pictures drawn or cut from magazines and glued-on items. Examples of items for a poster of the letter *l* include real or pictured leaves, lollipops, lemons, lists, lice, lettuce and liver (you're probably best not to glue on the real thing in some cases!).

Trying three-letter words with short vowels

After your child knows the sounds of individual letters, she should soon be able to read three-letter, short-vowel words. Does she know how to blend letters together? Is she comfortable with common two-letter chunks, like *at* and *an*? Is she eager to show you what she can do? The next test can help you find answers to these questions.

Test 7: Have your child read out the words in Table A-5. If you've helped her read words in chunks, you may want to encourage her to underline the last two letters in each word so that she remembers to sound out in chunks, like *c-at*, *c-ut* and *t-en*, rather than in all single letters.

Table A-5		Three-Letter Words with Short Vowels		
cat	hut	mop	van	ten
cut	kit	pan	fog	hen
ten	jam	big	cup	box
sun	log	pen	web	wax
mud	yes	win	rub	log

How to help: Buy (or make) easy workbooks such as the *Jolly Phonics Workbooks* by Susan M. Lloyd and Sara Wernham for your child to do. You can also play 'Change one letter'. Write a word like *bug* and make new words by changing one letter *(beg, big, bog, hug)*. Change the original word or the new words you make and see whether you can make ten words. Sound out as you play and let your child take charge. She holds the pen and finds all the answers; you give gentle hints.

Blending letters

After three-letter words, your child should be able to read short-vowel words with consonant blends. A *consonant blend* is two or more consonants, like *st*, *cl* and *str*, that sound out together, one letter blending into the next. You teach your child to recognise them as a distinct whole and blend together their individual sounds.

Test 8: Have your child read out the words in Table A-6. You may want to help your child underline or highlight blends beforehand.

Table A-6		Simple Words with Consonant Blends		
brag	glad	jump	best	lamp
stop	smell	frog	twist	dress
long	desk	bent	sink	strap
swim	drink	trust	snap	drop
trust	grip	stamp	cross	press

How to help: Using words from Table A-6 and other words that rhyme with them (like *drink*, *pink*, *stink*, *link*, *think* and *brink*), write a list of 100 words. Every night for ten nights, have your child read ten words to you from the list, top to bottom and then bottom to top. Then dictate them for her to write.

Diving into digraphs

After short-vowel words with blends, your child should be able to read short-vowel words with consonant digraphs (*ch*, *sh*, *th*, *ph* and *wh*). Unlike a blend (see the previous section), a *digraph* is a whole new and unique sound, not a sound made by blending each letter into the next.

Test 9: Have your child read out the words in Table A-7. (Notice that *th* has two pronunciations, like in *that* and *think*.)

Table A-7	Simple Words with Consonant Digraphs			
chips	shell	shed	then	chop
chin	shot	chat	graph	shut
flash	chick	chess	that	check
think	this	thin	chill	shrimp
when	shrink	smash	phantom	chimp

How to help: Do the same kind of reading and dictation that we describe for blends in the previous section. If she hates dictation, then make up sentences together and get her to write the word you're concentrating on. You can write the rest for her if she's getting tired. Or you could make it a fun activity by cutting up a sentence containing the words and putting them back together. You can extend this by then making it a dictation to be self-checked.

Testing for Independent Reading Skills

After your child masters the words we give you in the previous sections, she has good basic reading skills. Now she needs to master more complex skills. The following sections show the harder skills she needs, roughly in order. Have her read the words to you so that you can find her areas of weakness. Most children have basic independent reading skills – in other words, they read simple text by themselves – at age 7.

Have your child focus on one phonetic rule she's weak on for a week. Have her read lists of words every night. Dictate words to her every night. When you help your child often like this, in her areas of weakness, and keep activities short and fun, she moves forward.

Looking at long and short vowels

Test 10: Can your child read all the long and short vowels mixed in together in Table A-8? Short vowels sound like the *a* in *apple*, the *e* in *egg*, the *i* in *ink*, the *o* in *octopus* and the *u* in *up*. Long vowels make the same sound you hear when you say the vowel's name: *a* like in *ape*, *e* like in *eve*, *i* like in *ice*, *o* like in *oak* and *u* like in *uniform*.

If your child knows the rules of *Bossy e* and 'When two vowels go walking, the first one does the talking' (which we explain in Chapter 11), she may want to underline or highlight *Bossy e* (like in *came* and *fade*) and the two vowels walking (like in *stain*) before she reads.

Table A-8		Long and Short Vowels		
came	stain	fade	need	tape
game	fate	pan	hid	trap
spike	tap	made	pale	bean
best	hop	beg	drain	ride
spoke	maid	pole	rate	train
slime	cost	scrape	team	rain
sleep	strap	feel	hide	file
coat	fill	pain	hope	crept
soak	toast	task	felt	cream
slim	slip	sock	roast	weep

How to help: To fix the rules of *Bossy e* and 'When two vowels go walking, the first one does the talking' in your child's mind, teach one rule thoroughly before starting on the next. In Chapter 11, we provide instructions and plenty of word lists to help you accomplish this.

Getting the hang of y endings

When your child reads short-vowel words with consonant digraphs, she should also be able to read simple words with *y* endings. Words ending in *y* can be tricky for children with dyslexia because they make either a long *i* or *e* sound, and your child has to choose the right one.

Test 11: Have your child read out the words in Table A-9.

Table A-9		*y* Endings		
my	happy	silly	why	by
smelly	cry	windy	chilly	poppy
funny	foggy	fry	hungry	sly
ugly	skinny	dusty	sticky	rusty
crunchy	lumpy	bendy	boggy	sandy

How to help: Dictate words from Table A-8 for your child to write. To practise y-ending words more interactively, try this additional activity: Write out up to ten simple sentences, such as 'The tree is . . .', 'The man was . . .' and 'The soup is . . .'. Make copies of the sentences for you and your child. Referring to Table A-8, you and your child fill out answers (they can be silly) and try to guess each other's responses.

Sorting out vowel combinations

Test 12: Does your child know the sound-alike spelling chunks like *ou* and *ow*? In Table A-10 she gets *ou* and *ow*, *oy* and *oi* and *aw* and *au*. Have her read the words to you so that you can see whether she needs practice.

Table A-10		Sound-Alike Spelling Chunks		
loud	out	count	boy	prowl
orouch	lawn	proud	clown	shout
coil	owl	soil	draw	crown
straw	crawl	straw	jaw	paw
howl	law	toy	frown	town
clown	cloud	growl	claw	soil
foil	brown	round	boil	laundry
hawk	law	point	dawn	joy
mouth	found	sow	raw	flour
fawn	saw	house	sound	pound

How to help: Many speech sounds are spelled a few different ways (like *ew* and *oo*, *ee* and *ea* and *ay* and *ai*). To avoid confusing your child, show her one spelling thoroughly before introducing her to another. If one spelling's prevalent, like *tion* from the group *tion*, *sion* and *cian*, show her that one first.

Spotting soft and hard letters

Test 13: Words with soft and hard *c* and *g* sounds are mixed in together in Table A-11. Can your child distinguish between the soft and hard sounds? The soft sound of *c* is the sound of *s*, and the soft sound of *g* is the sound of *j*. The rule for deciding whether you have a soft letter on your hands is 'Soft *c* and *g* are followed by *i*, *y* or *e*', as in *city*, *cyst* and *cent*. Have your child read the words in Table A-11 to you so that you can see whether she has this rule firmly under her belt or needs more practice.

Table A-11		Soft and Hard Letters		
pace	pocket	spoke	place	ice
strange	angry	slice	face	dance
past	race	ragged	plunge	wage
germ	fence	rage	lice	lace
glad	cage	locket	last	wedge

How to help: If your child can't read the words in Table A-11 or isn't confident with them, go over the rule with her and have her read plenty of soft *c* and *g* words. Read a few words each day. When your child has had a lot of practice, show her Table A-11 again and, if she wants, have her mark the soft-letter words. If she still can't read the words, repeat the activity and be sure that she says the words out loud while looking at the letters. Have her mark the letters and read the words again. With plenty of regular practice, she gets better at cracking this pretty hard nut.

Watching out for silent letters

Test 14: Can your child spot and *not* pronounce silent letters like the *k* in *knot* and the *b* in *climb*? Table A-12 helps you find out. It has a mixture of regular words and words with silent letters in them, so your child's a pretty good reader if she can read the whole lot without making errors.

Table A-12		Silent Letters		
climb	yolk	west	wrong	wind
palm	pale	kneel	keep	knot
creep	calm	wrist	flight	flick
knob	pink	crumb	whistle	sight
high	habit	crisp	comb	clasp

How to help: If your child struggles with silent letters, introduce her to one silent letter at a time. In Chapter 12, we give you several silent-letter families (like the silent *k* family that includes *kneel*, *knife* and *knew*), so browse through it and take your time with the activities.

Placing vowels before r

Test 15: When a vowel comes before *r*, a special sound is made. You can hear the sound if you say *far*, *star* and *bar* out loud and then pronounce *a* (like in *apple*) and *r* (like in *rat*) separately. Do you hear how the pronunciation of *ar* isn't a straightforward blending of *a* and *r*? Good! The same thing applies to *er*, *ir* and *ur*, which all sound the same, and to *or*. Have your child read the words in Table A-13 to you so that you can see whether she know her *ur* from her *er* or needs more practice. So that she carefully looks and sounds out each word, we include some easy words that don't have the vowel + *r* combination. You may want to explain this fact and have her highlight the vowel + *r* combinations before she reads.

Table A-13		Vowels before *r*		
her	hidden	fleck	burn	brim
rust	shirt	grip	thirst	camp
stern	strap	sharp	shake	chart
harm	thorn	throat	hurt	churn
stale	scrape	stir	firm	film

How to help: Your child may find reading the words in Table A-13 easier if she first highlights the vowel + *r* combinations. If she still struggles after doing so, flip to Chapter 12. Run through the practice activities at your own pace and repeat them as often as you need. If you want, come back to Table A-13 for a retest.

Appendix B
Contacts and Resources

The great thing about finding information on dyslexia is that every kind of help and advice you ever need's within reach. We've delved deep into the Internet and run up a fearsome phone bill to give you exactly the right contacts. Here they are then – links and numbers that really do work.

 If you don't see a phone number in the resources in this chapter, the organisation concerned doesn't provide one. You may be able to get additional information (usually including an email address), or your local phone number, from its website.

Getting General Information Online or by Voice Mail

The contacts in the following sections give you info on just about everything you ever need to know about dyslexia (definitions, advocacy, parent courses, technology, legislature, local branches, ask the experts, FAQs and chat rooms). We tell you what we think are each one's special strengths.

Three general websites to start you off

This appendix is so chock-full of websites that you may be wondering where on earth to start. Start here. The websites in this section are easy to navigate, friendly in tone and really helpful (or we wouldn't have included them!).

- ✔ **LD Online:** www.ldonline.com
  This US website features forums, ask the experts, FAQs and in-depth information. Use the top menu bar to navigate and check out 'First person essays' to see what being dyslexic is like. (Our favourite essay's 'Upside down in a right sided world' by W. Sumner Davis, PhD.)

- ✔ **Dyslexia Parent:** www.dyslexia-parent.com
  This informative US website for parents also provides links to UK dyslexia associations.

✔ **I Am Dyslexic:** www.iamdyslexic.com
This uplifting site is written by a boy (diagnosed with dyslexia at 5) who struggled in school but went on to academic success. He shares his favourite tips, software and reviews of products.

Three big organisations

For information on just about anything to do with dyslexia, consult the big shots. The organisations we list here have big reputations, huge databases and plenty of connections. They may have the answers you need, and if not, they can connect you to someone who does.

British Dyslexia Association: www.bdadyslexia.org.uk
Helpline: 0118 966 8271
The BDA Helpline is probably the first port of call for most parents. The association also offers training courses and a limited amount of area-specific tuition – multisensory tuition mainly for adults but also a range of courses depending on the area, such as touch typing and maths.

Dyslexia Action: www.dyslexiaaction.org.uk
Voice mail: 01784 222 3000
Dyslexia Action is the UK's largest provider of dyslexia services. The website's easy to navigate (you won't get lost, we promise) and offers brief, to-the-point information about research, tuition, assessments and resources. Use the Contact Us page to seek out answers to any queries.

Helen Arkell: www.arkellcentre.org.uk
Phone: 01252 792 400
Email: enquiries@arkellcentre.org.uk
The Helen Arkell Dyslexia Centre (HADC) is a registered charity mainly covering the Surrey area. It employs educational professionals to help individuals with dyslexia and other specific learning difficulties, and provides training for people who wish to study the subject.

If you live in the Bristol area, the Bristol Dyslexia Centre is also worth contacting at www.dyslexiacentre.co.uk or 0117 973 9405.

The preceding organisations help adults as well as children, but if you're an adult with dyslexia, consider contacting The Adult Dyslexia Centre at www.adultdyslexiacentre.co.uk or 0207 388 8744. (Not to make things confusing, but the Adult Dyslexia Centre also offers services for children!). Try the Adult Dyslexia Organisation as well, which you can look up at www.adult-dyslexia-centre.co.uk. It also offers help and advice to adults.

Talking to Someone Directly

Sometimes a website isn't what you want, and a recorded telephone message isn't the answer either. You need to talk to a real live person in the here and now. You can forgo technology for a while and get that simple human touch by contacting the groups in this section.

- ✔ **The Advisory Centre for Education:** 0808 800 5793
  This valuable source of advice and guidance for parents offers a Special Education Handbook, which provides a useful summary of the law in regard to children with special needs.
- ✔ **British Dyslexia Association Helpline:** 0118 966 8271
- ✔ **The Citizens Advice Bureau:** Go to the website on `www.citizens advice.org.uk/index/getadvice.htm#searchbox` to find the phone number for your local centre.

Checking Your Child's Eyes, Ears and Mouth

You want to be sure that speech, hearing or vision problems aren't making your child's dyslexia worse. The websites in the following list provide direction on where you can get this important stuff checked out. See Chapter 4 for details on the importance of watching for vision, hearing and speech problems at an early age.

- ✔ **Optometrists:** For information on vision problems and a directory of optometrists, contact the Institute of Optometry by email at `admin@ioo.org.uk` or by phone on 0207 234 9641. Its address is Institute of Optometry, 56–62 Newington Causeway, London SE1 6DS.
- ✔ **Overlays and lenses:** To read about coloured lenses and overlays, check out the Irlen Syndrome site at `www.irlenuk.com` and also the Dyslexia Research Trust at `www.dyslexic.org.uk`.
- ✔ **Speech therapy:** For information on language problems and speech therapy, log on to `www.rcslt.org.uk`. For more general advice if you're worried about your child, go to the NHS Direct website at `www.nhsdirect.nhs.uk` or consult your GP.
- ✔ **Treatments via the ears:** To read about dyslexia treatments that involve playing filtered sounds to your child through earphones, visit the commercial site for Audiblox at `www.audiblox2000.com/dyslexia`.

Surveying Self-Tests

When you have your child assessed for dyslexia, you typically work with a specialist from the local education authority or an independent tester. However, if you want to get dyslexia tests for yourself, here are your connections. You can have your child take tests online, or you can download a test so that he takes it the paper and pen way. Either way, you may get the basic information you want without paying the high fees that psychologists charge. See Chapter 6 for full details on the assessment process.

- ✔ **The Bristol Dyslexia Centre** website at www.dyslexiacentre.co.uk offers a short online test.

- ✔ **The British Dyslexia Association** has an adult checklist at www.bdadyslexia.org.uk/adultchecklist.html that you can adapt for children. The website also has a checklist of indicators for children.

- ✔ Additional online tests are available on www.dyslexia-test.com or www.amidyslexic.com.

Local education authorities don't accept the results of these self-tests on their own as reliable indicators that your child needs a dyslexia assessment or special accommodations in class.

Focusing on Alternative Schooling and School Reading Programmes

Alternative schools offer programmes that you may not find in a state school, but that doesn't mean they necessarily provide special help for children with dyslexia. See Chapter 7 for details on selecting the best school for your child and then find your nearest schools by visiting the sites listed here. (Chapter 7 also has information on home schooling, including resources and materials.)

Schools

This section lets you search outside the lines. You can get in touch with private schools that may offer just the kind of curriculum you're thinking of for your child.

CReSTeD, the Council for the Registration of Schools Teaching Dyslexic Children, has a booklet that can help you find suitable specialist schools in your area.
Website: www.crested.org.uk
Phone: 01242 604 852

The Good Schools Guide has an excellent section on special educational needs.
Website: www.goodschoolsguide.co.uk

Montessori schools
Website: www.montessori.org.uk
Phone: 0207 493 8300

Steiner Waldorf Schools
Website: www.steinerwaldorf.org.uk
Phone: 01342 822 115

For general information about schools and education go to www.direct.gov.uk.

School reading programmes

Most schools have a reading programme in place. Get the full picture about a school's reading programme on its website or get a quick summary by phone. Either way, finding out how these programmes work and whether you can get support materials to use at home can be well worthwhile.

Jolly Phonics, Dandelion Readers, Jelly and Bean and Oxford Reading Tree are well-respected and widely used programmes. They are school-based programmes, but we cover other programmes that independent therapists and tutors use later in this appendix.

Davis Learning Strategies
Website: uk.dyslexia.com
Phone: 0870 443 9059

Jelly and Bean
Website: www.jellyandbean.co.uk
Phone: 01423 879 182

Jolly Phonics
Website: www.jollylearning.co.uk
Phone: 0208 501 0405

Oxford Reading Tree
Website: www.oup.co.uk
Phone: 01865 556 646

National Literacy Trust (this organisation offers great advice about all the different phonics-based reading programmes available)
Website: www.literacytrust.org.uk
Phone: 0207 587 1842

Reading Recovery
Website: www.ioe.ac.uk
Phone: 0207 612 6585

Laying Down the Law

Legal jargon and legal forms are heavy stuff. In this section, you get places you can go for legal advice and specialists you can call on to help you translate all the legal hoopla and SEN Statement procedure into everyday language. See Chapter 8 for more about your legal rights (and your child's).

- ✔ **The Children's Legal Centre:** Get advice on educational law and how to appeal to SENDIST at www.childrenslegalcentre.com.

- ✔ **Consumer Action Group:** Visit this forum for all kinds of legal advice, including SEN issues at www.consumeractiongroup.co.uk/forum/special-needs-disability-etc/123950-disability-sen-self-help.html.

- ✔ **IPSEA: The Independent Panel for Special Education Advice.** Find free and independent advice at www.ipsea.org.uk.

- ✔ **SEN Code of Practice:** For a free copy of the Code of Practice telephone 0845 602 260.

- ✔ **SENDIST:** Find information on the SEN tribunal process at www.sendist.gov.uk.

Finding Independent Programmes, Therapists and Learning Centres

Many of the places in the following sections have phone numbers and someone who answers them (not voice mail)! Call, talk and get local contacts – as easily as that! When you're trying to secure help outside school for your child with dyslexia, finding help is easy but narrowing down your options (whether to go to a clinic, therapist or tutor and whether you like the programmes they use) is much harder. Check out Chapter 9 for additional information about securing independent help.

Dyslexia programmes

Skip back a few pages to Chapter 20 for a rundown of independent treatments. I include telephone numbers and website addresses so that you can make a quick call or take a web surf. You probably have to call to get prices (they're usually not on the websites), and even then you may have to persevere. If you're told 'Prices are different for each child', hang on in there. You get to the cold figures in the end.

Therapists and tutors

The term 'consultant' usually signifies that the person using it is qualified and experienced. A 'tutor' is probably a more modest deal in these areas, but you must check qualifications, experience and all-round niceness on an individual basis. The Professional Association of Teachers of Students with Specific Learning Disabilities (PATOSS) is probably your first place to start looking; they hold a list of suitably qualified specialists in your local area. Go to www. patoss-dyslexia.org or telephone 01386 712 650 for more info.

Dyslexia centres

A local dyslexia centre can be an option for supplementing your child's education in school.

The Bristol Dyslexia Centre
Website: www.dyslexia centre.co.uk
Phone: 0117 973 9405

Dyslexia Action
Website: www.dyslexia action.org.uk
Phone: 01784 222 300
With 26 centres around the UK, you should be able to find a specialist teacher near you. The organisation also has outposts in many schools.

The Helen Arkell Dyslexia Centre
Website: www.arkell centre.org.uk
This centre is a good option if you live in the Surrey area.

General learning centres

If you're thinking of taking your child to a general learning centre, a quick call to the numbers we list here can save you a lot of time. The people who work in these centres are always happy to tell you about their programmes, but remember that as good as these centres sound, they're for all learners and *don't* focus solely on instruction for people with dyslexia.

Explore Learning
Website: www.explore

learning.ltd.uk
Phone: 01483 447 410

Kip McGrath Centres
Website: www.kip
mcgrath.co.uk
Phone: 01452 382 282

**Kumon Maths and
Reading Centres**
Website: www.kumon.
co.uk
Phone: 0800 854 714

Trying Technology

Are you stepping over CD-ROMs that your child used a few times and then threw aside with his karaoke machine and hand-held gaming device (it's six months old but technologically speaking obsolete)? Here are a few gizmos that, in technical life spans, have longevity. Chapter 9 has additional information on other gadgets that can help your child.

- **Books on tape:** Get books on tape by visiting the website for Listening Books at www.listening-books.org.uk or Calibre Books at www.calibre.org.uk.

- **CD-ROMs:** For a CD-ROM that's designed to fine-tune your child's auditory discrimination and phonemic awareness, check out Earobics at www.donjohnston.co.uk. For Kidspiration and Inspiration software, visit www.inspiration.com or www.dyslexic.com. For reviews of software, have a look at www.beingdyslexic.co.uk/reviews.

  The main supplier of technological aids and specialist software for supporting children or adults with dyslexia is Iansyst and you can find them at www.iansyst.co.uk.

- **Computers:** To buy used or reconditioned computers, check out www.pcworld.co.uk/recon-computers. Or go to www.mar.partners.extranet.microsoft.com for information about reconditioned Microsoft computers.

- **Print recognition software:** Text Help Read and Write Gold is probably the best software available for people with dyslexia. Purchase a copy at www.dyslexic.com.

- **Speech-to-text software:** For comparisons of Dragon NaturallySpeaking and Via Voice, go to www.dyslexic.com.

- **Spell checkers:** To find out about spell checkers, visit www.dyslexic.com.

- **Typing:** Check out English Type Junior and Senior at www.dyslexia action.org.uk or go to DI Trading.

Lending a Hand to Teenagers, Students and Adults

Plenty of information is available about university and finances and other grown-up matters. The information can be overwhelming, so in this section we give you a handful of easy-to-understand resources. See Chapters 16, 17 and 18 for more about helping teens, students and adults.

University entrance exams and other tests

Terms such as HAT and LNAT may sound like alphabet soup to you. To get the dish on these tests, sample these wholesome websites:

- **HAT and other tests:** Take a look at www.hero.ac.uk/uk/studying/ applying_to_university_or_college/interviews_and_ admissions_tests.cfm.

- **LNAT:** Visit www.lnat.ac.uk for practice tests and further information.

University and general educational information

If you want to know which universities have less focus on formal examinations or you want to know which university can train you in law but make allowances for your dyslexia, here are some helpful contacts:

- **Dyslexic Adult Link:** www.dyslexia-adults.com
  This US site gives some information about UK colleges and universities. For example, it cites Mansfield College, Oxford as having a positive policy towards specific learning difficulties. You can also find information about grants for UK students.

- **Open University:** www.open.ac.uk
  For a student with dyslexia who wants to work at his own pace, the Open University can be a great option.

- **Student Room:** www.studentroom.co.uk
  This excellent website has a forum for students to participate in and share knowledge. You also find good information about courses and degrees.

Financial assistance, grants and scholarships

University costs money – no surprise there. Here are a few places that can give you advice about how to pay for your studies and even how to reduce your costs:

- **Armed forces careers:** For students interested in careers in the forces and the various financial incentives they offer, go to www.scholarship-search.com. or directly to the particular forces website (for example, www.army.mod.uk).

- **Awards and scholarships:** For information on the various kinds of bursaries and scholarships available for university students from different organisations, have a look at www.scholarship-search.org.uk/pls/mon/hc_edufin.page_pls_user_studmoney?x=16180339&y=&a=220707.

- **Other sources of income:** Explore the website of the university or college you're interested in for further information about potential help. For example, many universities offer their own bursaries, employ students as ambassadors and provide work opportunities in the student union bar.

- Student loans and grants: Both www.studentfinancedirect.co.uk and www.ucas.co.uk/students/studentfinance give excellent advice on how to apply for various kinds of loans and grants. Also, www.direct.gov.uk has useful information.

Jobs and other life skills

If you're out of work and need help getting back into the groove, your local Jobcentre Plus can give you details of programmes designed to help. Its website is www.jobcentreplus.gov.uk.

Jobcentres Plus in conjunction with Dyslexia Action and the Shaw Trust offer the Pathways to Work scheme, which enables pre-screened individuals to be put forward for a Skills Profile that a specialist teacher carries out. The scheme includes 20 hours of specialist tuition. Find more information on www.shaw-trust.org.uk and www.jobcentreplus.gov.uk.

At-home dyslexia programmes

Adults with dyslexia and children too can improve their reading skills at home by working through any of the following programmes. The best approach is to have a calm and constructive friend to guide you, but you can choose to work alone if you prefer or can't find a willing ally. To make the right choice of programme, read the following brief descriptions and then visit the sites that interest you:

- **Units of Sound (Version 4.4).** Adult learners can effectively use this multisensory reading and spelling programme. A test places the learner on one of three stages for reading and spelling, and resources enable him to work independently on the computer. The programme builds reading accuracy, vocabulary, spelling, sentence writing skills, listening skills, visual skills and comprehension. Each of the three stages costs £90, or the complete set is available for £250 from DI Trading at www.dyslexia action.org.uk/store or at www.unitsofsound.net.

- **Units of Sound: Literacy that Fits.** The Literacy that Fits resource is a great home supplement to the larger Units of Sound programme. A simple placement test and an easy-to-follow guide lead you along the way. Although children can use the programme, the graphics are very adult-friendly. Like the full Units of Sound programme, the CD-ROM contains reading, spelling, memory and dictation programmes. The cost is £59 from DI Trading at www.dyslexiaaction.org/store or www.unitsofsound.net.

Index

● *E* ●

• O •

• P •

FOR DUMMIES®

BUSINESS

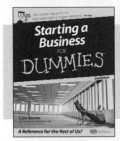

978-0-470-51806-9

Understanding Business Accounting For Dummies

978-0-470-99245-6

978-0-470-75626-3

FINANCE

978-0-470-99280-7

978-0-470-99811-3

978-0-470-69515-9

PROPERTY

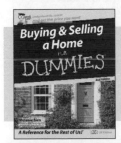

978-0-470-99448-1

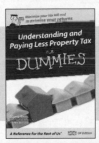

978-0-470-75872-4

978-0-7645-7054-4

Backgammon For Dummies
978-0-470-77085-6

Body Language For Dummies
978-0-470-51291-3

British Sign Language
For Dummies
978-0-470-69477-0

Business NLP For Dummies
978-0-470-69757-3

Children's Health For Dummies
978-0-470-02735-6

Cognitive Behavioural Coaching
For Dummies
978-0-470-71379-2

Counselling Skills For Dummies
978-0-470-51190-9

Digital Marketing For Dummies
978-0-470-05793-3

eBay.co.uk For Dummies,
2nd Edition
970-0-470-51007-0

English Grammar For Dummies
978-0-470-05752-0

Fertility & Infertility For Dummies
978-0-470-05750-6

Genealogy Online For Dummies
978-0-7645-7061-2

Golf For Dummies
978-0-470-01811-8

Green Living For Dummies
978-0-470-06038-4

Hypnotherapy For Dummies
978-0-470-01930-6

13902_p1

FOR DUMMIES®

A world of resources to help you grow

UK editions

SELF-HELP

978-0-470-01838-5

978-0-7645-7028-5

978-0-470-75876-2

Inventing For Dummies
978-0-470-51996-7

Job Hunting and Career Change
All-In-One For Dummies
978-0-470-51611-9

Motivation For Dummies
978-0-470-76035-2

Origami Kit For Dummies
978-0-470-75857-1

Personal Development All-In-One
For Dummies
978-0-470-51501-3

PRINCE2 For Dummies
978-0-470-51919-6

Psychometric Tests For Dummies
978-0-470-75366-8

Raising Happy Children For
Dummies
978-0-470-05978-4

Starting and Running a Business
All-in-One For Dummies
978-0-470-51648-5

Sudoku for Dummies
978-0-470-01892-7

The British Citizenship Test
For Dummies, 2nd Edition
978-0-470-72339-5

Time Management For Dummies
978-0-470-77765-7

Wills, Probate, & Inheritance Tax
For Dummies, 2nd Edition
978-0-470-75629-4

Winning on Betfair For Dummies,
2nd Edition
978-0-470-72336-4

HEALTH

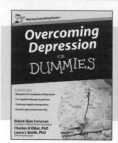

978-0-470-69430-5

978-0-470-51737-6

978-0-470-71401-0

HISTORY

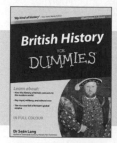

978-0-470-99468-9

978-0-470-51015-5

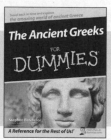

978-0-470-98787-2

FOR DUMMIES

LANGUAGES

978-0-7645-5194-9

978-0-7645-5193-2

978-0-471-77270-5

MUSIC

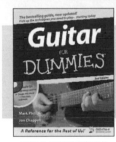

978-0-7645-9904-0

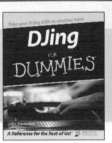

978-0-470-03275-6
UK Edition

978-0-7645-5105-5

SCIENCE & MATHS

978-0-7645-5326-4

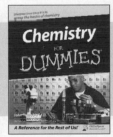

978-0-7645-5430-8

978-0-7645-5325-7

Art For Dummies
978-0-7645-5104-8

Baby & Toddler Sleep Solutions For Dummies
978-0-470-11794-1

Bass Guitar For Dummies
978-0-7645-2487-5

Brain Games For Dummies
978-0-470-37378-1

Christianity For Dummies
978-0-7645-4482-8

Filmmaking For Dummies, 2nd Edition
978-0-470-38694-1

Forensics For Dummies
978-0-7645-5580-0

German For Dummies
978-0-7645-5195-6

Hobby Farming For Dummies
978-0-470-28172-7

Jewelry Making & Beading For Dummies
978-0-7645-2571-1

Knitting for Dummies, 2nd Edition
978-0-470-28747-7

Music Composition For Dummies
978-0-470-22421-2

Physics For Dummies
978-0-7645-5433-9

Sex For Dummies, 3rd Edition
978 0 470 04523-7

Solar Power Your Home For Dummies
978-0-470-17569-9

Tennis For Dummies
978-0-7645-5087-4

The Koran For Dummies
978-0-7645-5581-7

U.S. History For Dummies
978-0-7645-5249-6

Wine For Dummies, 4th Edition
978-0-470-04579-4

13902_p3

FOR DUMMIES®

Helping you expand your horizons and achieve your potential

COMPUTER BASICS

978-0-470-27759-1

978-0-470-13728-4

978-0-471-75421-3

DIGITAL LIFESTYLE

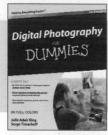
978-0-470-25074-7

978-0-470-39062-7

978-0-470-17469-2

WEB & DESIGN

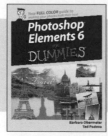
978-0-470-19238-2

978-0-470-32725-8

978-0-470-34502-3

Access 2007 For Dummies
978-0-470-04612-8

Adobe Creative Suite 3 Design Premium
All-in-One Desk Reference For Dummies
978-0-470-11724-8

AutoCAD 2009 For Dummies
978-0-470-22977-4

C++ For Dummies, 5th Edition
978-0-7645-6852-7

Computers For Seniors For Dummies
978-0-470-24055-7

Excel 2007 All-In-One Desk Reference
For Dummies
978-0-470-03738-6

Flash CS3 For Dummies
978-0-470-12100-9

Mac OS X Leopard For Dummies
978-0-470-05433-8

Macs For Dummies, 10th Edition
978-0-470-27817-8

Networking All-in-One Desk Reference
For Dummies, 3rd Edition
978-0-470-17915-4

Office 2007 All-in-One Desk Reference
For Dummies
978-0-471-78279-7

Search Engine Optimization For
Dummies, 2nd Edition
978-0-471-97998-2

Second Life For Dummies
978-0-470-18025-9

The Internet For Dummies, 11th Edition
978-0-470-12174-0

Visual Studio 2008 All-In-One Desk
Reference For Dummies
978-0-470-19108-8

Web Analytics For Dummies
978-0-470-09824-0

Windows XP For Dummies, 2nd Edition
978-0-7645-7326-2